KOINE EIRENE

UNIVERSITY OF HULL PUBLICATIONS

KOINE EIRENE

General Peace and Local Independence in Ancient Greece

T. T. B. RYDER

Lecturer in Classics in the University of Hull

Published for the UNIVERSITY OF HULL *by the*

OXFORD UNIVERSITY PRESS

LONDON   NEW YORK   TORONTO

1965

Oxford University Press, Amen House, London E.C.4

GLASGOW NEW YORK TORONTO MELBOURNE WELLINGTON
BOMBAY CALCUTTA MADRAS KARACHI LAHORE DACCA
CAPE TOWN SALISBURY NAIROBI IBADAN ACCRA
KUALA LUMPUR HONG KONG

PRINTED IN GREAT BRITAIN
AT THE UNIVERSITY PRESS, OXFORD
BY VIVIAN RIDLER
PRINTER TO THE UNIVERSITY

PREFACE

IT is a commonplace for writers on Greek History to acknowledge in their prefaces their great debt to the writings of their predecessors, but it is just and not any less so in a study of *Koine Eirene*, although it is a subject of comparatively recent growth. It was indeed only in the thirties that the observations first made about the meaning and importance of *Koine Eirene* by Wilhelm in 1900 were seriously followed up; but during that decade Momigliano, Hampl and Accame in particular laid the foundations of all subsequent work in this field. My own debt to these and others should be apparent even in footnotes which have been kept within reasonable bounds.

It is one of the justifications for writing this book (the scope and purpose of which are explained in the Introduction) that the work done on *Koine Eirene* has received scant recognition in the more general type of book on Greek history and civilization; Bengtson's *Griechische Geschichte* is the notable exception, but English readers for instance, who find the fundamentals of this subject taken for granted in the learned journals, have little to guide them except the references in Griffith's chapter on the Greek Historians in *Fifty Years of Classical Scholarship* and in Ehrenberg's *The Greek State*.

Though I would claim some novelty in my subject, I must confess to being unashamedly old fashioned in my treatment of Greek proper names. These, with the normal exception of some Aegean island-states, have been latinized and even to some extent anglicized through my preference for describing a state by the name of its inhabitants. I have, though, followed a good modern custom in eschewing, except in a few cases where it should cause no confusion, the use of op. cit. in the footnotes; books are referred to with a title, sometimes abbreviated, though full information is given in first references and in the Bibliography. Art. cit. is used, but all references to articles, except a few within individual appendixes, include the name of periodical with number and date of volume.

This work has grown out of my Cambridge Ph.D. dissertation of 1956 and its foundation was laid in the three years 1952-5, when my first university and King's College were most generous in their support of my efforts; with like generosity my second university has seen to its publication. Of those who have read earlier versions of it, I should like to mention Professor H. D. Westlake and Dr. A. H. McDonald, who gave valuable and stimulating advice at important moments, and especially Sir Frank Adcock, who first set me on the track of *Koine Eirene* and with generous and lively interest has afforded me constant encouragement.

But my greatest debt of gratitude is owed to three people. Mr. G. T. Griffith, who since the thirties has held, as it were, a watching brief for British scholarship over the study of *Koine Eirene*, supervised my early endeavours and has been ever ready over the years to read, criticize and encourage; he scrutinized the main body of this work in typescript. Mrs. A. M. R. Strachan gave unsparingly of time and care in reading the proofs and in doing so did much more than merely find misprints that had eluded all others. These two have saved me from many errors and infelicities, though the one would not agree with all my conclusions or the other approve all my usages and all surviving faults must be laid at my door. The third is my wife, who, though she has been spared having to read the unfinished work, has none the less nurtured it by urging me on and ministering to my needs; she richly deserves its dedication.

T. T. B. R.

Hull
January 1965

CONTENTS

LIST OF ABBREVIATIONS

Abh. Berlin	*Abhandlungen der Preussischen Akademie der Wissenschaften*: Philosophisch-historische Klasse.
A.J. Arch.	*American Journal of Archaeology.*
A.J. Ph.	*American Journal of Philology.*
Ath. Mitt.	*Mitteilungen des Deutschen Archäologischen Instituts*: Athenische Abteilung.
A.T.L.	*The Athenian Tribute Lists*, by B. D. Meritt, H. T. Wade-Gery, and M. F. McGregor, 4 vols. (Princeton, 1939–53).
B.C.H.	*Bulletin de correspondance hellénique.*
C.A.H.	*Cambridge Ancient History.*
C.Q.	*Classical Quarterly.*
Class. Phil.	*Classical Philology.*
Ditt. *Syll.*	W. Dittenberger, *Sylloge Inscriptionum Graecarum* (3rd ed., Leipzig, 1915–24).
IG	*Inscriptiones Graecae.*
J.H.S.	*Journal of Hellenic Studies.*
Jahreshefte Österr. Arch. Inst.	*Jahreshefte des Österreichischen Archäologischen Instituts in Wien.*
Rev. d'étud. anc. (grec.)	*Revue des études anciennes (grecques).*
Rh. Mus.	*Rheinisches Museum für Philologie.*
Riv. di filol.	*Rivista di filologia e di istruzione classica.*
S.E.G.	*Supplementum Epigraphicum Graecum.*
Sitzb. Berlin (München)	*Sitzungsberichte der Preussischen (Bayerischen) Akademie der Wissenschaften*: Philosophisch-historische Klasse.
Sitzb. Wien	*Sitzungsberichte der Akademie der Wissenschaften in Wien*: Philosophisch-historische Klasse.
Tod	M. N. Tod, *Greek Historical Inscriptions*, 2 vols., vol. i, 2nd ed. (Oxford, 1946–8).

INTRODUCTION

THE simple and obvious translation of the Greek phrase *Koine Eirene* is Common Peace; but these two words have not as a phrase acquired a special meaning in twentieth-century English. That they have not is perhaps one of the accidents of journalism, for the phrase was coined by a prominent statesman in a significant speech. On 22 January 1917 President Woodrow Wilson addressed the United States Senate and told that body what he thought it must be the nation's purpose to achieve, if she were compelled to go to war. 'There must be', he said, 'not a balance of power, but a community of power, not organized rivalries, but an organized Common Peace.'

This Peace was to be a peace in which all nations should share equally, enjoying complete independence and guarding it jealously, not a peace dictated by victors to vanquished, but 'peace without victory'. This last phrase was the one which was afforded wider currency, and Common Peace was forgotten, never yet to become one of the meaningless slogans of modern international politics.[1]

To the Greeks, though, at least in the fourth century B.C., *Koine Eirene* had a generally accepted technical meaning such as Common Peace in modern English lacks. The examples of the use of the phrase known from extant literature and inscriptions are not, however, very numerous and it is convenient at this point to list them and so from them to show what Common Peace meant to the Greeks.

I. FOURTH-CENTURY SOURCES

1. Andocides iii. 17: 'you are dealing with *common peace* and freedom for all the Greeks' (recommending peace-proposals at Athens in 391).
2. Restoration of '*the common peace*' as a description of the Peace of 387/386 in line 13 of the decree of the Athenian people proposed by Aristoteles in 377; restoration proposed by

[1] The text of Wilson's speech was given by *The Times*, 23 January 1917, pp. 9–10.

S. Accame, *La lega ateniense nel secolo IV a.c.* (Rome, 1941), p. 51, and accepted by M. N. Tod, *Greek Historical Inscriptions*, vol. ii, no. 123.

3. Inscription, Tod 145, lines 5–6: 'the Greeks have settled their differences with a view to *common peace*' (one letter restored) and line 3 '. . . to those who share in *common peace*' (*peace* restored) (referring to the Peace of 362/361).

4. Aeschines iii. 254: '. . . with those who violate *the common peace*' (referring to the Peace of 338/337).

5. Pseudo-Demosthenes xvii. 2: 'from the very treaty and the oaths concerning *the common peace*' (referring to the Peace of 338/337).

6. Pseudo-Demosthenes xvii. 4: 'contrary to the oaths and to the treaty that was written in *the common peace*' (referring to the Peace of 338/337).

7. Pseudo-Demosthenes xvii. 17: '. . . who mock *the common peace*' (in a passage discussing the Peace of 338/337).

8. Inscription, Tod 177, lines 20–21: 'I will make war against anyone who transgresses *the common peace*.' The phrase *the common peace* restored originally by A. Wilhelm, 'Attische Urkunde', *Sitzb. Wien*, clxv, no. 6 (1911), but not universally accepted (part of oath to the Peace of 338/337.)

II. LATER AUTHORS REFERRING TO THE FOURTH CENTURY

1. Plutarch (first to second century A.D.)
   Life of Phocion c. 16: '. . . proposed that the city should participate with the Greeks in *the common peace* and in the synhedrion' (referring to the Peace of 338/337).

2. Diodorus Siculus (first century B.C.)
   i. xv. 5. 1: 'The Greeks were enjoying *the common peace* of Antalcidas' (Peace of 387/386).
   ii. xv. 38. 1–2: '. . . to urge the cities *to conclude common peace* . . .; . . . the Greeks . . . all *concluded* the peace' (Peace of 375).
   iii. xv. 45. 2: '. . . no longer respecting *the common peace that had been concluded*' (Peace of 375).
   iv. xv. 50. 4: '. . . calling upon the Greeks . . . *to conclude*

common peace . . .; . . . all the cities except the Thebans *concluded common peace*' (Peace of 371 at Sparta).

v. xv. 51. 1: 'because they had all *concluded the common peace*' (Peace of 371 at Sparta).

vi. xv. 70. 2: '. . . to urge the Greeks . . . *to conclude common peace*; . . . when *the common peace* was rejected . . .' (proposals of 368).

vii. xv. 76. 3: '. . . persuaded the Greeks . . . *to conclude common peace* with one another' (Peace of 366/365).

viii. xv. 89. 1: '. . . (the Greeks) having *concluded common peace*' (Peace of 362/361).

ix. xv. 90. 2: '. . . because the Messenians had been included in *the common peace*' (Peace of 362/361).

x. xv. 94. 1: 'though the Arcadians had agreed on *common peace* . . . they adhered to the oaths for only one year' (Peace of 362/361).

xi. xvi. 60. 3: 'the Amphictyons laid down regulations . . . and other matters affecting due respect for the gods and *common peace* and concord among the Greeks' (the settlement after the defeat of the Phocians in 346).

xii. xvii. 9. 5: 'calling on them to share in *the common peace* of the Greeks' (Peace of 338/337).

xiii. xx. 46. 6: '. . . preferring to maintain *common peace* with all' (after the Peace of 311).

III. OTHER REFERENCES (outside the scope of this work)

1. Polybius iv. 3. 8: '. . . because *the common peace* among the Greeks which had been arranged by Antigonus was still in force' (referring to a settlement between 224 and 222).

2. Fragment of an inscription of Mylasa, end of second–beginning of first century (*B.C.H.* (1888), 8): '*of the common peace*' (four letters restored) (reference unknown).

3. Livy xxix. 12 (following Polybius): 'the Epirotes . . . sent ambassadors to Philip about *common peace* (*de pace communi*)' (Peace of Phoenice, 205).

The list shows that in fourth-century authors and inscriptions the phrase occurs in Andocides once, in Aeschines once, in Pseudo-Demosthenes xvii thrice, in one inscription twice, in another inscription probably, in a third inscription possibly:

seven certain cases, including one official document. The two other official documents contribute a 'probable' and a 'possible' respectively, making nine cases the highest number possible. The phrase does not occur at all in Demosthenes' own speeches, in Isocrates' political pamphlets, or in Xenophon's histories, which between them form by far the greater part of the contemporary political and historical sources for the period.

The other uses of the phrase relative to the fourth century appear in authors writing several centuries after it, one in Plutarch's *Lives* and fourteen in Diodorus' *World History*. Diodorus thus furnishes well over half the examples, but this fact is not so discouraging as it may seem at first sight. It is true that he wrote as late as the first century B.C. and that he was clearly without great intelligence or even competence, but, unlike Plutarch who tended to use a variety of sources without notable discrimination, he made his task easier by following, where possible, one principal source at a time for a particular period. For Greek affairs in Book xv (which goes down to 360 B.C.) he followed, and greatly abbreviated, the contemporary fourth-century historian Ephorus;[1] and in Book xv ten of his fourteen references to Common Peace are found. Nothing that is known of Diodorus' ability or his methods suggests that he was clever enough or adventurous enough to impose a common interpretation on various events not so linked in his sources. So, certainly, Common Peace here goes back to Ephorus and must be taken seriously.

Of the thirteen passages in which the phrase Common Peace is used by Diodorus, in seven (nos. ii–viii) he says that the Greeks *concluded* (or were urged *to conclude*) Common Peace, using some part of the verb συντίθεμαι; in these cases he evidently gives to a peace treaty the name Common Peace. Moreover, in all the other cases but three (nos. xi–xiii), though not actually describing the conclusion of a treaty of peace, he seems to refer to one. Plutarch's one use of the phrase also indicates a treaty and of the fourth-century examples two of those in Demosthenes xvii do so quite explicitly, while in the inscription, Tod 145, a

---

[1] Cf. C. A. Volquardsen, *Untersuchungen über die Quellen der griech. und sizil. Geschichte bei Diodoros XI. bis XVI.* (Kiel, 1868), and E. Schwartz, *P.–W.*, s.v. Diodoros (38), cols. 679–82.

treaty is being referred to and the fact that the phrase Common
Peace is repeated suggests that there too it is being used of the
treaty itself.

In view of this large proportion of cases referring to a treaty of
peace we must conclude that to the Greeks of the fourth century
κοινὴ εἰρήνη meant primarily a General Peace *treaty*, that is a
particular kind of peace treaty. The phrase could also mean a
state of general peace, the product, as it were, of a peace treaty
or treaties which left Greece at present without wars; and it
may have originally meant only that. In a valuable study of
the uses of the word εἰρήνη,[1] B. Keil has shown that it certainly
meant only a state of peace, the opposite of war (πόλεμος), right
down to the beginning of the fourth century; up to that time
treaties were called truces (σπονδαί, συνθῆκαι) or cessations of
war (διάλυσις πολέμου, &c.) and the first that was called a
Peace (as it was also the first to be called Common Peace) was the
King's Peace of 387/386. By 362/361 the phrase Common Peace
is apparently used in official documents for a treaty of peace,
and according to some scholars as early as 377. It is reasonable
to suppose that in common parlance this usage had already been
established for some years before it was taken over into the
official language; but even so it cannot be determined whether
the phrase would have been understood as meaning a particular
sort of treaty when Andocides used it in 391. Then there had
not even been a Common Peace treaty, though the actual terms
that Andocides was advocating would have constituted one.
At all events, once the phrase was used to describe a particular
kind of peace treaty, it would be hard for anyone to use it
comprehensibly for a state of general peace without calling to
mind a Common Peace treaty and so without being taken to
mean a state of peace produced by such a treaty or regarded as
being regulated by its principles.

This argument that the name Common Peace was given to
and used almost entirely with reference to a particular kind of
peace treaty should not obscure the fact that treaties which
some people called Common Peace were not so called by others.
The silence of Demosthenes, Isocrates and Xenophon has
already been noted. These authors and others allude to and
discuss the treaties which Ephorus (Diodorus) calls Common

---

[1] *Εἰρήνη, Ber. über die Verh. der Königl. Sächs. Ges. der Wiss.* lxviii (1916), no. 4.

Peace, giving them either no special name or a different one; but at times they clearly recognize one or other of the features which to us distinguish Common Peace treaties, and at times they furnish us unwittingly with evidence that a particular treaty should be called Common Peace.

The two features which Diodorus' notices of the treaties show to be essential to what his source called Common Peace treaties are the following: first, that their principal clause laid down that all Greek states should be free and autonomous; second, that the treaties were made between all the Greeks, that is to say that they were not bilateral agreements limited to the two sides fighting a war, but were agreements of a general nature applicable to all Greeks equally, whether or not they had taken part in the preceding war. A detailed examination of Diodorus' accounts of the treaties and of the accounts and references in our other literary and epigraphical sources shows that his source, Ephorus, was right in seeing a series of similar general peace treaties in the fourth century; and that these two features were their distinguishing mark.

A detailed examination of this kind is the necessary first stage of any study of Common Peace; its result will be to determine which treaties should rightly be deemed Common Peace treaties and which not. Much work has already been done on these lines, but the nature of the evidence and the lack of generally accepted conclusions make it impossible to take anything for granted, and the appendixes to this book contain the necessary detailed discussions. The criteria there used are the two features mentioned above, with a third added, that to qualify for the title a treaty should in fact have been accepted by the vast majority of the leading Greek cities.

The conclusions are largely favourable to Diodorus. His evidence is prima facie compelling where he depends on Ephorus; and in that book it is to a great extent confirmed. He leaves out altogether one treaty, that of 371 at Athens (it may or may not have been recorded by Ephorus), and he seems to have been led by a confused reading and overcompression of his source into describing a Common Peace treaty which did not exist (366/365). Outside Book xv one can be less sure what his sources meant when they passed on the phrase Common Peace to him; but at least he has badly treated them, or been badly treated by them, in the case of the treaty of 338/337 which he describes as Common Peace only in retrospect.[1]

But, although Common Peace almost always referred directly or indirectly to a peace treaty formally concluded and recorded on stone, a study of Common Peace cannot be limited to an examination of the content of these treaties or to a discussion of their legal implications. For either of these subjects, what can be determined about the historical circumstances of the treaties and about the policies and aspirations of the Greek states which concluded them is essential evidence; conversely the fact that Common Peace treaties were so often concluded or proposed in the fourth century suggests that they may constitute one of the themes around which the complicated history of Greek interstate politics in that century can best be understood; while the dominance of treaties in the fourth century based on the general acceptance of the principle of small-state independence indicates that the part played by that principle in fifth-century history may help to illuminate its role in the fourth.

This book has these wider purposes, and its main body consists first of an examination of the history of the fifth century for events and ideas that may shed light on the conclusion of the first Common Peace treaty in the fourth and then of an account in chronological order of the treaties and their role in the history of the Greek states in the fourth century, from the first proposal in 392 to the failure of Antigonus Monophthalmus' policy of freedom in Greece in 300.

[1] Diodorus no. xii (xvii. 9. 5) was given above as one of three examples which could not at first sight be said to indicate a treaty, but, once it is established that κοινὴ εἰρήνη usually means a treaty and that the Peace of 338/337 was such a treaty, it seems obvious that Diodorus here does refer to that Peace.

I

The Antecedents to the King's Peace; the Greek States and the Principle of Autonomy

THE first Common Peace treaty, the King's Peace of 387 B.C., concluded the so-called Corinthian War which had broken out in 395 between the Spartans and their allies on the one side and the Athenians, Thebans, Corinthians and Argives, supported at first by the King of Persia, on the other. The King's Peace was preceded during the course of the war by two separate attempts to conclude treaties which would have been essentially similar to it and would have qualified for the description Common Peace. This chapter on the antecedents to the King's Peace will therefore consider events down to the outbreak of the Corinthian War, and this war with the two abortive proposals of Common Peace will be considered in the next chapter with the conclusion of the King's Peace itself.

The most important innovation in the treaties proposed in the Corinthian War and in the King's Peace was the essential stipulation that all cities great and small should be autonomous. The chief part of a chapter on the antecedents of the King's Peace must therefore be concerned with an examination of the part played in Greek interstate relations by the principle of autonomy before the beginning of the Corinthian War.

But there were two other features of the King's Peace which were unprecedented in peace treaties and which are worthy of passing notice. First, it was multilateral, that is, it was not simply an arrangement of mutual give and take between the two groups of states that had fought the Corinthian War, but it was applicable to all cities equally; second, it was concluded without time-limit.

These two features were not, as far as is known, expressed in words and written into the treaty. If the treaty had been drafted by men whose chief concern was to produce a comprehensive solution of the problem of interstate relations (and the next chapter will show that it certainly was not) these points might have been made explicit. They were indeed implicit in the general recognition of the principle of autonomy for all, which applied to all Greek states whether or not they had been involved in the war and which, considered as a principle of eternal validity, had no time-limit; and the absence of any term of years in the provisions of the treaty would, as will be seen, have made this latter point clear enough.

It is worth while noting that the King's Peace was the first multilateral treaty of peace between the Greek city-states, if only to observe that earlier peace treaties concluding wars on as large or larger scale than the Corinthian War and concerned with the interests of a large proportion of the cities had certainly not been of this nature.

The Thirty-Years Peace of 446/5, which brought to an end the first war between the Athenians and the Peloponnesian states, was a bilateral agreement between the Spartans and the Athenians; the Argives' request to be included in it was refused, and, more important, most at any rate of the allies of the two contracting states were probably not consulted, though their interests were deeply involved and their rights were to some extent defined in the treaty itself.[1] The Peace of Nicias of 421, which ended the first ten years of the great Peloponnesian War, again was a simple bilateral arrangement between the Spartans and the Athenians; it left the allies of the Athenians for the most part subject to their direction, while its failure to satisfy the allies of the Spartans led directly to its collapse.[2] Further, there is no reason to suppose that on the four other occasions during the Peloponnesian War on which the Spartans proposed peace they were thinking of anything but a bilateral treaty of this sort.[3] Finally, at the end of the war, when the Athenians surrendered in 404, the Spartans gave them terms, but no wider arrangement was made to establish the rights and position of the

[1] There is no full record of the treaty's terms. For the Argives, see Paus. v. 23. 4; a clause which acknowledged the right of both cities to deal with their own allies as they wished may be inferred from Thuc. i. 35. 2, taken with 40. 5 and 43. 1; in general, cf. A. W. Gomme, *A Historical Commentary on Thucydides*, vol. i (Oxford, 1945), p. 348.

[2] Thuc. v. 18, esp. ss. 1 and 11, and subsequent narrative.

[3] In 426 (Aristoph. *Ach*. 652–4; cf. F. E. Adcock, *C.A.H.*, vol. v (Cambridge, 1927), pp. 226–7); in 425 (Thuc. iv. 16 ff., esp. 20. 4); in 410 (Diod. xiii. 52); in 406 (Aristotle, *Ath. Pol.* 34. 1).

former members of the Athenian alliance, while the interests and aspirations of the Spartans' own allies were again largely ignored.[1]

This series of bilateral agreements between the Spartans and the Athenians only reflected the dominance of the two cities within their two alliance systems, and the alliances themselves, though uniting numerous cities, were not truly multilateral in form. The Peloponnesian League had originally grown out of a series of bilateral treaties between the Spartans and other Peloponnesian states, and, though a procedure was evolved by which the allies were consulted as a body before a war, the Spartans retained the final word and the allies were never linked to one another by the same obligations as tied them to the Spartans.[2] The Athenian alliance had been an organization of many states from the start, complete with a system of determining and collecting contributions to the common effort, but the pattern of alliances seems to have been similar to that of the Peloponnesian League;[3] again representatives of the allies met, in the earlier decades of the League's existence, to approve policy, but again nothing could be done without the Athenians.[4]

It was not surprising, then, that the two great states dominated Greek international relations in the fifth century; and this dominance was the chief reason why what chances there were of some general system being established to maintain peace and security came to nothing. For instance, after the Persian Wars the alliance of Greek states which had been formed in 481 to fight the impending invasion remained in existence. It was an organization that had some claim to be panhellenic and was not simply an extension of the Peloponnesian League or a

[1] Xen. *Hell.* II. ii. 19–20; cf. Plut. *Lys.* 27.

[2] Cf. J. A. O. Larsen, 'The Constitution of the Peloponnesian League', *Class. Phil.* xxviii (1933), 267 ff. He suggests that the system of consultation was instituted between the events of Hdt. v. 74 ff. and those of v. 91 ff. ('Sparta and the Ionian Revolt', *Class. Phil.* xxvii (1932), 132 ff.)

[3] Cf. J. A. O. Larsen, 'The Constitution and Original Purpose of the Delian League', *Harv. Class. Stud.* li (1940), 183.

[4] Cf. *A.T.L.* = B. D. Meritt, H. T. Wade-Gery, and M. F. McGregor, *The Athenian Tribute Lists* (Princeton, 1939–53, 4 vols.), vol. iii (1950), p. 227. N. G. L. Hammond, *A History of Greece to 322 B.C.* (Oxford, 1959), p. 256, goes too far in describing the League as 'bicameral'; the Athenian people effectively had a veto on decisions of the Council of Allies, but probably had no formal standing.

combination of it and an Athenian-led alliance, and it might
have been possible to have preserved through it the spirit of
unity fostered by the victories of 480–479.[1] In fact, it ceased
to be panhellenic in 479 when the Spartans refused to allow the
Asiatic Greeks to be admitted to it, partly because they could
not control such an extended organization; while the Athenians had rejected their proposal to transfer the Asiatic Greeks
to the lands of medizing states in central Greece, partly because their own leadership would thereby be threatened.[2]
Subsequently the alliance soon became a dead letter, when first
the Spartans abandoned the war against Persia and then both
the Spartans and the Athenians began to assert their leadership
in their respective spheres by superior force.

Later, in about 450, Pericles' proposals of a panhellenic
conference to discuss common action to secure, among other
things, the maintenance of peace was rejected by the Spartans,
principally, it is likely, because to accept it would be an
acknowledgement of the Athenians' claim to lead Greece.[3]

Against this pattern of Greek inter-state relations after the
Persian Wars can be set three, possibly four, examples of what
would now be classifiable as multilateral treaties of peace, all
so remote in time or space that they are not likely to have
influenced Greek politicians or theorists (if there were any) in
the early fourth century.

First, the mutual undertaking of the member-states of the
Delphian Amphictyony 'that they would raze no city of the
amphictyonic states nor shut them off from flowing water either
in war or in peace; that if anyone should violate this oath they
should march against such a one and raze his cities'. Though
this oath was known to Aeschines, whose quotation of it is our
only source of knowledge of it, the Amphictyony had ceased
to have much political importance after the Persian Wars.[4]

Second, the pacification concluded among the Sicilian states

[1] On the alliance, cf. P. A. Brunt, 'The Hellenic League against Persia', *Historia*, ii (1953), 135 ff., against *A.T.L.* iii. 183 ff. On the prospects of unity, cf. esp.
J. A. O. Larsen, 'Federation for Peace in Ancient Greece', *Class. Phil.* xxxix (1944),
152 ff.

[2] Hdt. ix. 106.

[3] Plut. *Per.* 17; on the Spartans' motives, cf. esp. *A.T.L.* iii. 280.

[4] Aeschines ii. 115 (trans. C. D. Adams, Loeb Class. Lib., 1919). On this oath
and on other multilateral arrangements before 400, cf. F. Wüst, 'Amphiktyonie,
Eidgenossenschaft, Symmachie', *Historia*, iii (1954), 129 ff.

after the conference at Gela in 424, which seems to have been multilateral and applicable to the whole island (as may also have been the general agreement mentioned by Diodorus in his account of events in Sicily in the year 461/60);[1] but this treaty was very much an *ad hoc* arrangement and not, it seems, based on any general principle, and its contribution to political theory is not likely to have formed part of the western Greeks' intellectual exports to the homeland.[2]

Third, the agreement imposed on the Asiatic Greek cities after the Ionian Revolt, by which they undertook to submit disputes to arbitration and to refrain from ravaging one another's land.[3] One modern commentator[4] has gone so far as to call this agreement 'in basis a Common Peace'; but what went on in Persian-governed Ionia would hardly interest the other Greeks, while the Common Peace part of the King's Peace was not drafted by the Persians and its chief value to them was not that it would decrease the chances of inter-city warfare in Greece.[5]

The fact that the King's Peace was the first Greek peace treaty known to us which did not include a time-limit is of some interest when viewed in connexion with Keil's discoveries, already referred to,[6] of the development in the usages of the word $\epsilon i \rho \eta \nu \eta$. Keil pointed out that in the fourth century the Greeks began to use this word for a treaty of peace itself as well as for the state of peace produced by a treaty, whereas previously they had used it only for the latter and had referred to the treaty of peace as a truce or a cessation of hostilities. The old terminology belonged strictly to a period when war was the normal state of affairs and the new to one when peace was no longer the exception. So, as Keil pointed out, in the fifth century peace treaties were made for a stated number of years, that of 446/5 for thirty, the Peace of Nicias for fifty (both these were called truces) and so on, whereas in the fourth century the King's Peace is found to have no time-limit; and it was this

---

[1] Diod. xi. 76. 5.

[2] Thuc. iv. 65. 1–2; H. D. Westlake, 'Hermocrates the Syracusan', *Bull. John Rylands Lib*. xli (1958–9), esp. 244–5, sees a possible connexion with the Common Peace idea.

[3] Hdt. vi. 42. 1.

[4] I. Calabi, *Ricerche sui rapporti tra le poleis* (Florence, 1953), p. 33.

[5] See below, Chapter II.   [6] Above, p. xv.

treaty which the Greeks first called a Peace, εἰρήνη, in the official language of peace treaties, though the word had already been used with the new meaning by Thucydides, Lysias and Andocides and once in an official document in the decree of the Athenian people concerning the Samians passed in 405.[1]

This may be a case of terminology following far behind general thought or of our sources giving us a false picture, but it is probably fair to say that people were thinking more widely than before that peace was the right state of affairs and that peace agreements should aim at some sort of permanent settlement; and that, if this belief existed, it must have had some marginal effect, if not on the form taken by the King's Peace, at least on the acceptability of its terms to some of those whose political aspirations were not directly furthered by them.

The idea that individual cities ought to enjoy freedom and autonomy was nothing new to the Greeks in the early fourth century. This feeling had of course grown up with the system of city-states and was part of the unwritten law of Greek interstate relations. The Amphictyonic oath mentioned above reflected a general idea that it was atrocious to destroy utterly another city; it could happen, though, that the destruction of a city was justified by its impiety, as was the case with Crissa (destroyed by the Amphictyonic states in about 600), and it is also not clear how far memories went back on this subject; the Spartan subjugation of Messenia was still obvious and its history probably well known, but Athens must have been regularly identified with Attica and Sparta with Laconia and the processes by which the Spartans won control of Laconia and the Athenians unified Attica were in all likelihood largely forgotten.[2] But at the beginning of the fifth century the notion of city-state independence was applied to the contemporary

---

[1] Thuc. v. 17. 2; Lysias xiii. 5, &c.; Andocides iii. 4, &c.; Tod [= M. N. Tod, *Greek Historical Inscriptions*, 2 vols., vol. i, 2nd ed. (Oxford, 1946–8)] 96, v. 22; and cf. Keil, art. cit. 49 ff.

[2] G. L. Huxley, *Early Sparta* (London, 1962), pp. 21 ff., dates the conquest of Laconia to the period between the middle and the end of the eighth century B.C. The tradition about this conquest comes through Pausanias (see Huxley, p. 19) and is absent from our fifth-century sources. In 399 the Eleans raised the question of the *perioeci* (cf. below, p. 19) after the Spartans had taken their arguments about autonomy further back into history than before. The Messenians, on the other hand, were always known as separate people (cf. Thuc. i. 101. 2; Hdt. v. 49. 8, ix. 35. 2, &c.).

world, in which, in any case, it was very difficult to capture a city itself and even harder to keep it or its inhabitants in permanent subjection.[1]

It is against this notion of what was proper and of what was possible that one should see the readiness of Greek states in the early fifth century to enter into alliance organizations which from the beginning were likely to be dominated by the leading city. Of course there were positive stimuli to the smaller cities to sacrifice some independence in return for increased security. In the Peloponnese there was the predominant military power of the Spartans and also a community of race and interest between the Spartans and the Dorian ruling classes in some other states; in the Aegean after 480 there was, above all, fear of the Persians, and there were also the power and the prestige of the Athenians. But the allies of the two leading states can hardly have foreseen at this stage that the Spartans and the Athenians would choose to become, or in the case of the Athenians would be able to become, such unsatisfactory leaders.

The obligation of the Spartans' allies to supply troops for brief campaigns on land was not especially irksome; but later there were to be longer and more distant expeditions, and, moreover, Spartan leadership was to prove unreliable and at times almost treacherous. The allies of the Athenians in the Delian League actually chose in many cases the method of contribution to the common cause, the payment of fixed annual tribute, which was to prove a constant irritation and to furnish the means of Athenian domination, by increasing their own weakness and the naval strength of the Athenians. It is worth emphasizing this point, that the Athenian ability to control the Aegean and the Asiatic coast with a fleet was something beyond reasonable expectation; indeed in 479 the Spartans had so much doubted the ability of the homeland Greeks to protect the Asiatic cities, even with their goodwill, against the Persians that they had proposed their removal to central Greece.[3] So, because they thought that the Persian menace was something unlikely to be removed and because they had no great fear of the Athenians, the cities of the Aegean basin were prepared both to bind

---

[1] Cf, for instance, A. R. Burn, *The Lyric Age of Greece* (London, 1960), p. 34.
[2] Thuc. i. 96. 1 and 99, with Gomme's notes, and *A.T.L.* iii. 229 ff., 244 ff.
[3] Hdt. ix. 106.

themselves solemnly in perpetual alliance with Athens and to extract from the Athenians no specific guarantees of their independence.[1]

The one known guarantee of autonomy of this period, that made to the Plataeans in 479 by the assembled Greeks,[2] is a special case. The Plataeans had been under considerable pressure from the Thebans in the sixth century to join in the federation of Boeotia and, though they had then obtained Athenian protection and could still expect it, they were in a vulnerable position and their own loyalty and the Thebans' medism in the Persian invasion made the general sentiment favourable to a special gesture.

In the period after the Athenians had established close control over their allies and had come into conflict with the Spartans and their Peloponnesian allies, there are a few examples of guarantees of autonomy being extracted from the Athenians for individual cities as a concession; these guarantees resulted from the exigencies of war, and two of them were among the provisions of peace treaties made with the Spartans.

The first of them was the guarantee of the autonomy of the Aeginetans included in the Thirty-Years Peace of 446/5.[3] What exactly this concession meant is not clear; the Aeginetans had to continue paying tribute to the Athenians[4] and by 432 were claiming that the guarantee was not being honoured,[3] but at any rate it was something not vouchsafed to the other allies of the Athenians. Then, in the Peace of Nicias, the Athenians agreed that six cities in Chalcidice which Brasidas had won over should be autonomous, provided that they paid tribute on the Aristidean scale.[5] Again it is not clear what this concession meant; whatever it was, the Chalcidians too were not satisfied, though again it was something not given to the other allies.[6]

---

[1] Permanent alliance: Plut. *Arist.* 25. 1; Aristotle, *Ath. Pol.* 23. 5; cf. J. A. O. Larsen, art. cit., *Harv. Class. Stud.* li (1940), 187 ff. It is sometimes held, e.g. by *A.T.L.* iii. 228, Larsen, art. cit. 186, 191, that the autonomy of the allies was guaranteed; of the texts cited to support this view, Thuc. i. 97. 1 need mean no more than that the allies were in fact independent and Thuc. i. 98. 4 probably means that the Naxians were enslaved 'contrary to established usage', cf. A. H. M. Jones, *Athenian Democracy* (Blackwell: Oxford, 1957), p. 64.

[2] Thuc. ii. 71. 2.   [3] Thuc. i. 67. 2.

[4] *A.T.L.* ii, lists nos. 10, 12, 13, 14, 15, 22 show that they paid between 445-432.

[5] Thuc. v. 18. 5.

[6] The meaning of autonomy is discussed more fully below, pp. 20 ff.

Of the other three examples, two certainly were the indirect result of Spartan successes in the Peloponnesian War. First, the Athenian inscription which records the ratification of the terms on which the Selymbrians renewed their alliance with the Athenians in 410 reveals a stipulation that they should be autonomous and should establish their constitution in whatever way they ordained;[1] from which it appears that in the then state of Athenian power they were able to insist on some definite undertakings in return for alliance, as indeed Xenophon's narrative suggests.[2] Unfortunately this is the only case of re-entry into the Athenian alliance in this period of which any details are known; there are no other relevant inscriptions and Xenophon was not apparently interested in the terms of such agreements. Not very different from this case was the concession of autonomy made to the newly established democratic govern-ment in Samos in 412; a concession made to a reliable ally at a time of crisis when reliability was at a premium, and one which was an exclusive privilege and must have meant something concrete, though again it is not known what.[3]

Finally, another inscription provides fragmentary informa-tion of an agreement between the Athenians and the Myti-leneans some time after the end of the Mytilenean revolt of 428–427, in which, it appears, it was laid down that the Myti-leneans should be autonomous.[4] Though there can be no certainty, this agreement looks like a conciliatory move by which the Athenians remitted some of the rigours imposed in 427, perhaps a result of anxieties about Brasidas' victories or about the attitude of the Chians.[5]

These examples illustrate first the obvious truth that support for the more or less subject allies of rival states could be a useful weapon in big-power politics. How soon the Spartans began to use this weapon against the Athenians is, however, not clear. It should not be supposed that the Athenians' leadership

[1] Tod 88 (= *S.E.G.* x. 132), vv. 5–7.   [2] *Hell.* i. i. 21.

[3] Thuc. viii. 21, who gives no details; an inscription, *S.E.G.* xiv. 9, connected with this concession, adds nothing.

[4] Tod 63 (= *S.E.G.* x. 69), vv. 11–12.

[5] On the Chians, Thuc. iv. 51 (winter 425/4). Gomme, '*IG* i². 60 and Thucydides iii. 50. 2', *Robinson Studies*, ii. 334 ff., suggests that the concession went so far as the restoration of their lands to the Mytileneans; B. D. Meritt, 'Athenian Covenant with Mytilene', *A.J. Ph.* lxxv (1954), 362 ff., while not agreeing with Gomme on this point, speaks of a 'restoration of political autonomy' (p. 364).

of their allies necessarily appeared, even to Peloponnesian oligarchs, unduly oppressive as early as the various events which modern commentators would identify as the points of no return in the conversion of Delian League into Athenian Empire; and it is likely that the Spartans, through weakness, sloth, or fellow feeling (they themselves exercised leadership), were prepared to acquiesce in a fair degree of Athenian domination outside the Peloponnese.

There is no suggestion in our admittedly scanty sources that the Spartans tried to attack Athenian power through the Athenians' allies during the first war which broke out in 459; they refused overtures from the Persians,[1] left to their fate the Euboeans, whose revolt had greatly assisted their success in 446,[2] and then made a treaty with the Athenians in which they won concessions for the Aeginetans alone of the maritime allies and gave to the Athenians the right to deal with all their other allies as they wished.[3] They may, it seems, have wanted to assist the Samians against the Athenians in 441/40[4] and they chose to make an issue of Athenian action against Potidaea in 432,[5] but it was not until the eve of the great Peloponnesian War, when they had already decided to fight, that they proclaimed themselves the defenders of Greek freedom, calling on the Athenians to leave the Greeks autonomous.[6]

According to Thucydides, though his critics would disagree, this stand won the Spartans general sympathy;[7] but they were not in a position to back it with active help for the Athenians' allies. Potidaea was not relieved and the Mytileneans, in the speech reported by Thucydides, appear mistrustful of the Spartans' will as much as of their ability to help, justifying at length their decision to secede from the Athenians.[8] The failure of Alcidas to reach Mytilene and the treatment meted out by him and other Spartans to non-Athenians they met in the Aegean,[9] and perhaps the execution of the Plataeans, must have harmed the Spartans' reputation as liberators, but the successes of Brasidas and the guarantee of autonomy which he

---

[1] Thuc. i. 109. 3. [2] Thuc. i. 114. 2–3. [3] Cf. above, p. 2, n. 1.
[4] The Corinthian story in Thuc. i. 40. 5.
[5] Thuc. i. 139. 1. [6] Thuc. i. 139. 3.
[7] Thuc. ii. 8. 4; criticism by G. de Ste Croix, 'The Character of the Athenian Empire', *Historia*, iii (1954–5), 1 ff.
[8] Thuc. iii. 9 ff. [9] Thuc. iii. 32. 2, cf. ii. 67. 4.

brought with him and to which he adhered seem to have done much to restore it.[1] Even so, before he ever started for Chalcidice, the Spartans had been willing, after their initial defeat at Pylos, to make peace with the Athenian empire untouched,[2] and in the Peace of Nicias, though they were able to obtain guarantees for six cities which he had won over, they agreed to hand back to the Athenians one other, Amphipolis, and there was no concession to the main body of the allies.[3] Subsequently the Melians were left to be conquered and help for the Syracusans, though in the end effective, was minimal and late.

None the less, in 412 the enemies of the Athenians in the Aegean still looked primarily to the Spartans to help them to grasp the opportunity of Athenian weakness and their response this time was eager, though unskilful. But they were quickly compelled again to compromise their position by purchasing Persian assistance with a recognition of the King's sovereignty over the Asiatic Greeks.[4] This surrender, and their dependence on the Persians, worried the conscience of some Spartans even as late as 406,[5] and after their principal benefactor, Cyrus, with their discreet support, had tried and failed to take the Persian throne, they were able in 399 honourably to defend the Asiatic Greeks against Artaxerxes.[6]

But, though Agesilaus took over the war with the Persians in 395 in something of a crusading spirit[7] and rejected compromises which would have left the Asiatic Greeks in some degree of subservience,[8] the past conduct of the Spartans suggested that they might easily change their policy towards the Persians. Meanwhile in the Aegean their treatment of the former allies of the Athenians did not in general confer on them the sort of freedom they had expected—the imposition of harmosts and decarchies was widespread and disliked[9]—and they were in fact to lose their power in the Aegean at the beginning of the Corinthian War. Even so, much of the tyranny could be blamed on Lysander and, once he had gone, a different situation, in

---

[1] Esp. Thuc. iv. 81.   [2] Thuc. iv. 16 ff.   [3] Thuc. v. 18. 5.
[4] Thuc. viii. 58, superseding earlier drafts (viii. 18 and 37).
[5] Xen. *Hell.* i. vi. 7.   [6] Ibid. iii. i. 3 ff.
[7] Ibid. iii. iv. 3-4.   [8] Ibid. iii. iv. 5, 11 and 25 ff.
[9] Diod. xiv. 10. 1-2; cf. H. W. Parke, 'The Development of the Second Spartan Empire', *J.H.S.* l (1930), 37 ff., esp. 50 ff., and M. Cary, *C.A.H.* vol. vi (Cambridge, 1927), pp. 27 ff.

which circumstances did not make it inevitable that Athenian or other control be replaced by Spartan, could still make effective in this area a Spartan stand on behalf of freedom and autonomy.[1]

In one of the principal fields of their foreign policy, then, their rivalry with the Athenians, the Spartans had come to use the defence of small-state freedom and autonomy as a diplomatic weapon, both to enhance their own prestige, in the eyes of gods as well as of men, and to win actual concessions from the Athenians in peace treaties.

As to their relations with the other Peloponnesian states, the Spartans claimed that their allies, unlike those of the Athenians, were autonomous and for the most part those that spoke for the allied states would have agreed with them. They could, and did at times, disagree with Spartan policy towards the Athenians and they did not thereby provoke repressive measures. But the Spartans did also exploit the autonomy principle in their relations with these states, to weaken both their potential enemies, the Argives, and also some of their stronger allies.

They had probably, for instance, for long afforded to the Myceneans and Tirynthians protection against the Argives, and this had helped them to remain independent. Certainly in the Persian Wars these cities sent contingents to the Peloponnesian armies,[2] while the Argives were suspected of medism and sent nothing; and afterwards the absorption of these two states by the Argives is probably to be connected with the troubled position of the Spartans in the decade after 470.[3]

It is also generally assumed that the Spartans would have prevented, if they could, the synoecism of Elis which took place at about this time,[4] though many years before they had helped the Eleans to extend their territories to the south and east.[5] The Spartans were probably also anxious to prevent further centralization of the Arcadian communities; another episode in

---

[1] While Lysander was still alive, the decarchies were removed and replaced with 'ancestral constitutions', a reform which Lysander regarded as a rebuff to himself (cf. Xen. *Hell.* III. iv. 2).

[2] Hdt. vii. 202, ix. 28. 4, and Tod 19, vv. 17, 20.

[3] Diod. xi. 65 (Mycenae), Paus. v. 23. 3 (both).

[4] Diod. xi. 54. 1; cf. Gomme, i. 427, and W. G. Forrest, 'Themistocles and Argos', *C.Q.* N.S. x (1960), 229 ff.

[5] After the second Messenian War—Strabo viii. 3. 30 (355 and 358).

the post-Persian Wars crisis was the battle of Dipaea fought against 'all the Arcadians except the Mantineans', and it is fair to assume that the Spartans were faced with an incipient confederation of this group of their northern neighbours, actively hostile to themselves.[1]

Another attempt to combine some of the Arcadian communities, this time with the Mantineans, caused the Spartans serious anxiety at the time of the Peace of Nicias; here the Spartans, it seems, countered with the demand that one group affected, the Parrhasioi, should be left autonomous and then took the field to secure their independence.[2] At this same time they were having trouble with the Eleans, who had absorbed Lepreum during the Archidamian War and had refused to take the oaths to the Peace of Nicias; here again they based their action on the demand that the autonomy of Lepreum be respected.[3]

It is indicative of the importance attached by the Spartans to this method of weakening the other Peloponnesian states that the truce agreed between them and the Argives in the winter of 418/17 and quoted by Thucydides included a stipulation that 'the cities in the Peloponnese, both small and large, be autonomous in accordance with their ancestral traditions',[4] a stipulation that was repeated soon after in the draft alliance between the two cities.[5] As the Argives had been in alliance with both the Mantineans and the Eleans, this stipulation was of particular significance and showed Argive acceptance of the Spartan interpretation of the autonomy principle—in these two cases, that is, for it is surely not to be supposed that the restitution of Mycenae and Tiryns was contemplated. Though the accord between the Spartans and the Argives soon broke down and the Argives again became the allies of the Athenians, the Spartans were able to force the Mantineans to come to terms and to give up their hegemony of neighbouring communities.[6] As for their quarrel with the Eleans, they had secured the disputed territory of Lepreum and presumably they now readmitted the Eleans to their own alliance. In 399, though, they were apparently seeking a means of humbling them and demanded that they

---

[1] Hdt. ix. 35. 2 ; cf. H. B. Mattingly, 'The Date of Plato's Symposium', *Phronesis*, iii (1958), 31 ff., esp. 33, and W. P. Wallace, 'Kleomenes, Marathon, the Helots and Arcadia', *J.H.S.* lxxiv (1954), 32 ff.

[2] Thuc. v. 29. 1, 33 ; cf. Mattingly, art. cit., 34 ff.   [3] Thuc. v. 31.

[4] Thuc. v. 77. 5.   [5] Thuc. v. 79. 1.   [6] Thuc. v. 81. 1.

should leave autonomous not only Lepreum but the other border communities too; the Eleans refused, but after two years of warfare were forced to comply.[1]

The Spartans thus had constantly used the excuse of protecting the autonomy of the small Peloponnesian communities to limit the power of their larger allies and were still doing so within three years of the outbreak of the Corinthian War. It has indeed rightly been pointed out that the autonomy 'in accordance with ancestral traditions' which was hallowed in the treaties with the Argives is a concept to be closely linked with the principle of autonomy for all proposed by the Spartans in the Corinthian War; referring to the Spartans' terms in 391 Andocides speaks of the 'ancestral peace' being extended to all the Greeks.[2]

Whereas the Spartans applied the principle of autonomy in the Peloponnese to prevent confederations, they seemed to follow the opposite course in their relations with the Boeotians in the later fifth century, supporting the Thebans, who had been trying to establish a degree of control over the other cities at least since the end of the sixth century.

At an earlier stage, immediately after the Persian Wars, the Spartans had joined in the oath to protect the Plataeans against attack and had gone beyond the views of most other Greeks in proposing first the removal of the Thebans and other medizers from their lands to make room for the Greeks from Asia, and then their exclusion from the Delphian Amphictyony.[3] The increased power of the Athenians, though, made an association with the Thebans, who were bitter enemies of the Athenians, a useful counter-measure and the Spartans' intervention in central Greece in 457, whatever its original purpose, probably had the effect of strengthening Theban control of Boeotia,[4] though this effect was cancelled out within three months by the Athenian victory at Oenophyta. Ten years later the Spartans took no part apparently in the expulsion of the Athenians, a movement carried out not in Thebes but in western Boeotia,

---

[1] Xen. *Hell.* iii. ii. 21–31.

[2] Andoc. iii. 27 linked with Thuc. v. 77. 5 and 79. 1 by S. Payrau, 'Sur un passage d'Andocide', *Rev. d'étud. anc.* lxiii (1961), 15 ff.

[3] Hdt. ix. 106, Plut. *Them.* 20.

[4] Diod. xi. 81; Thuc. i. 107 is silent on this point.

and one which perhaps brought the Orchomenians temporarily to the front in Boeotian affairs.[1]

In the early years of the Peloponnesian War the Spartans helped the Thebans to capture Plataea and then condemned the prisoners to death; the Thebans in return rendered them good service at Megara and in the Delium campaign, but in doing so strengthened their own position in Boeotia and there may well have been an element of mistrust in the refusal of the Spartans to respect Theban wishes in the Peace of Nicias. Certainly the Thebans double-crossed them in the subsequent diplomatic exchanges, and no doubt fear of Theban ambitions was one of the reasons why the Spartans refused to destroy Athens in 404, as the Thebans and others demanded;[2] and subsequent Theban support of the Athenians exiled by the Thirty seemed to justify this fear.[3] Their support for the Thebans had been an expedient in the struggle with the Athenians; with that struggle now over and the Thebans causing disquiet, the resistance of other Boeotians to Theban supremacy afforded opportunities, which the policy of the Spartans in the Peloponnese suggested they were not likely to let slip.

The Spartans, then, in the last part of the fifth century had paid frequent lip-service to the principle of small-state autonomy, which they had exploited against their enemies both large and small; it remains to see how their enemies reacted to this Spartan propaganda and whether they were able to return the fire by exploiting the principle themselves.

The real character of the Athenian empire and the general opinion of it at Athens are controversial topics into which it would be unsuitable to enter at length here. Thucydides believed that the empire was a tyranny and that Athenian leaders, such as Pericles and Cleon, acknowledged it to be one;[4] but one modern school of thought believes that Thucydides' opinions, expressed in his own comments on events and in the speeches, can be refuted from the evidence of his own objective narrative, and that in fact, because the Athenians supported the

---

[1] Thuc. i. 113; cf. J. A. O. Larsen, 'Orchomenus and the Formation of the Boeotian Confederacy in 447 B.C.', *Class. Phil.* lv (1960), 9 ff.

[2] Xen. *Hell.* II. ii. 19 ff.

[3] Ibid. II. iv. 1–2, 30; cf. III. v. 5.

[4] Cf. esp. Thuc. ii. 63. 2 (Pericles), iii. 37. 2 (Cleon), and his own comments at ii. 8. 4 and viii. 2. 2.

democratic parties in the allied cities, their leadership was popular with the majority of the populations of those cities and was challenged only when minority pro-Spartan aristocratic groups held control.[1]

If this latter interpretation is correct, the Athenians could have argued either that their allies were autonomous or that, if they were not, they had willingly given up their autonomy and did not regret it. It does, however, seem an extreme view for several reasons. First, it takes too poor a view of Thucydides' judgement and honesty and is not in accord with the most cogent explanation of his method in composing the speeches, that he followed what to the best of his knowledge was actually said;[2] second, it neglects the likelihood that in many of the allied cities there was a considerable body of moderate opinion inclined to prefer independence to achieving party-political aims at the price of subservience to either Athens or Sparta;[3] third, because it is hard to see how the Athenians could have conceded autonomy to the Aeginetans in the Thirty-Years Peace, to the Chalcidian cities in the Peace of Nicias or to the Samians in 412, if they publicly asserted that their allies' autonomy had not been unjustly infringed. None the less, the majority of people in many of the allied cities had probably been satisfied with obtaining security from the Persians and from other local enemies at the price of the annual tribute and the loss of an independent foreign policy. Certainly both this security provided by Athenian leadership and the spread of democratic government were justifications of this empire which were put forward in the fourth century.[4]

It is, however, fair to say that there was opposition to Athenian supremacy in the allied cities in a quantity and of a nature to make it relevant to ask whether at any time of stress the Athenians, when under democratic government, made or contemplated making any large-scale concessions to the allies to confirm their loyalty. The oligarchic leaders of the 411 revolution certainly suggested and partly put into effect a plan to

---

[1] Expounded by G. de Ste Croix, art. cit., *Historia*, iii (1954–5), 1 ff., and by A. H. M. Jones, *Athenian Democracy*, ch. iii.

[2] Thuc. i. 22. 1 with Gomme's interpretation.

[3] On these two points, cf. D. W. Bradeen, 'The Popularity of the Athenian Empire', *Historia*, ix (1960), 257 ff.

[4] Cf. A. H. M. Jones, *Athenian Democracy*, p. 66, with references in n. 109.

remove the democratic governments of allied cities as well as of Athens itself, and its ostensible purpose was to prevent revolts;[1] its effect in Thasos, where Thucydides reports the sequel, was to open the way to pro-Spartan extremists[2] and the experiment died with the power of its instigators.

But, as to other times, there is no sign of any relaxation of control in the difficult periods of the Archidamian War, except perhaps, as has been seen, some small concessions to the Mytileneans,[3] and the general picture is one of higher tribute and tighter regulations (with some lowering of the tribute after the Peace of Nicias).[4] In the crisis of 413–412 there was the grant of autonomy to the Samians already noticed,[5] but this appears to have been exceptional. After the expulsion of the oligarchs there may have been a policy of giving favourable terms to cities re-entering the alliance, but Selymbria is the only case to afford evidence of it;[6] the tribute had been replaced in 413 by the 5-per-cent. tax on trade, a measure, it seems, born of financial stringency rather than of liberalization,[7] but it was restored in 410.[8] In general it seems likely that within the limitations imposed by enemy action the Athenians for the most part exercised as rigid a control over their allies in the last few years of their empire as at any time before.

There are some signs that the Athenians, like the Spartans, invoked the autonomy principle to weaken their stronger allies by protecting smaller communities against absorption. It is reasonable to suppose that any larger city attempting to incorporate a smaller which had been separately enrolled in the alliance and was separately assessed for tribute would have met with the opposition of the Athenians, who could invoke their treaty obligations to the smaller.

There is no clear example of this sort. The movement of union in 432 between Olynthus and some small neighbouring

---

[1] Thuc. viii. 48. 5.   [2] Thuc. viii. 64.   [3] Above, p. 9, n. 5.

[4] Cf. the reassessments of 428 (the lost A8, see *A.T.L.* i. 197), of 425/4 (A9 = Tod 66 = *S.E.G.* x. 75, cf. *A.T.L.* iii. 345, and Gomme, vol. iii (Oxford, 1956), pp. 500 ff.) and of 421/20 (the fragmentary A10, see *A.T.L.* iii. 347–53); stricter collection of tribute is provided for in A9 and in *IG* I² 65 (= D8 in *A.T.L.* i. 166). Some would also put the Coinage Decree in the late 420's—e.g. Tod 67 commentary and H. B. Mattingly, 'The Athenian Coinage Decree', *Historia*, x (1961), 148 ff.

[5] Above, p. 9, with n. 3.   [6] Above, p. 9, with n. 1.

[7] Thuc. vii. 28. 4, who gives the motive.   [8] *A.T.L.* i, list no. 46 and A13.

towns, which had been separately assessed in recent years, though not always, was in any case not the cause of Athenian hostility, but the first stage of a revolt anticipating Athenian repressive measures.[1] Here, though Thucydides called the new state the Chalcidians, the Athenians refused to recognize it as anything more than the city of the Olynthians;[2] and the special provision in the Peace of Nicias for the integrity of Mecyberna, Sane and Singus was probably directed against the Olynthians' centralizing policy.[3]

In 428 a report that the Mytileneans were planning a synoecism of the Lesbian cities, brought to them by some Methymneans who were not in favour of it, was one of the things that made the Athenians force the showdown which led to the Mytilenean revolt; and the abandonment of the synoecism was one of the demands rejected by the Mytileneans.[4] The Lesbian cities still contributed ships and had never paid tribute at all, but they had been assessed and, presumably, assessed separately. The cities continued their separate existence after the end of the revolt; further, the Mytileneans were deprived of their settlements on the Asiatic mainland, which were thereafter assessed separately for tribute.[5]

There are other examples of the separate assessment of communities previously assessed together—the process known as *apotaxis*—beginning with the Chersonese in 447/6, but there is no accompanying literary evidence in these cases to show that the various parts were separated politically from the centre, and the changes were probably intended chiefly to increase revenue.[6]

Outside their Aegean empire the Athenians certainly justified their intervention in Sicily in 427 by the pretext of protecting the Leontinians, as allies and fellow Ionians, against the Syracusans, though, according to Thucydides, many of them even then had wider ambitions;[7] and one of the professed objects of the great expedition of 415 was to restore their city to

---

[1] Thuc. i. 58; for the assessment records, see Gomme, i. 203 ff.

[2] For details, see Gomme, i. 204 ff.

[3] Thuc. v. 18. 6; cf. Gomme, i. 206, n. 1.   [4] Thuc. iii. 2. 3, 3. 1.

[5] Thuc. iii. 50. 3; assessed as Ἀκταῖαι πόλεις in A9 and A10.

[6] *A.T.L.* iii. 59 (Chersonese), 195–6 (on *apotaxis* generally).

[7] Thuc. iii. 86; cf. H. D. Westlake, 'Athenian Aims in Sicily, 427–424 B.C.', *Historia*, ix (1960), 327 ff.

the now dispossessed Leontinians.[1] In the funeral oration in Plato's *Menexenus* (published soon after the King's Peace) the Athenians are said to have fought in Sicily for the freedom of Leontini;[2] they are said too to have fought at Oenophyta for the freedom of the Boeotians.[3] Athenian backing for the Plataeans is well attested, and there is some reason to believe also that, just as the Spartans probably favoured Theban supremacy in Boeotia at this stage, the Athenian victory in 457 made all the other cities independent of Thebes,[4] though the democratic governments which they supported were failures[5] and the movement against the Athenians in 447 was conducted in the cities of western Boeotia and not in Thebes.

There is also some evidence that the Athenians were aware of the possibilities of turning against the Spartans their own criticisms of empire. In his last speech before the outbreak of the Peloponnesian War Pericles, as reported by Thucydides, told the Athenian people to reply to the final Spartan demand: 'We shall leave the cities autonomous if they were when we made the treaty' (i.e. they are no less autonomous now than they were in 445) 'and when they (the Spartans) too allow their own cities to be autonomous not in the way that suits themselves, but according as each one wishes.'[6] At this late stage Pericles was seeking only to score a debating-point and in fact some of the Spartans' allies were noticeably more eager for war than they were themselves. But in 421 it was one of the merits of Nicias' policy of making peace and alliance with the Spartans that it almost persuaded some of the leading Peloponnesian allies that their lot was as bad as that of the Aegean cities. It is even possible that, when the Argives, prompted by the Corinthians, called for allies to join a third force outside both Athens and Sparta, the new alliance was proclaimed to be the right alignment for truly independent states; its first adherents were the Eleans and the Mantineans, current victims of the Spartans' autonomy policy, who may well have countered diplomatically with their own interpretation of autonomy.[7] In 399 the Eleans, according to Pausanias,[8] answered the Spartans' demand that

---

[1] Thuc. vi. 8. 2.   [2] *Menex.* 242E.   [3] Ibid. 242A.
[4] Diod. xi. 81 ; cf. Gomme, i. 317–18.
[5] Ps.-Xen., *Ath. Pol.*, iii. 10–11.   [6] Thuc. i. 144. 2.
[7] Thuc. v. 27 ff., and esp. the invitation to any *autonomous* city in 27. 2.
[8] Paus. iii. 8. 2.

they should leave their border districts autonomous by telling them in turn to free their *perioeci*; a truculent gesture, significant of future events, for after the Athenians had purged themselves and through the Second Confederacy become the protectors of freedom, there was a brief moment in 371–370 when the Peloponnesian states were convinced that the Athenians and no longer the Spartans could best protect their interests.[1]

This examination of the few cases in which small cities received guarantees of autonomy by treaty and of the extent to which the two leading states protected or professed to protect their freedom shows that few of them obtained solid benefits, and that what they did receive was entirely subject to the whims of one or both of the leading states.

The advantages of a guarantee were further decreased by the fact that autonomy was very hard to define. Basically an autonomous city was one where the people were governed according to their own laws and not according to any dictated from elsewhere. The most obvious way in which such dictation could occur was as the result of successful armed attack. So the Greeks guaranteed to the Plataeans in 479 that no one should 'make an expedition against them unjustly or to enslave them' (i.e. even a just expedition should not go so far as enslavement);[2] and in the Peace of Nicias it was stated that the Athenians should not 'bear arms with evil intent' against the six Chalcidian cities, provided that they paid the stipulated tribute.[3]

But this simple undertaking did not go very far for the members of the organized alliance-systems that emerged in the fifth century. As far as we know, the Athenians used force against comparatively few of the allied cities, and in most cases after the state had already seceded; certainly many of those who thought that their cities had lost their autonomy had never seen the Athenian fleet approach in anger.

Of course the very act of joining a large-scale alliance meant the surrender of an independent foreign policy, especially where the alliance treaties were concluded for ever and there was no explicit right of secession. A system of consultation through a council of representatives existed both in the Peloponnesian League and in the Athenian alliance; and such a system, if it

---

[1] Below, Chapter IV, pp. 71 ff.   [2] Thuc. ii. 71. 2.
[3] Thuc. v. 18. 5.

worked, could give the individual city some say in the alliance's policy. But the practice of making decisions by majority vote greatly reduced its value to the protesting ally and it is pretty clear that the council of allies in the Athenian alliance had ceased to have any significance some time before its meetings were no longer held.[1] Yet it remains probable that some of the tyrannical actions by which the Athenians seem to have imposed their own wishes on the allies were in fact approved by a majority of them—such as, for instance, the suppression of the Naxians, the removal of the treasury from Delos to Athens in 454, the tightening-up of tribute-collection in the early 440's (and the coinage decree, if it belongs there), the transfer of certain legal cases from the allied cities to Athens and even the decision to support Miletus against Samos in 441.[2]

Systems of consultation, then, were likely to be unreliable whenever one city had a great preponderance of power; but experience suggested perhaps to those in the smaller cities who cherished independence that undertakings not to take specified actions might prove to be a more effective reinforcement of a guarantee of autonomy extracted from a powerful ally. So, in the fourth-century Athenian confederacy organized in 378, the allies were to be free of tribute and from the imposition of foreign governors and garrisons, and the Athenians promised not to reintroduce the system of cleruchies, settlements of Athenian citizens on the land of allied cities.[3]

The payment of tribute by those allies who could not furnish ships and men had been part of the original organization of the Delian League,[4] and the assessment of each city's contribution had been generally approved;[5] subsequently additional cities had chosen to pay tribute rather than to continue to supply ships and men.[6] These changes, though, were a direct cause of weakening the power of the allies and strengthening that of the Athenians, and the payment of tribute became the most

---

[1] Cf. the Mytileneans' views in Thuc. iii. 10. 5.

[2] Plut. *Arist.* 25. 2 says that the Samians proposed the transfer of the treasury; Plut. *Cimon* 11. 1 speaks of the Athenians 'prosecuting and punishing' cities which fell down on their contributions of ships and men, a process which at this stage can only have been carried out before the Council of Allies. On the Samian Revolt, cf. Jones, *Athenian Democracy*, p. 69 with n. 127.

[3] *IG* ii². 43 = Tod 123, vv. 21 ff.　　　　　　　　[4] Thuc. i. 96. 1.

[5] Plut. *Arist.* 24. 1–2.　　　　　　　　Thuc. i. 99. 3; Plut. *Cimon* 11.

obvious and to some the most irksome feature of subservience; an impression heightened by the fact that the Athenians naturally took away the ships of cities with whom they had trouble, such as Naxos and Thasos. Thucydides at any rate believed the payment of tribute to be incompatible with autonomy, for he classifies the allies as either tribute-paying or autonomous,[1] and it may be supposed that this belief was widespread at the end of the century. It should be noted, though, that in the Peace of Nicias it was laid down that the six Chalcidian cities whose autonomy was guaranteed were to pay tribute to the Athenians on the original Aristidean scale[2] and that in 395 Tithraustes proposed to Agesilaus that the Greek cities in Asia should be autonomous, but should pay tribute at the old rate (i.e. at the rate fixed by Artaphernes after the Ionian Revolt).[3] These stipulations may perhaps be regarded as conscious exceptions to what was felt to be the rule or alternatively may reflect a 'compromise' view that payment of tribute at a fixed rate, freely agreed, was compatible with autonomy, but when the rate was arbitrarily raised by the collecting city (as the Athenians had certainly done in the Archidamian War)[4] it became an infringement of autonomy. It can at least be doubted whether before the Corinthian War a guarantee of autonomy could have been taken to include a guarantee against tribute where nothing was laid down about it.

The imposition of governors and garrisons upon individual cities does not seem to have been a widespread practice in the Athenian empire, though it may have increased in the closing stages of the Peloponnesian War and it became the chief feature of Spartan domination after it. Again the presence of governors and garrisons could on occasions be justified as being requested by the local government for security against internal disorder or external attack—as were probably the earliest Athenian examples, those at Erythrae and Miletus in the 450's and at Samos in 441/40;[5] and certainly the Spartan garrison in Athens

---

[1] e.g. ii. 9. 4, vii. 57. 3–4.
[2] Thuc. v. 18. 5.
[3] Xen. *Hell.* iii. iv. 25.
[4] Above, p. 17, n. 4.
[5] For Erythrae and Miletus, cf. *A.T.L.* iii. 252 ff.; for Samos, Thuc. i. 115 (the oligarchic exiles fled to the mainland to fetch Persian help and did in fact return with overwhelming force).

in 404.[1] None the less the presence of a governor or garrison was an obvious symbol of foreign power and the general attitude to garrisons at the beginning of the fourth century is best illustrated from the promise made to the Aegean cities by Pharnabazus and Conon in the opening year of the Corinthian War that they would 'not fortify their citadels, but would leave them autonomous'.[2]

Garrisons were not only a symbol of subservience, but they had to be fed. Though cleruchies represented a less obvious garrison, the price of their maintenance was much greater, for the Athenian settlers were normally established on land expropriated from local citizens. It is true that on some occasions at least the land used was that of exiled oligarchic opponents of the new popular government[3] and that on others the establishment of the cleruchy was marked by a reduction of the annual tribute;[4] and so it is possible, or even likely, that the cleruchies were sent with the full agreement of the local pro-Athenian government. But the presence of foreign settlers on a city's lands was a ready grievance (not least to those who had hoped to profit from the sudden departure of land-owners) and, though nothing in the way of a formal definition is available, it was clearly widely believed that a city which had them had forfeited its independence.[5]

Apart from the direct affront which these three potentially tyrannical tools of leadership made to the spirit of independence, where it existed, they also afforded means by which the influence of the leading state might indirectly affect the internal political equilibrium in the smaller cities. The mere presence of governor and garrison or of cleruchs could obviously make a difference even if there was no positive interference. So Brasidas, in his speech at Acanthus,[6] seems to try to dispel the fear that, even

---

[1] Xen. *Hell.* II. iii. 13.

[2] Ibid. IV. viii. 1; cf. Tod 114 (of the year 387/6), where the Athenian people are said to have voted that the Clazomenians should be 'free, as the Athenians are, without paying tribute and without receiving a garrison or governor' (vv. 22–25: autonomy is not itself mentioned—the word used is ἐλευθέρους).

[3] Euboea—Plut. *Per.* 23. 4 with discussion by *A.T.L.* iii. 294 ff. (but note Gomme's dissent, i. 344 ff.); Lesbos—a reasonable inference from Thuc. iii. 50. 1–2, cf. Gomme's note.

[4] Andros, Naxos, Chersonese, Chalcis, Eretria—*A.T.L.* iii. 286 ff.

[5] Cf. fourth-century reactions in Isocr. iv. 107; Tod 123, vv. 25 ff.; Diod. xv. 23. 4.   [6] Thuc. iv. 86. 4 ff.

if he carried out the undertaking of the Spartan government to leave cities which he won over autonomous, his presence in the city and the force of his personality could tilt the balance in favour of the oligarchs—which is what seems to have happened shortly before at Megara.[1] The payment of tribute meanwhile bore more heavily on the wealthier citizens and so weakened them, while any failure or tardiness in paying gave the collectors an opportunity for interference.

Interference of some sort in the domestic politics of the allied city was undoubtedly a widely feared consequence of an alliance with a leading state; to show that it did occur in the Athenian empire there is no need to go so far as to believe that it was Athenian policy to set up democracies in all the allied cities, though some ancient commentators thought so.[2] Where they had trouble, the Athenians naturally tried to secure the future by strengthening the power of their friends.[3] Elsewhere there are no known cases of political interference for its own sake; but clearly the organization, and even the very existence, of the alliance favoured the popular parties, who could always exploit the threat of Athenian interference and who might expect to be supported in political law-suits submitted to Athenian courts.[4] The Athenians at least strongly encouraged the development of democratic governments, just as the Spartans strongly encouraged the maintenance of oligarchies in the Peloponnesian states.

So the charter of the second Athenian confederacy included the provision that the allies should have the constitutions of their choice,[5] and a similar provision had been added to the guarantee of autonomy given to the Selymbrians in 410.[6] The value of this definition of autonomy, though, remained doubtful, in so far as there might be various views on what constituted a city's choice and so more opportunities for interference from without.

---

[1] Thuc. iv. 74.

[2] e.g. Lysias ii. 56; Isocr. iv. 104–6; Aristotle, *Pol.* 1307^{b}22; the first two were *defending* the Athenians' record.

[3] Cf. *A.T.L.* iii. 149 ff., and Gomme, i. 380 ff.

[4] Cf. the comments of Ps.-Xen., *Ath. Pol.* i. 16.   [5] Tod 123, vv. 20–21.

[6] Tod 88, vv. 6–8.

II

The Corinthian War and the King's Peace

I. THE EARLY YEARS

THE Spartans had begun the Corinthian War with high hopes of success. They had readily seized upon the chance offered by an appeal from the Phocians of settling their account with the Thebans and may even have hoped to involve the Athenians and curb their growing independence.[1] But the absence of Agesilaus and his army in Asia, the speed with which the alliance of Thebans, Athenians, Corinthians and Argives was formed against them, and the strong reaction of the Persians to Agesilaus' successes—in first using their money to help build the Greek alliance and then bringing their fleet into the Aegean—speedily threw the Spartans back on to the defensive; and the defeat of their fleet at Cnidus and the military stalemate at the Isthmus meant that they now had to rely on their diplomatic skill in winning over Persians and Greeks to achieve any conclusion to the war commensurate with their original aims.

As far as their relations with the Persians were concerned, the most obvious move for the Spartans was some recognition of the King's sovereignty over the Greek cities in Asia; and, though it is possible that Agesilaus' campaigns in Asia had made him reluctant to approve such a move,[2] the history of the previous twenty years suggests that the Spartans in general were not likely to find it difficult. In Greece there were a number of factors which made a renewed application of the policy of defending small-state autonomy an attractive proposition. The Thebans' leadership in Boeotia was especially susceptible to this sort of attack; at the beginning of the war before his defeat and death at Haliartus, Lysander had detached from them the Orchomenians,[3] and later events were to show that

---

[1] Xen. *Hell.* III. v. 5, cf. Plut. *Lys.* 27; for the attitude to the Athenians, cf. E. Meyer, *Theopomps Hellenika* (Halle, 1909), p. 87.

[2] Cf. esp. Xen. *Ages.* i. 36 ff.; Plut. *Ages.* 15.   [3] Xen. *Hell.* III. v. 6.

there was enough opposition in the other cities for the Spartans to work on. In Corinth the anti-Spartan group had not easily triumphed; in 392 they not only had to conduct a massacre of their opponents, but also had to protect their position by seeking a union between their city and Argos, the first stage of which was carried out soon after the massacre.[1] This union was an obvious target for an autonomy policy.

In the Aegean too it might achieve some success. The conduct of the Spartans after the defeat of the Athenians had been unpopular, and there was little prospect of their ever recreating a naval empire; but something might be done to prevent the Athenians taking their place. After Cnidus the islanders had not fallen into the arms of Conon and Pharnabazus so easily as might have been expected, and they obtained promises that their autonomy would be respected and that their citadels would not be garrisoned;[2] the Spartans would have had enough general information of the mood of these islanders to be able to exploit any mistrust of Athenian ambitions. There were grounds for mistrust; for, though there is no evidence for putting the organization of a new Athenian alliance in the Aegean, with the reintroduction of the 5-per-cent. tax on trade, before the abortive peace negotiations of 392–391,[3] an Athenian, Conon, was at the head of the Persian fleet and was, by the end of 392, actively using it in the Athenian interest;[4] while at Athens, though there was condemnation of the fifth-century empire, the chief disposition was to defend the city's record and imperialism was by no means extinct.[5]

[1] Xen. *Hell.* IV. iv. 1 ff.; cf. G. T. Griffith, 'The Union of Corinth and Argos', *Historia*, ii (1950), 236 ff., and D. Kagan, 'Corinthian Politics and the Revolution of 392 B.C.', *Historia*, xi (1962), 447 ff.

[2] Xen. *Hell.* IV. viii. 1.

[3] The only inscription which throws light on Athenian relations with an island state previously under Spartan control (Tod 110, assigned by Tod to the years 394–390) shows the Athenians guaranteeing the autonomy of the smaller city in general terms (vv. 12–13).

[4] Xen. *Hell.* IV. viii. 9 ff.

[5] Three works published at Athens in the decade after the end of the Peloponnesian War discuss Athenian imperialism—Thucydides' *History*, Lysias xviii, and Isocrates xvi. Thucydides (the relevant parts of whose work may have been written years earlier) in general condemned not the Athenian empire itself, but its excesses and blunders; Lysias and Isocrates are concerned with the share of the blame for the Sicilian catastrophe due to Nicias and Alcibiades; neither regards imperialism as stupid in itself. On these works cf. P. Treves, 'Note sulla guerra corinzia' *Riv. di filol.* N.S. XV (1937), 113 ff.

On the other hand, the actual policy of those who were in effective power at Athens was moderate,[1] and may have suggested to the Spartans that peace-proposals which left the Athenians with their full independence and some honour, while they bore heavily on their mainland allies, might succeed in rekindling feelings of affinity that had on occasions glimmered in the fifth century, and so in detaching them from the coalition.

By 392, it can be said, the main lines to be followed by Spartan diplomacy must have been clear enough. There remained the problem how to pursue both at once without spoiling them: how to persuade the King that a recognition of his right to rule the Asiatic cities was of value when it came from a state that professed to defend the independence of small cities, and how to prevent the recognition of Persian claims from undoing any advantage derived from the stand on behalf of freedom. The solution was to persuade the Persians that the application of the autonomy principle in Greece would suit their interests and to secure a general Greek participation in the cession of the Asiatic cities.

II. THE CONFERENCE IN ASIA MINOR

The first of the peace conferences in the Corinthian War was in the spring of 392,[2] and the only account of it is that of Xenophon:[3]

The Spartans, hearing that Conon was rebuilding their fortifications for the Athenians out of the King's money and by maintaining his fleet from the King's resources was bringing the islands and the

---

[1] e.g. in the Demaenetus affair (*Ox. Hell.* i. 1–3), in officially refusing Timocrates' money (*Ox. Hell.* ii. 2; Xen. *Hell.* III. v. 1) and, perhaps, in offering to arbitrate between Spartans and Thebans (Paus. iii. 9. 11); on Athenian politics in this period, cf. P. Cloché, 'Notes sur la politique athénienne au début du IVme siècle', *Rev. d'étud. anc.* xliii (1941), 16 ff.

[2] On the chronology of the first part of the Corinthian War and the priority of this conference, see Appendix XII.

[3] It is not mentioned by Andocides in Or. III, where he reports on a conference held at Sparta which in turn is not mentioned by Xenophon. It will be seen in the next section that the terms proposed at these conferences, though similar, were different, and it is the general view that there were separate negotiations. Beloch, *Griechische Geschichte*, vol. iii (2nd ed., Strasbourg, 1922–3), ii. 220, and V. Martin, 'Le traitement de l'histoire diplomatique dans la tradition littéraire du IVme siècle', *Museum Helveticum*, i (1944), 13 ff., have suggested that one set of peace terms was proposed in Asia and (despite Xenophon) discussed at Sparta.

coastal cities over to the Athenians, thought that, if they explained these things to Tiribazus, the King's general, he would either come over to their side or at least stop maintaining Conon's fleet. With this intention they sent Antalcidas to Tiribazus with instructions to explain these things and to try to make peace between Sparta and the King. But when they heard of this, the Athenians in turn sent ambassadors . . . and they summoned ambassadors from the allies to come with them, and they came from the Boeotians, from Corinth and from Argos.[1]

It is clear thus far that the Spartans intended to enter into purely bilateral discussions with Tiribazus, but found themselves at an international conference which included their Greek enemies also.[2]

When they were there, Antalcidas told Tiribazus that he had come to seek peace for Sparta with the King and the sort of peace that the King had long wanted: the Spartans were not opposing the King's claim to the Greek cities in Asia and it would be enough for them if all the islands and the other cities should be autonomous. 'And yet', he said, 'if these are our wishes, why would the King make war or spend his money against us? For it is not possible for the Athenians to attack the King without our leadership or for us to do so, if the cities are autonomous.' Antalcidas' words were very pleasing to Tiribazus as he heard them. . . .[3]

Antalcidas proclaimed his mission, to seek peace between the King and the Spartans, but the actual terms he proposed were of a general nature and fully implemented would have brought a general pacification in Greece; they amounted in fact to the first proposal of a Common Peace agreement on the basis of autonomy for all.[4]

It is, though, not difficult to see why the Spartan proposals for a separate peace with the Persians should have been of general application, and concerned apparently with the organization of Greece rather than with the ending of the war.[5]

[1] *Hell.* iv. viii. 12–13.

[2] On the Spartans' intentions, cf. U. Wilcken, 'Über Entstehung und Zweck des Königsfriedens', *Abh. Berlin*, 1941, no. 15, p. 10.

[3] *Hell.* iv. viii. 14–15.

[4] Identified with Common Peace by F. Hampl, *Die griechischen Staatsverträge des 4 Jahrhunderts* (Leipzig, 1938), pp. 85 ff., and A. Heuss, 'Antigonos Monophthalmos und die griechischen Städte', *Hermes*, lxxiii (1938), 161.

[5] It was just this apparent contradiction that led Martin to believe that these terms were discussed at the Sparta conference.

The terms proposed, as Antalcidas said and Tiribazus evidently agreed, would have given the King what he wanted—control of the Greek cities in Asia and a guarantee, in the principle of autonomy, that no one city could dominate the Aegean, a point made by Antalcidas in the part of his argument quoted directly by Xenophon. The principle of autonomy would also suit Spartan interests in Greece. With Persian backing the Spartans would be strong enough to prevent the principle being applied to their own disadvantage in the Peloponnese and at the same time to apply it to the disadvantage of their enemies, all of whom were, as has been seen, open to this sort of pressure.

It was, in fact, the autonomy principle to which, according to Xenophon, the enemies of the Spartans would not agree. His narrative continues with a passage where the correct reading has been irretrievably lost, but which must have reported the displeasure of the Persians' allies with Antalcidas' suggestions, for he proceeds with an explanation of their stand:

> For the Athenians were afraid to agree that the islands should be autonomous, lest they should be deprived of Lemnos, Imbros and Scyros, and the Thebans, lest they should be compelled to leave the Boeotian cities autonomous, and the Argives did not think that they would be able to have Corinth as Argos, as they wanted, if such a treaty and agreement were concluded.[1]

In face of this declared opposition Tiribazus thought it unwise to take any overt action without the King's approval. He supplied Antalcidas with money, arrested Conon, and then went up to the King to seek guidance. The King's reply was to supersede him with Struthas, who, Xenophon says, remembered what Agesilaus had done in Asia Minor and supported the Athenians.[2] The King had evidently decided that at this stage it would be more dangerous to rebuild Spartan naval power than to leave the Athenians unmolested.

The King may indeed have had some misgivings about the restoration of Athenian influence in the Aegean, but things had not yet gone very far and the Athenian attitude to his claims in Asia Minor seems to have been respectful. Although the Athenians had probably not formally recognized the King's right to rule the Asiatic Greeks and may not have even formally

---

[1] *Hell*. iv. viii. 15. [2] Ibid. 16 ff.

allied themselves to the Persians,[1] there is no evidence to suggest that they had interfered on the mainland or that they organized the alliance of island and Asiatic cities[2] (Ephesus, Cnidus and Iasos included) known to us from coins, an alliance which seems to belong to the beginning of this war and to have been a product of the Persian campaign against the Spartans. The Athenians had once before liberated the Asiatic Greeks from the Persians, and were known to have special feelings of affinity with the Ionians; but, though they might be expected to have resisted a general recognition of the King's rights, such as Antalcidas proposed, there is nothing in Xenophon's account to suggest that they made an issue of it at the meeting with Tiribazus.

In spite of this silence it has been argued, on the strength of a passage in Plato's *Menexenus*, that the negotiations with Tiribazus broke down through an Athenian refusal to sign away the Asiatic Greeks and not primarily for the reasons given by Xenophon.[3] In that dialogue Socrates is made to report Aspasia as saying in her funeral oration that

The King wished to desert us (the Athenians); so he demanded the surrender of the Greeks on the mainland, whom the Spartans before had given over to him, as the price of his continuing his alliance with us and the other allies, thinking that we would refuse, and so he would have an excuse for deserting us. In the case of the other allies he was mistaken; for the Corinthians, Argives, Boeotians and other allies were willing to hand them over to him and made an agreement and swore that, if he would supply them with money, they would hand over the Greeks on the mainland. But we alone could not bring ourselves to hand them over or to swear to an agreement.[4]

The value of the *Menexenus* as an historical source is certainly questionable, but, if it is accepted that there must have been some factual basis for this account, it remains hard to believe that the Athenians and their allies could have had this difference of opinion openly before Tiribazus and Antalcidas, for neither seems to have tried to exploit it by seeking to divide the Greek

---

[1] As 'Aspasia' said in Plato, *Menex.* 245A.

[2] R. von Scala, *Die Staatsverträge des Altertums* (Leipzig, 1898), no. 105; B. V. Head, *Historia Nummorum* (2nd ed., Oxford, 1911, reprinted London, 1963), pp. 267, 573, 604, 616, 621, 638. Discussed by G. L. Cawkwell, 'The ΣYN Coins Again', *J.H.S.* lxxiii (1963), 152 ff. with references to earlier articles.

[3] By H. Bengtson, *Griechische Geschichte* (2nd ed., Munich, 1960), p. 261.

[4] 245 B.C.

allies, and the Athenian attitude, if thus made clear, would surely have alienated the King. This latter objection applies also to the alternative suggestion[1] that the refusal to surrender the Asiatic Greeks was expressed not at the negotiations in Asia, but by the people at Athens on their ambassadors' return, and that it is their refusal which is described by Philochorus, who says that in 392/1 the Athenians would not accept the peace which the King had sent down by Antalcidas, because it was written in it that the Greeks who dwelled in Asia should all be included together in the King's household.[2] Philochorus was almost certainly talking about the terms proposed by Antalcidas to Tiribazus, but his details are muddled; the King 'sent down' the peace terms subsequently in 387/6, but not in 392; and in any case the Athenian delegation had already rejected Antalcidas' terms at the meeting in Asia. It remains possible that there was a difference of opinion between the Athenians and their allies about the Asiatic cities, but that the delegations kept it quiet; they all regarded the Spartan interpretation of the autonomy principle as intolerable, and so by objecting to it let their opposition appear united.

III. THE CONFERENCE AT SPARTA

Within a few months of Antalcidas' failure in Asia there was another conference, this time at Sparta, to discuss an end to the war and a settlement of Greece. Chronological indications are too vague for it to be determined whether the Spartans offered new terms in the hope that what Tiribazus did for them before his replacement and their own capture of Lechaeum near Corinth had induced second thoughts in their enemies or whether they decided on a fresh approach after Struthas' arrival made it clear that the King for the moment was still against them.[3]

---

[1] By Wilcken, art. cit., *Abh. Berlin*, 1940, p. 11, followed by Bengtson, l.c.

[2] Ap. Didymus vii. 20; the passage goes on: 'and they also exiled the ambassadors who had agreed on the terms in Sparta'; and the whole is used by Martin (l.c. on p. 27, n. 3) to support his argument that a single set of terms was proposed in Asia and discussed at Sparta. But it is scarcely possible to argue from so brief a notice that Philochorus was not talking about two conferences.

[3] Cf. Appendix XII.

The terms proposed by the Spartans are known to us only from the speech which one of the Athenian ambassadors, Andocides, made to recommend them on his return home.[1] But, though Andocides spoke *ex parte* and displayed a distressing ignorance of fifth-century history, it is clear enough from what he said that the terms were certainly not the same as those proposed by Antalcidas in Asia.

There is, for instance, nothing in the speech to suggest that the Spartans proposed a formal surrender of the Asiatic Greeks to the King. Of course it is possible that Andocides kept silent on a subject that would certainly have aroused hostility. But at one point[2] he so emphasizes the military achievements of the Spartans that he seems to wish to represent them as capable of victory on land without Persian help; and, though he warned the Athenians against relying on Persian assistance without question or limit and against the risk of offending the King by a new imperialism,[3] he did not really try to put the fear of the King into their hearts. Even if Struthas had now taken over, Tiribazus' attitude would have been sufficient justification for such warnings.[4]

This time, moreover, the Athenians were to be allowed to retain Lemnos, Imbros and Scyros,[5] and the Thebans had apparently to recognize the autonomy, not of all the other Boeotian cities, but only of the Orchomenians (which, according to Andocides, they were prepared to do).[6] It is clear, though, that the autonomy principle was kept as the basis of the proposed settlement,[7] and its retention is of special significance, if the Persians did have no part in these negotiations. In the previous discussions the autonomy principle had been a shrewd proposal, which when applied would meet Persian fears of a strong Greek power in the Aegean, but which in its application would probably require Persian assistance against the opposition

---

[1] Or. III. [2] Cc. 18, 19. [3] C. 15.

[4] Apart from Martin, who believed that the terms given in Xenophon were discussed at Sparta, S. Accame, *Ricerche intorno alla guerra corinzia* (Turin, 1951), pp. 111 ff. (who puts this conference second) and Wilcken, art. cit., *Abh. Berlin*, 1940, pp. 8 ff. (who puts it first), have thought that a recognition of Persian rights was included here. Against them, cf. A. Momigliano, 'Per la storia pubblicistica sulla κοινὴ εἰρήνη nel IV secolo a.C.', *Annali di Pisa*, II. v (1936), 106 ff., and R. E. Smith, 'The Opposition to Agesilaus' Foreign Policy', *Historia*, ii (1954), 278.

[5] Cc. 12, 14. [6] Cc. 13, 20. [7] Cc. 14, 19.

of the Spartans' enemies; now, when, it seems, Persian interests were not in question, the Spartans kept the principle, though it had already been once rejected by their enemies. They were prepared to make concessions on details to the Athenians and to the Thebans, but were evidently convinced that the autonomy principle served their own best interests in Greece. Their championship of it could well have already won them fresh support in areas threatened by Theban or Athenian expansion, and its establishment would curb the extension of Athenian power in the Aegean and perhaps provide an excuse for further pressure upon the Thebans, once the Orchomenians were securely independent.

It is just possible that the Spartans hoped to use the autonomy principle to bring some marginal pressure on their enemies from within their cities by evoking panhellenic or pacifist idealism. Andocides did make the points that a just peace was better than war,[1] that it was not right to continue a war after victory to destroy an enemy[2] and that the proposed peace would bring peace and freedom common to all Greeks;[3] it was here that he used the phrase 'common peace', though it is not likely that it had yet become a technical term for a general treaty based on the principle of autonomy.

But Andocides' chief purpose was to show to the Athenians that to continue the war was inexpedient and most of his arguments were addressed to those who would judge every situation on its merits; and it is a fair inference that the Spartan proposals were rejected not simply because they had a poor advocate—Andocides was probably a supporter of oligarchy, almost certainly a sympathizer of the Spartans—though he was later exiled for his pains,[4] but because the Athenians believed it worth while to prolong the war and to avoid a settlement which might tie their hands in the Aegean. They and their allies indeed continued to hold the Spartan land-forces at the Isthmus, while at sea they gradually extended their influence without serious Spartan opposition or any immediate sign of Persian reaction.

[1] C. 1. [2] Cc. 15–16. [3] C. 17, cf. c. 34.
[4] Philoch. ap. Didym. vii. 20.

IV. THE KING'S PEACE

In the next two years the new Athenian alliance in the Aegean began to assume some resemblance to the fifth-century empire. The 5-per-cent. tax on trade, which had temporarily replaced the tribute in 413, was revived,[1] and Athenian fleets began to roam the seas interfering in the internal affairs of island cities.[2] This activity, exaggerated no doubt by oligarchic exiles, must in any case have alarmed the Persian authorities, but the Athenians went further and opposed Persian interests in Cyprus and, probably, in Clazomenae. In Cyprus, the king Evagoras rebelled against his overlord, the Great King, in 390. He was an old friend of Athens, and at once the Athenians sent out a squadron of ten ships to help him; this squadron was intercepted by the Spartan admiral Teleutias and there were no damaging consequences.[3] Early in 387 another Athenian force sailed for Cyprus,[4] and at the same time the Athenians were interfering in Clazomenae, part of whose lands were on the Asiatic mainland, though they were perhaps careful to recognize the King's predominance (and indeed gave firm guarantees to the Clazomenians themselves that they would not exact tribute—only the 5-per-cent. tax—or install a governor and garrison).[5] Whatever the truth of this incident, Clazomenae was linked with Cyprus in the terms of the subsequent King's Peace[6] and the specific inclusion there of these two areas among his possessions shows how seriously the King regarded the Athenian action. It was primarily to protect his own interests that he now changed over to the Spartan side and started the train of events which culminated in the conclusion of the King's Peace.

The Spartans had apparently continued their diplomatic pressure on the Persians, for now, Xenophon says, 'Antalcidas

---

[1] Diod. xiv. 94. 2; Tod 114, v. 8.

[2] Xen. *Hell.* IV. viii. 25 ff.; though cf. Tod 114 (below, n. 5) for readiness to give guarantees of non-interference.

[3] Diod. xiv. 98; Xen. *Hell.* IV. viii. 24.   [4] Xen. *Hell.* v. i. 10 ff.

[5] Tod 114 concerns a settlement with the Clazomenians, firmly dated in 387/386; for the 5-per-cent. tax, cf. vv. 7–8; for the guarantees, cf. vv. 22–25; the Clazomenians are to have a free hand with settlers at Chytum on the mainland (vv. 8–13); there may be a reference to the King's rights in v. 26, where Tod accepts Wilhelm's restoration . . . κύριον εἶ]ναι βα[σιλέα. . . .

[6] Xen. *Hell.* v. i. 31.

came down with Tiribazus' (significantly restored to authority at Sardis) 'having brought it about that the King would fight along with the Spartans, if the Athenians and their allies were not willing to accept the peace in the way he said.'[1] Antalcidas had evidently secured the King's agreement to the terms on which he would, if necessary, support the Spartans to produce a peace in Greece. These terms, as subsequently made known, differed in details from those offered by Antalcidas to Tiribazus in 392. The King was to have the Greek cities in Asia (to which Cyprus and Clazomenae were added), and the other Greek cities were to be autonomous, though Lemnos, Imbros and Scyros were now to remain in Athenian possession; and the King now backed his terms with a threat to use force against anyone who did not accept them.[2] This threat showed the change in the King's position: by approving these terms he committed himself to precisely such action in support of the Spartans as he had been unwilling to take, when he was informed of Antalcidas' proposals in 392.

Though armed with this threat, Tiribazus does not seem, from Xenophon's account, to have summoned the Greeks to hear the terms first, and then to have begun a campaign to speed their response; perhaps he wanted, as before, to be sure of damaging the Athenians in war. He at once helped Antalcidas to carry out a successful naval offensive in the Aegean, which set the Athenians in fear of another Aegospotami, and at the same time the Spartans prepared to invade the Argolid. At this point Tiribazus announced that those who wanted to hear the terms which the King had sent down should present themselves, and they all came 'swiftly'.[3]

The satrap now read out the terms. The Greek delegates must have then put them in the normal form of a treaty[4] and sent back some of their number to submit the proposed settlement to their several cities.[5] Representatives then assembled at Sparta, where Agesilaus, who had not apparently been concerned with the negotiations at Sardis, took over the administration of the peace and the application of its general terms to particular points of dispute in Greece. Here he was able to

---

[1] Xen. *Hell.* v. i. 25.   [2] Ibid. 31; cf. Diod. xiv. 110. 3.
[3] Xen. *Hell.* v. i. 30.
[4] Cf. Wilcken, art. cit., *Abh. Berlin*, 1940, pp. 15 ff.
[5] Xen. *Hell.* v. i. 32.

enforce the Spartan interpretation of the autonomy principle, that the Boeotian cities should be independent of Thebes, that Corinth should be separate from Argos, and that Athens' new hegemony in the Aegean should be dissolved. The Thebans claimed the right to take the oath to the Peace on behalf of the Boeotians, but succumbed to the threat of exclusion from the treaty and of imminent Spartan invasion; the anti-Spartan leaders in Corinth were likewise constrained to send the Argive garrison away, and themselves fled at the prospect of the return of their exiled enemies.[1] The Athenians, on the other hand, are not said to have offered any objection at this stage; they had suffered from the combined power of the Spartans and the Persians, and they had the consolation of retaining Lemnos, Imbros and Scyros as well as their rebuilt fortifications and their ships.

Agesilaus thus obtained the oaths of the leading Greek cities to the treaty, and the King, satisfied that he would not have to fight to impose his terms, also swore to observe them.[2] So the King's Peace evolved from the interaction, and ultimately from the reconciliation of Spartan and Persian interests, and was finally concluded and ratified. The account of this process has made it clear that this was not an agreement worked out by men who sought a settlement of the problems of inter-state relations in Greece and has explained the paradox that the first Common Peace, the first of the series of general peace treaties based on the principle of autonomy for all cities, should have been linked with a general recognition that one group of Greek cities, those in Asia, should be not free, but subject to the rule of the King of Persia.

NOTE ON PANHELLENISM AND PACIFISM IN THE FIRST YEARS OF THE FOURTH CENTURY

THERE is little doubt that at the beginning of the fourth century city-state patriotism and class interest were the chief factors affecting the

---

[1] Xen. *Hell.* v. i. 32–34.

[2] Cf. Wilcken, 'Philipp II von Makedonien und die panhellenische Idee', *Sitzb.* (*Berlin*), 1929, p. 293; Hampl, *Die griechischen Staatsverträge*, p. 12; and S. Accame, *La lega ateniense del sec. IV a.C.* (Rome, 1941), p. 2. Both in the alliance between Athens and Chios (Tod 118) and in Aristoteles' decree (Tod 123) the King is expressly stated to have sworn to the treaty. For a contrary view, see F. Nolte, *Die historisch-politischen Voraussetzungen des Königsfriedens* (Bamberg, 1923), p. 4.

opinions held on foreign policy by citizens of the Greek states. None the less, the feeling that the Greek peoples should be united and the desire for peace for its own sake were emotions which, though they could overlap with patriotism and class interest, could have had some special influence, especially where these more selfish interests were not directly involved.

It might be supposed that the attempts between 392 and 386 to reach a general peace settlement in Greece on the basis of autonomy for all would have commended themselves to those whose opinions were coloured by panhellenic sentiments. But since the Persian Wars the devotees of Greek unity had tended to see it taking the form of a common struggle against barbarian foes; and these attempts to conclude a general peace, so far from being the first steps in such a struggle, were associated with the surrender of the Asiatic Greeks to the Persians and the invocation of the Great King as the arbiter of Greek disputes. Moreover, the principle of autonomy now being consecrated was directly opposed to the sort of leadership demanded by a panhellenic war effort.

It was possible, it seems, for the feeling of kinship with fellow Greeks to take a less militant form, and so be more in accord with the idea of a general peace. Andocides, for instance, asserted as a generally accepted axiom that wars should be fought only when one is being wronged oneself or is helping those who are being wronged, and that they should be fought to victory and not to destruction,[1] and this sentiment would have made for compromise; though it would be dangerous to believe that the Spartans were moved chiefly by this sort of ideal in saving Athens from destruction in 404 and from severe defeat in 387.

There was not the same conflict between the idea of general peace with local autonomy and pacifism; and, if it were possible to prove that at the beginning of the fourth century more people than ever before were feeling that war was an evil and peace a boon for all Greeks and not just for themselves, this increasing sentiment could be said to have played some part in preparing the way for the King's Peace.

There is little doubt that the incentives to selfish pacifism—wealth, trade and war-weariness in its manifold forms—were growing more pressing on the Greeks in general, and they were probably at their strongest now after the toils of the Peloponnesian War, and before the use of mercenary armies became widespread. To this extent Greek states were less ready to use war involving themselves as an instrument

---

[1] Andoc. iii. 13 ff.; cf. Diod. xiii. 24. 3—speech of Nicolaus at Syracuse in 413, though its authenticity is doubtful.

of policy. But there is less certainty about the growth of pacifist idealism. The apparent development in the use of the word $\epsilon i \rho \dot{\eta} \nu \eta$, which has been discussed above,[1] should indicate a growing feeling that peace rather than war was the normal condition of Greek international life. Beyond that, it may be noteworthy that there are several examples from the forty years before the King's Peace of politicians commending peace as the best state of affairs;[2] and it would seem that praise of peace was now an acceptable sentiment likely to bring some advantage to the speaker. But whether it appealed to selfish or idealistic pacifism is another matter. Moreover, the absence of instances of this sentiment from an earlier period does not prove that it was not then voiced, as there is very little evidence of what politicians did say before the second half of the fifth century. Reviews which have been made of other literary references to peace are necessarily inconclusive.[3] There are certainly more pacific sentiments expressed in the plays of Euripides than, say, in the plays of Aeschylus, but this fact does not compel the conclusion that more people entertained pacifist feelings in Euripides' time than in Aeschylus', or even that Euripides himself was more pacifist than Aeschylus. Pindar may have deified Peace and made her the daughter of Right and the sister of Justice and Equity,[4] but in doing so he did nothing new, for Hesiod had done it long before.[5]

[1] Pp. xv, 5 ff.

[2] Thuc. ii. 61. 1 (Pericles), iv. 62. 2 (Hermocrates); Diod. xiii. 29. 4 (Gylippus) (?); Herodes, περὶ πολιτείας 11; Andoc. iii. 1.

[3] W. E. Caldwell, *Hellenic Conceptions of Peace* (New York, 1919); W. Nestlé, 'Der Friedensgedanke in der antiken Welt', *Philologus Suppl.* xxxi, no. 1 (1938).

[4] *Olympians*, xiii. 6 ff.

[5] *Theogony*, 901 ff.

III

The Period of Spartan Dominance and the Foundation of the Second Athenian Confederacy

THE King's Peace had been devised by the Spartans as an acceptable basis for Persian intervention, had been presented to the Greeks by the King of Persia and had been enforced by the Spartans, backed by the threat of Persian power. It was, then, naturally suited primarily to the interests of the Spartans and Persians, to whom the principle of city-state independence was a means rather than an end.

Apart from the circumstances of its establishment, the King's Peace, considered as an instrument for preserving peace and independence throughout Greece, had obvious deficiencies in its provisions. True, the principle of autonomy was for the first time stated and approved; but it at once raised three important questions: first, what did freedom and autonomy mean; second, how far were freedom and autonomy to be pressed, that is to what extent should existing states be dismembered in this cause; third, what would happen in the event of an alleged breach of the treaty.

As far as can be seen from scanty evidence, the Peace produced almost no answers to these questions. Though some of the properties of autonomy, such as freedom from foreign garrisons and from the obligation to pay tribute to another city, were coming to be accepted in current thinking, it seems that none was specified in the treaty.[1] On the second point, the Athenian possession of Lemnos, Imbros and Scyros, which had for long been inhabited almost entirely by Athenians, was a stated exception to the autonomy rule; otherwise it was laid down that cities should 'possess their own territory', but this additional general principle simply raised the further question, what was a city's own territory.[2]

---

[1] See Appendix I.
[2] For the existence of this clause, see Appendix I.

On the third point, a city which had bound itself by oath to a multilateral treaty of this kind was presumably under some sort of obligation to do something to uphold the peace in the case of any quarrel between any two other cities. Previous peace treaties had been only bilateral, and so any breach of the treaty had concerned all (that is, both) parties directly; an oath to uphold the treaty merely bound the swearers not to break it, and there were no tiresome third parties. But these new obligations, though no doubt felt to exist, were not defined in the King's Peace.[1]

This vagueness in the provisions for the future maintenance of the peace is, then, partly to be accounted for by its novelty; and so too the failure to define or delimit autonomy was perhaps due partly to inexperience. But both deficiencies were due much more to the fact that the treaty was not drafted by people who wanted to draft a permanent settlement of Greece; a fact which cannot be too often emphasized in an age when the organization of collective peace and security has been the object of much theorizing, and of not a little practical effort.

The King of Persia was not chiefly concerned with the maintenance of peace and justice in Greece. The Spartans hoped to derive further political profit from the autonomy clause, which they were in a position to exploit against their rivals, and they spent the next few years doing so. They did not require a rigid definition of autonomy in the treaty, which might prove embarrassing; it suited them better to be able to issue their own interpretation *ad hoc* for any particular occasion. This was what they did when dealing with the Thebans and the Corinthians in the application of the Peace, in which there was nothing stated about close federations or about these particular cases. Later they took action against the Olynthians' federation in the same way, when it suited them, though they ignored other

---

[1] It has been thought, on the strength of the King's threat in the rescript (Xen. *Hell.* v. i. 31) and of Isocrates' description of him as 'protector of the peace' (iv. 75), that the King was named in the treaty as its guarantor—cf. Scala, *Die Staatsverträge des Altertums*, no. 121; Nolte, *Die hist.-pol. Voraussetzungen des Königsfriedens*, pp. 13 ff.; and Momigliano, 'La κοινὴ εἰρήνη dal 386 al 338 a.C.', *Riv. di filol.* n.s. xii (1934), 483 ff. But the threat applied only to the initial conclusion of the treaty, not to the future, and Isocrates was speaking only in general terms; see below, p. 41, and cf. Hampl, *Die griechischen Staatsverträge*, p. 11; Accame, *La lega ateniense*, pp. 1–2; Heuss, art. cit., *Hermes*, lxxiii (1938), 163 note; and H. Berve, review of F. Taeger's '*Der Friede von 362/1*', *Gnomon*, ix (1933), 301.

federal states, such as that of the Achaeans,[1] which caused them no trouble.

Yet for all its deficiencies, there were solid gains in the King's Peace for those in the smaller cities who wished to be free of the leading powers. For the first time the autonomy of all cities, large and small, had been recognized in a treaty ratified by the leading states and by the King; and in most cases the independence now achieved was at least more genuine than that which the Spartans had brought to the cities of the Aegean in the Peloponnesian War. The newly formed Athenian alliance in the Aegean was broken up—those that remained allies of the Athenians had to make a positive choice to do so and were exceptional[2]—and the cities did not pass in turn under Spartan or Persian rule. It may be assumed too that, until the Spartan attack on Thebes in 382, the lesser Boeotian cities enjoyed some degree of independence from Spartan protection as well as from Theban leadership.[3]

These benefits, though, depended to a great extent on the goodwill of the Spartans and the Persians. In the absence of a Spartan fleet of any permanent consequence the island cities probably felt that they had most to fear from a recrudescence of Persian imperial ambitions; but such fears were later shown to have been groundless. Isocrates, attacking the King's Peace in the *Panegyricus* in 380, declared that it had put all Greece in the King's power;[4] but his support of the autonomy principle was not part of a plan to divide and conquer, but a means of preventing any Greek state becoming strong enough to dominate the Aegean. The King threatened to enforce his settlement in the first instance, but he did not guarantee it against any future breach of the peace, and he himself swore to observe it; he was interested in Greek disputes only in so far as they affected his position, and in the event his intervention in Greek affairs can be detected only once in the sixteen years down to 370.[5]

---

[1] On the federal state of the Achaeans cf. J. A. O. Larsen, 'The Early Achaean League', *Robinson Studies*, ii (1953), 809.

[2] Isocr. xiv. 28.

[3] On the position in Thebes and Boeotia at this time cf. P. Cloché, *Thèbes de Béotie* (Namur, 1952), pp. 112 ff.

[4] iv. 120–1.

[5] To promote the Peace of 375—Diod. xv. 38; cf. Appendix II.

Nevertheless the threat of Persian power remained a useful weapon for the Spartans and, while it was not used but was still threatening, one which the Spartans would more readily abuse in their own interests. The position of the Spartans was indeed a very powerful one. Militarily their supremacy was again unchallenged, and they had brought the Thebans to heel by the mere threat of invasion. Their prestige as champions of freedom had been greatly enhanced[1] and their interpretation of autonomy to the disadvantage of the Thebans, the Argives, the Corinthians and the Athenians was evidently widely accepted.

If the Spartans had rested content with these successes and had themselves respected the treaty by which the present situation was guaranteed, they might well have inaugurated a long period of peace in Greece under their own leadership. It seems from our scanty sources that at first opposition to the settlement was concerned chiefly with the surrender of the Asiatic Greeks. Diodorus says that the Athenians, the Thebans and certain others of the Greeks agreed to this surrender much against their will.[2] Xenophon has nothing to say on this subject, but two other works, Plato's *Menexenus* and Lysias' *Olympic Oration*, the latter hard to date and the former hard to evaluate as evidence, may perhaps shed some light on immediate reactions to the treaty.

The *Menexenus* belongs to some time within a year or two after the King's Peace, to which there seems to be a clear, though not explicit, reference in the historical survey.[3] The work consists largely of a funeral oration over Athenian war-dead, which 'Socrates' has heard from 'Aspasia'. The tenor of this oration is such that most of those who accept the work as Plato's regard it as satirical,[4] though the ancients without exception took it perfectly seriously.[5] It is illuminating to compare Plato's historical survey with that in Lysias' *Funeral*

---

[1] Cf. Xen. *Hell.* v. i. 36.

[2] Diod. xiv. 110. 4.

[3] 245E; the date is generally agreed, though for an earlier date cf. Treves, art. cit., *Riv. di filol.* N.S. xv (1937), 135 ff.

[4] Cf., for instance, M. Méridier, introduction in *Platon V* (Budé ed., Paris, 1931); G. Mathieu, 'Les premiers conflits entre Platon et Isocrate et la date de l'Euthydème', *Mélanges Glotz*, ii (1932), 555 ff.; A. E. Taylor, *Plato: the Man and his Work* (London, 1926), p. 43.

[5] See P. Huby, 'The Menexenus Reconsidered', *Phronesis*, ii (1957), 104 ff., for a review of the ancient references.

Oration, a genuine speech to be dated about 390.[1] There is considerable similarity of approach. Both writers deal in the same way with the Athenians' part in the Persian Wars, with the formation of their League, with the blessings brought by them to the cities of the Aegean, with the civil strife of 404, and with the generosity of the Athenians in joining their former enemies in the Corinthian War.[2] Where Plato is significantly different is in his emphasis on the care which the Athenians have shown for the freedom of the Greeks from one another: they fought at Tanagra for the freedom of the Boeotians, in Sicily for the freedom of Leontini.[3] These references to freedom have seemed to some critics too absurd to be taken seriously, and are one of the chief features regarded as caricature; but in fact Athenian leadership was seriously defended in this way.[4] Plato also attempts to show that in the recent war the Athenians did not co-operate with the King of Persia purely for their own interests and that they alone at one point (in 392) stood up for the freedom of the Asiatic Greeks;[5] again he seems to be putting the best possible interpretation on Athenian actions, though not an absurd one. These two special emphases suggest a reaction to the two parts of the King's Peace which was not ridiculous but rational, and which Plato either simply observed in the Athenian politicians and public[6] or wished to commend to his readers;[7] first, a realization that the autonomy principle had come to stay and that the Athenians should adjust their picture of themselves and their history to it, and second that there was need to clear the city's honour of any share in the disgrace of the betrayal of the Asiatic Greeks.

Lysias' *Olympic Oration*, of which a few chapters survive, is

---

[1] Cf. J. Walz, 'Der lysianische Epitaphios', *Philologus Suppl.* xxix. 4 (1936), 51 ff.

[2] Lysias, ii. 20–70; *Menex.* 239D–245A.   [3] 242A, 243A.

[4] Cf. Jones, *Athenian Democracy*, p. 66.   [5] 245.

[6] It has been suggested that Plato was simply indulging in 'fine writing' with no political purpose—cf. Grote, *Plato and the Other Companions of Socrates*, vol. iii (London, 1867), pp. 1 ff.; and Wilamowitz, *Platon*, vol. i (3rd ed., Berlin, 1929), pp. 265 ff.; and that he was campaigning for war-orphans—cf. Huby, art. cit., *Phronesis*, ii (1957), 112 ff.

[7] Taeger, *Der Friede von 362/1* (Stuttgart, 1930), pp. 13 ff., suggests a serious political purpose, to promote panhellenic ideas. C. H. Kahn, 'Plato's Funeral Oration: the Motive of the *Menexenus*', *Class. Phil.* lviii (1963), 220 ff., appeared since this passage was completed; its conclusion seems similar to Taeger's (which is not referred to), though argued in greater detail.

put by Diodorus at the festival of 388, but internal evidence suggests that it was delivered in 384.[1] The Olympic festival was naturally an occasion when the speaker would air acceptable panhellenic sentiments, and Gorgias is known to have done so at an earlier festival.[2] Whether he went beyond vague and general exhortations is not known, but the surviving chapters of Lysias' speech show that he made specific attacks on those who seemed to him to menace Greece, and that he suggested steps to be taken. The main weight of his assault fell on Dionysius of Syracuse, against whom his speech produced an angry demonstration;[3] but he also appealed to the Greeks to protect their kinsmen against barbarians, who, he said, controlled many cities.[4] Here he was surely referring to the Asiatic Greeks, for he went on to point out that the quarrels of the Greeks had benefited the King of Persia, who had become ruler of the seas, because he was the source of money.[5] Attacks on the King, then, and on those clauses of the Peace that gave him the Asiatic cities are acceptable at a panhellenic gathering; but not apparently attacks on the Spartans, for, while the Athenians are nowhere mentioned, the Spartans are censured only by an expression of surprise that, being rightly the leaders of the Greeks, they take no action against Dionysius or the King.[6] Yet Lysias, though a metic, was as loyal to the Athenian democracy as any man, and in his *Funeral Oration* had been most eloquent in its defence.

At this stage, then, in the late summer of 384 the Spartans' prestige as the champions of freedom was unimpaired and the deficiencies of the King's Peace remained for the moment obscured. The Spartans had probably already attacked Mantinea, and split the city up into its component villages.[7] By 380, though, when Isocrates published his *Panegyricus*,[8] this

[1] Diod. xiv. 109. 3; the date 384 was first proposed by Grote, who deploys the arguments at length (*History of Greece* (new ed., London, 1888), vol. iii, p. 72, n. 2—arguments from the history of the Greek homeland; vol. ix, p. 34, n. 1—arguments from the career of Dionysius).

[2] Cf. H. Diels—W. Kranz, *Fragmente der Vorsokratiker*, vol. ii (6th ed., Berlin, 1952), 82 A. 1 (4), p. 272 and 82 B. 7–8a, p. 287; the date is unknown.

[3] Ss. 3, 5, Dionysius' ὑπόθεσις and Diod. l.c.

[4] S. 3.   [5] S. 5.   [6] S. 7.

[7] 385 seems the best year for the war with Mantinea (cf. Underhill, *Xenophon Hellenica*, Introduction, pp. lviii ff.), though 384 cannot be altogether ruled out.

[8] The *Panegyricus* was almost certainly not delivered at an Olympic festival; but

action had become but the first episode in a series of aggressive moves; they had seized the Cadmea, the citadel of Thebes, by treachery in time of peace, had twice interfered in Phlius and were still besieging the city, and at the request of the Acanthians, Apollonians and Amyntas of Macedon had sent an army to the far north, had broken up the Olynthian League and were besieging Olynthus itself.

These events constituted a quite remarkable course of action for a state that had been traditionally conservative, and had so recently presented itself as the protector of small-state autonomy. Thucydides could say of the Spartans that they were never quick to go to war;[1] but the victory over the Athenians and the empire that it had brought them had done no more than whet the appetite of many for power and Diodorus' judgement that the Spartans were now by nature lovers of power and warlike in their decisions[2] is less unfair on this generation than on their forefathers. Yet, though the Spartans consistently pursued an aggressive policy and, as a result, in time forfeited their prestige as defenders of freedom, it is still relevant to inquire to what extent this policy was opposed at Sparta, and how far attempts were made to justify these various actions by representing them as carried out in the best interests of Greece as a whole and in support of the principles of the Peace.

Diodorus gives in general terms a picture of conflict between the two kings who reigned in the years immediately after the Peace. He observes that

Agesipolis was just and peaceful . . ., and said that they should abide by their oaths, and should not enslave the Greeks contrary to the common agreement. He argued that the Spartans would come into disrepute, if, having made over the Greeks in Asia to the Persians, they should themselves scheme against the cities in Greece, when they had sworn in the common agreement to preserve their autonomy. Agesilaus, on the other hand, was a lover of war and a man of action and aimed at a dominion over Greece.[3]

This picture of conflict, though no doubt oversimplified, is confirmed by Xenophon's comment on the reaction of Agesilaus to the news of Agesipolis' death in 380: 'when Agesilaus heard

the condition of Greece described in c. 126 obtained in 380—cf. chronological study of Underhill, l.c.

[1] Thuc. i. 118. 2.   [2] Diod. xv. 5. 1.   [3] Diod. xv. 19. 4.

this, he did not, as one might have expected, rejoice over the news as over the death of an adversary.'[1] The kings were apparently personal friends, and this fact suggests that Agesipolis' policy was inspired not entirely by jealousy or by mistrust of Agesilaus' ambitions, but in part, as Diodorus says, by a genuine belief that the Spartans should respect the peace terms.

Xenophon also says that Agesipolis was friendly towards the Spartans' allies,[2] and, although he was in command against the Mantineans and against the Olynthians,[3] there is no reason to connect him with the aggressive foreign policy of his city, and indeed it is possible that opposition on his part led to his military appointments; on the second occasion at any rate he was accompanied by a watchful commission of thirty Spartiates. It is noteworthy that, when the Mantineans surrendered, the terms were fixed not by Agesipolis, the general on the spot, but by 'the Spartans', that is the people, advised, no doubt, by the ephors, and that Agesipolis enabled the pro-Argive Mantineans to depart under safe-conduct.[4] On the first occasion that the Spartans interfered in Phlius the ephors were responsible;[5] on the second Agesipolis, who had recently commended the Phliasians for their loyalty,[6] was away in Chalcidice, and the ephors declared war with the approval of Agesilaus.[7] When the ambassadors of Acanthus and Apollonia sought help against the Olynthians, the Spartans in general, it is said, were eager to intervene, but nothing is known of the attitude of Agesipolis.[8] Finally, the case of the seizure of the Cadmea: Xenophon makes out that the *coup* was suggested in the first instance by the Theban Leontiades to the Spartan commander Phoebidas, and that the news of it caused surprise and indignation at Sparta, even among the ephors; but Agesilaus, with the aid of Leontiades, persuaded the Spartans to keep what they had gained.[9] According to Diodorus, the 'Spartan authorities' gave secret orders to Phoebidas to seize the Cadmea, if an opportunity occurred; the Spartans then actually fined Phoebidas, but kept the Cadmea.[10] Whatever the truth, both versions reveal more considerable opposition to the policy of aggression than on the

[1] Xen. *Hell*. v. iii. 20. [2] Ibid. 9. [3] Ibid. ii. 3, iii. 8.
[4] Ibid. ii. 5, 6. [5] Ibid. 8, 9. [6] Ibid. iii. 10.
[7] Ibid. 13; cf. Plut. *Ages*. 24. 2; Xen. *Ages*. ii. 21.
[8] Xen. *Hell*. v. ii. 20.
[9] Ibid. 25–35. [10] Diod. xv. 20.

other occasions considered, but here again Agesilaus and his associates carried their view.[1]

To turn to the pretexts for Spartan actions: Xenophon can find nothing better to say of the Spartans' motives in attacking the Mantineans than that they had decided to punish those of their allies who had been unfaithful in the war.[2] The Mantineans had certainly been unenthusiastic,[3] but it is hard to see how the Spartans could have justified by reference to the Peace the dismemberment of the city into the villages that had existed before the synoecism, unless perhaps they professed to be securing autonomy for these villages (which they did choose to treat as separate entities for the supply of troops to the Peloponnesian army), and their action was in any case inconsistent with their original demand that the Mantineans should simply dismantle their walls.

The Phliasians had also misbehaved in the war,[4] but the occasion for Spartan intervention was an appeal from some of their supporters who were now in exile;[5] these men may have suffered injustice, and it may have been possible for the Spartans to base their action on the Peace, though there was nothing explicitly stated in it about the internal stability of the autonomous cities. On the second occasion the former exiles again appealed for aid, and Agesilaus asserted that he had come to 'help those who had been wronged'.[6]

When the ambassadors of Acanthus and Apollonia came to the Spartans for help, they had a reasonable complaint in that the Olynthians were trying to coerce their cities into a league; and, according to Xenophon, they did appeal to the principle of autonomy, though they also tried to frighten the Spartans into war by exaggerating the power of the Olynthians, whom they alleged to be about to join with the Athenians and the Thebans.[7] The Spartans, for their part, were eager for war, but, as they submitted the decision to their allies,[8] it is likely that they professed to be defending freedom.

---

[1] On the differences between Agesilaus and Agesipolis at this time, esp. over Phlius and Olynthus, see Smith, art. cit., *Historia*, ii (1954), 279 ff.

[2] *Hell.* v. ii. 1.   [3] Cf. ibid. iv. v. 18.

[4] Cf. ibid. ii. 16, but note iv. 15 and vii. 3.

[5] Ibid. v. ii. 8.   [6] Ibid. v. iii. 10, 14.

[7] Autonomy—ibid. ii. 14, comparison with Boeotian cities—ibid. 16; Athenians and Thebans—ibid. 15.   [8] Ibid. 20.

According to Diodorus, the seizure of the Cadmea brought the Spartans into immediate disrepute in Greece.[1] They certainly made some attempt to justify their action. They arraigned Ismenias, the leader of the anti-Spartan politicians in Thebes, before a court on which all their allies were represented, and accused him of 'barbarism', collaboration with the Persians, and especially of having taken money from Timocrates in 395.[2] It is not known if they accused him specifically of intriguing with the Olynthians,[3] who had probably been branded as the enemies of the Peace and of autonomy, or of any fresh designs on the independence of the Boeotian cities, but they may well have claimed that their occupation of the Cadmea was necessary for the maintenance of the Peace, for they bade the Athenians not to receive Theban exiles, as they had been declared 'the common enemies of the allies'.[4] Ismenias was condemned and executed, but the Athenians gave refuge to the exiles.

Soon afterwards the Spartans refounded Plataea on territory which in 427 they themselves had given to the Thebans after Plataea had been captured; it was obviously open to them to plead that they were restoring the autonomy of Plataea (an argument later to rebound on them in the case of Messene) and there is some evidence that they did so.[5]

The Spartan leaders, then, made some attempt to justify their actions during the years 386–380 by reference to the terms of the King's Peace, but it is hard to see how they could have convinced an unprejudiced observer and they certainly went beyond what some of their own citizens thought proper. But, whatever their moral standing, their military supremacy was now even more secure and such that it could be shaken only if a rival power were able to supplant them effectively as the protectors of the peace.

The most obvious rival was Athens. The Athenians had been cowed by the naval campaign of 387 in which Tiribazus had

---

[1] Diod. xv. 20. 2. [2] Xen. *Hell.* v. ii. 35.
[3] He seems to have had a decree passed forbidding Thebans from joining the expedition against Olynthus—Xen. *Hell.* v. ii. 27. [4] Plut. *Pelop.* 6. 3.
[5] The refounding is not described by Xenophon, who brings the Plataeans and their city into his narrative without introduction at v. iv. 10; Pausanias (ix. 1. 4) shows that it was after the King's Peace, and it was more probably after the seizure of the Cadmea than before it. Isocrates' *Plataicus* (xiv) shows that the Plataeans thought themselves as much entitled to freedom and autonomy as any state.

joined with the Spartans, and seem not to have disputed the line taken by Agesilaus at Sparta in enforcing the King's Peace and to have acquiesced in the dissolution of their new alliance in the Aegean. They were allowed to retain Lemnos, Imbros and Scyros, and they were not deserted by (of their existing allies) the Chians, the Byzantines and the Mytileneans;[1] but it must have been clear enough to them that of all the Greeks they had most to fear from the King, for he in turn feared most any attempt to rebuild an empire in the Aegean. There was a danger too that the Spartans might feel inclined to try to re-establish the relationship between the Athenians and themselves which had existed before the Corinthian War, the rebuilding of the defences of Athens and the rebirth of the fleet. The official policy of the Athenians, therefore, continued for these next six years to be a correct attitude to the Peace. Though they were already in 386/385 seeking to extend their influence in areas where they thought that Persian or Spartan interests were not involved,[2] they were careful not to provide their late enemies with a *casus belli*. When they renewed their alliance with the Chians in 384, they anxiously affirmed that it in no way infringed the Peace or the interests of the King or of any of the Greeks.[3] They refused a request for help from the Mantineans 'preferring not to transgress the common treaty'[4] (by making war on the Spartans), and, if they did, as was alleged, conclude an alliance with the Olynthians, they did nothing to succour them.[5] Thus the existence of the Peace constituted an additional discouragement which prevented the Athenians from bringing succour to the victims of Spartan aggression; yet it also prevented them from taking precipitate action before they were prepared for war and, more important, enabled them to some extent to purge the stain of their former imperialism.

The Athenians' first known act of defiance against the Spartans was when they refused to close their frontier to the exiles from Thebes. This refusal may be taken as an indication of increasing Athenian determination to check the Spartans and of

---

[1] Isocr. xiv. 28.
[2] Honours were voted to Hebryzelmis, King of the Odrysian Thracians—cf. Tod 117, where v. 21 mentions Athenian ships.
[3] Tod 118, esp. vv. 8–24.   [4] Diod. xv. 5. 5.
[5] The allegation—Xen. *Hell.* v. ii. 15; Tod 119, which records such an alliance, might be dated here—cf. Tod's commentary.

growing confidence of doing so (even if at the same time pledges to the Olynthians were being ignored) and it can reasonably be said that in 380, when Isocrates published his *Panegyricus*, the problem of foreign policy most eagerly discussed at Athens was not whether Athenian primacy should be reasserted but how. It is as an answer to this second question that the *Panegyricus* should be regarded.

The *Panegyricus* purports to be what Lysias' *Olympic Oration* was, an address to the Greeks assembled at Olympia. It does, however, seem more likely, from what is known of Isocrates and from the style of the work, that it was a pamphlet written to be read; and further examination of both form and content gives the impression that it was intended to be read chiefly by the Athenians.[1] Its avowed purpose—and the theme of its opening and closing chapters—is still, like that of Lysias, to make the Greeks unite against the Persians, with the suggestion, moderate for an Athenian, that they should do so under the combined leadership of the Athenians and the Spartans. The argument is supported by a long defence of the Athenians' claim to leadership on the basis of past services and a condemnation of Spartan policy, especially since the King's Peace; and this defence of the Athenians and attack on the Spartans are so drawn out and strongly worded as to make one think that what Isocrates really wanted was the sole leadership of the Athenians, and not a combination with the Spartans at all, and that his subject was not so much the future of Greece as a whole as the future policy to be followed by the Athenians in their efforts to recover their former position.[2]

But, granted that the *Panegyricus* is addressed to a public naturally hostile to the Spartans, it is still of some value for assessing the standing of the Spartans among the other Greeks in general; for Isocrates' advice on future Athenian policy must have rested to some extent on his estimate of Greek opinion. His chief criticism of the King's Peace is of course directed at the surrender of the Asiatic Greeks to the Persians, and at the fact that the King was permitted to dictate terms to the Greeks of

[1] Cf. esp. H. Ll. Hudson-Williams, 'Isocrates and Recitations', *C.Q.* xlii (1949), 65 ff., and E. Buchner, *Der Panegyrikos des Isokrates* (Historia Einzelschriften ii, 1958).

[2] The difference between the opening and closing chapters and the rest of the work is well shown by Buchner, op. cit., pp. 1–10.

Europe;[1] and, it seems, he thought that the Athenians' best policy was to use feeling against the Persians and the suggestion of a panhellenic war as a means of extending their influence. But there is also, as has been said, outspoken criticism of the role of the Spartans, not only for their readiness to betray the cause of the Asiatic Greeks to Persia and to call in the King to redress the balance in the homeland, but also of their cynical exploitation of the principle of autonomy to extend their own power in Greece. 'So far are the cities from freedom and autonomy that some are under tyrants, some under harmosts, some destroyed, and some fallen to barbarians', he wrote,[2] and later listed the crimes of the Spartans against the Mantineans, the Thebans, the Olynthians and the Phliasians.[3]

In the event fear of the Spartans rather than of the Persians induced the cities of the Aegean to join the Athenians and the confedcracy which was founded three years later was directed specifically against Spartan encroachments on autonomy, while respecting the right of the King to rule the Asiatic Greeks. But this movement in favour of the Athenians came only after further demonstrations of Spartan aggressiveness, and, though there must have been some resentment against the Spartans for Isocrates to think of exploiting, the talk of a panhellenic war against the Persians which he and no doubt others indulged in was likely only to keep alive the widespread mistrust of Athenian ambitions. On the one hand, the Persians had not interfered in the homeland or in the Aegean since the King's Peace, and might seem to be a declining menace; on the other, a combined war fought in and to the east of the Aegean would bring with it the dangers not only of Persian counter-attack but also of Athenian leadership that might again prove too exacting.

At any rate, whatever the feeling about Spartan aggressiveness, in 380 there was no significant change in the relative positions of the Spartans and the Athenians. Olynthus and Phlius fell to the Spartans; and at this point both Xenophon and Diodorus summarized the situation, emphasizing the apparent security of the Spartans' supremacy. Xenophon observed significantly that the Athenians, the only city of any strength not yet subject to the Spartans, were deserted;[4] Diodorus that the Athenians were 'unpopular with the Greeks because of their

---

[1] Cf. esp. cc. 175–80.   [2] C. 117.   [3] C. 126.   [4] *Hell.* v. iii. 27.

policy of sending cleruchies to the lands which they subdued', a badly abbreviated version of what was perhaps in Ephorus an account of lingering memories of fifth-century imperialism.[1]

There are, however, some indications that the Spartans were becoming nervous about increasing hostility in Greece. Phlius and Olynthus were treated with comparative clemency. At Phlius Agesilaus decided that a committee of fifty pro-Spartan exiles and fifty of their opponents should settle the affairs of the city under the protection of a Spartan garrison;[2] however unfair to the Spartans' opponents this arrangement was in practice, it appeared more just than those made at Mantinea and Thebes. The Olynthians had already lost their confederacy before the Spartan advance; now they were compelled only to conclude an offensive and defensive alliance with the Spartans on much the same conditions as those the Athenians received in 404.[3] Agesilaus and the ephors seem to have agreed over the lenient treatment of the Phliasians, and so there is no reason to suppose that the king did not still control foreign policy or that these measures were not calculated moderation.[4]

But, though the Spartans seem to have felt the breeze of unpopularity, they appear, like Isocrates, to have thought that their bad reputation was due to a great extent to their co-operation with the Persians. When at about this time the Persian admiral Glos, who was in rebellion against the King, asked the Spartans for help, offering them money and assistance in Greece, they made an alliance with him.[5] They had refused a similar request from Evagoras of Cyprus a year or two earlier,[6] but now, according to Diodorus, they were glad of a chance to attack the King, because they were becoming unpopular in Greece for their surrender of the Asiatic Greeks;[7] certainly Glos' capacity to provide the financial and other help that he

---

[1] Diod. xv. 23. 4.

[2] Xen. *Hell.* v. iii. 21–25.

[3] Ibid. 26; cf. II. ii. 20.

[4] Cf. Smith, art. cit., *Historia*, ii (1954), 274 ff., whose silence on the settlements with Phlius and Olynthus (see p. 280) suggests that he does not connect them with the opposition.

[5] Diod. xv. 9. 3 ff.; for the date and for the veracity of this account, see Ryder, 'Spartan Relations with Persia after the King's Peace; a Strange Story in Diodorus 15. 9', *C.Q.* N.S. xiii (1963), 105 ff.

[6] Isocr. iv. 134–5; Theopompus frag. 101 (Oxford).

[7] On Spartan motives, cf. Ryder, art. cit., and Beloch, *Griechische Geschichte*, III. i. 99.

promised cannot have been taken very seriously. Glos and his successor in revolt, Tachos, soon died;[1] the alliance was never implemented and the Spartans withdrew from the affairs of Asia.

Almost at once the train of events which was to swing the balance of power against the Spartans began. In the late summer of 379 Theban exiles from Athens carried out a successful revolution in Thebes and forced the Spartan garrison to retire under a truce. The Spartans reacted strongly and, claiming no doubt that their supporters were the legal government of Thebes, at once sent an expedition into Boeotia, and, when this withdrew without achieving decisive success, they left garrisons in some of the cities of southern Boeotia.[2]

These garrisons stationed in cities whose autonomy the Spartans claimed to protect were, no doubt, excused with the plea of military necessity; if this plea was justified anywhere, it was so here, as later events were to show. But the garrisons none the less constituted a continuous threat to the Thebans, at least to the peaceful working of their land, and, as it turned out, to the Athenians also.

The Athenians had acted with caution throughout. A force under two of the Strategi had advanced to the border with the returning exiles, and on the day after the *coup* moved up to Thebes; but the Athenians did no fighting and even intervened to prevent some of the pro-Spartan Thebans from being killed.[3] The force then retired, and during the Spartan invasion Athenian troops watched from the frontier and did nothing.[4] The Thebans now asked for an alliance but were refused, and pro-Theban politicians were attacked in the courts; one of the two generals who had led the force to Thebes was executed and the other exiled.[5] The Spartans followed up this diplomatic victory by sending an embassy to Athens, but, while it was there, Sphodrias, who was in Boeotia as harmost of Thespiae, made a raid by night into Attica with the intention of seizing the Piraeus. Sphodrias was foiled by daylight, but his plan was sufficiently clear and the Athenians at once complained to the Spartan embassy; they denied their government's responsibility and promised that Sphodrias would be punished. But when his

[1] Diod. xv. 19. 1. [2] Xen. *Hell.* v. iv. 1–18. [3] Ibid. 10, 12.
[4] Ibid. 14. [5] Plut. *Pelop.* 14; Xen. *Hell.* v. iv. 19.

behaviour was investigated at Sparta, he was acquitted of all blame.[1]

Agesilaus was certainly the chief instrument of his acquittal, but he may not have prompted him in the first place, and even if he did, he would not have hesitated to abandon him after failure and to judge the case solely from his view of Sparta's best interests.[2] He evidently believed that this was a good time to fight Athens as well as Thebes,[3] for he must have realized that to acquit Sphodrias would drive the Athenians into war. In agreeing with his judgement the Spartans not only made a serious miscalculation of the military situation, but forfeited much of what remained of their prestige as protectors of the peace and of autonomy. The Athenians now declared the Peace broken and allied themselves to the Thebans;[4] and when they called on all those not under the rule of the King to help in making the Spartans leave the Greeks autonomous and in upholding the King's Peace, the response of the islanders was at once enthusiastic.[5]

[1] Xen. *Hell.* v. iv. 20–33; cf. Diod. xv. 29. 5–6; Plut. *Pelop.* 14. 2 ff.; and *Ages.* 24. 3 ff.

[2] No ancient authority gives the initiative to Agesilaus. Xenophon (*Hell.* v. iv. 20) and Plutarch (*Pelop.* 14. 3) make the Thebans approach Sphodrias, wishing to drive the Athenians into war; but Sphodrias had only to report the approach for the Spartan diplomatic pressure on the Athenians to be greatly strengthened. Diodorus (l.c.) says that the other king, Cleombrotus, inspired Sphodrias; certainly Xenophon gives a connexion between him and Sphodrias (ibid. 25). Smith, art. cit., *Historia*, ii (1954), 280 ff., points out that at least one of the Spartan embassy to Athens—Etymocles—was a supporter of Agesilaus and two of them went on the embassy in 370/369, and suggests that Agesilaus wanted an alliance with the Athenians, but Cleombrotus prompted Sphodrias to thwart him. But Agesilaus' subsequent conduct then becomes a mystery. A possible explanation is that no one inspired Sphodrias, but he fancied himself another Phoebidas (cf. Plut. *Ages.* l.c.).

[3] Cf. Lysander in 395 (above p. 25).

[4] Xen. *Hell.* v. iv. 34; Diod. xv. 29. 6, &c. Diodorus' report (xv. 28. 5) of an alliance between the Athenians and the Thebans concluded before Sphodrias' raid, which is accepted by Cloché, *Thèbes de Béotie*, pp. 117–23, and by A. P. Burnett, 'Thebes and the Expansion of the Second Athenian Confederacy', *Historia*, xi (1962), 2 ff., is probably due to the later myth that the Athenians liberated Thebes; at any rate it was not effective, for, though it followed the trial of the generals, it was itself followed by further negotiations between the Athenians and the Spartans and the Athenians were prepared at first to overlook Sphodrias' raid.

[5] The foundation of the Second Confederacy is a notorious omission in Xenophon's *Hellenica*. There is an account in Diod. xv. 28. 2–5, but the best evidence is found in the preserved decree of Aristoteles (Tod 123) and in other inscriptions recording individual alliances.

The Athenians' claim, which is found expressed by later writers and speakers,[1] to be the liberators of the Thebans and the defenders of Greek freedom was not wholly valid. The Athenians had sympathized with the Theban democrats, had sheltered them in exile, and had given them useful help in the revolution, but they had not dared openly to go to war with the Spartans, until appeasement could be of little further use; though they may have proposed to their existing allies the formation of some sort of confederacy before the Sphodrias incident, the confederacy was not actually formed until the summer of 378 and was not thrown open to all Greeks and barbarians, except those under the King, until February/March 377.[2] But in spite of their tardiness in taking action, the Athenians had strictly adhered to the Peace since 386 and the instantaneous success of their appeal testified to the respect in which their new role as protectors of freedom was held by the islanders. The latter were in no very serious danger of Spartan interference,[3] yet within a few years most of them had overcome their fears of Athenian imperialism. By 372 about seventy cities had joined the confederacy.[4]

The islanders wanted the King's Peace to be maintained as the basis of Greek international relations. That they were prepared to believe that the Athenians could be entrusted with its protection was due principally to the skill of Athenian diplomacy and the vigour of Athenian action, to the correct Athenian behaviour of the past nine years and to the stringent obligations which the Athenians laid on themselves to respect the autonomy of their allies and to eschew the policies that had turned the Delian League into an empire. Apart from special restrictions on the Athenians, designed mainly to prevent a repetition of the cleruchy system,[5] the charter of the confederacy contained a closer definition of the autonomy guaranteed by the Peace and

[1] Cf. Isocr. xiv. 6, 29; Dem. xvi. 14.

[2] Tod 123 is securely dated to this time; on the earlier moves, cf. Accame, *La lega ateniense*, pp. 27 ff.; F. H. Marshall, *The Second Athenian Confederacy* (Cambridge, 1905), pp. 14 ff.

[3] The Spartans controlled Olynthus and may also have occupied Sciathos and other islands thereabouts (cf. Diod. xv. 30. 5), perhaps in connexion with operations against Olynthus (cf. Smith, art. cit., *Historia*, ii (1954), 280 ff.).

[4] Diod. xv. 30. 2 gives this figure; cf. the incomplete list in Tod 123, vv. 79 ff.; Accame, *La lega ateniense*, pp. 70 ff., counts sixty-nine cities.

[5] Tod 123, vv. 25–46.

now reaffirmed. Any city which joined was to be 'free and autonomous and in possession of its own territory, governed according to the constitution of its choice, and free from the imposition of tribute or of a foreign governor or garrison.'[1] Primarily, no doubt, intended as safeguards against Athenian imperialism, these definitions were also to be regarded as supplementing the general guarantee of freedom and autonomy contained in the King's Peace, which the confederacy was set up to preserve; and so in a sense they were a condemnation of the Spartan interpretation of the Peace, for the Spartans had interfered in the constitutions of the Thebans and of the Phliasians and had put garrisons in both these cities.

At the time of the King's Peace the Spartan view that the character of Athenian leadership in the Aegean was inconsistent with the principle of autonomy for all had prevailed and the Athenian alliance had broken up. The formation of the confederacy was an attempt to adapt the old form of hegemonial alliance, which small cities still needed for their security, to the new system of autonomous states. The attempt was made partly by the safeguards described, whether general guarantees of the rights of allies or special restrictions on the Athenians, and partly by a new system for reaching decisions. Decisions had to be made by both the Council of the Allies, which met at Athens and on which each city had one vote, and the Athenian people meeting separately,[2] and, though the allies swore to do concerning peace and war what seemed good to the Athenian people and to the Council of the Allies,[3] they were protected both by the dual nature of the legislature and by the safeguards in the charter, which were immutable even by the legislating process laid down. This system gave to the allies a greater and more secure share in the making of policy than had been enjoyed by the allies at even the most liberal periods of the Peloponnesian League; there the council of allies was called only to ratify or to refuse to ratify the decisions of the Spartan people, while here the allies were at times given only a subject for discussion[4]

---

[1] Tod 123, vv. 20–25.

[2] Cf. esp. Tod 127 (alliance between Athens and Corcyra), also Tod 133 and 144 and Aeschines ii. 60 ff., iii. 69 ff., 74 ff. See Accame, *La lega ateniense*, pp. 112 ff., where variant opinions are cited in notes on pp. 113–14, and Hampl, *Die griechischen Staatsverträge*, pp. 126 ff.   [3] Cf. Tod 127, vv. 32–36.

[4] As in 346 before the Peace of Philocrates (cf. Aeschines ii. 60, iii. 68 ff.).

and normally debated a motion presented by the Athenian Boule, before it was passed to the Athenian people,[1] and there the presidency was held not by one of the allies, as here,[2] but by the Spartan ephors.

Thus learning from the experiences of their fathers the new allies furnished themselves with constitutional safeguards against Athenian tyranny. They could be comforted too by the obvious fact that the Athenians were a good deal less strong than in the fifth century, and that Athenian ambitions seemed to have moderated; ideas of a panhellenic war against the Persians, for instance, had been renounced and, as has been seen, 'those under the King' were expressly excluded from the confederacy,[3] which appears to have had at any rate the tacit approval of the King.

Though the confederacy was founded on fear of the Spartans and the first part of its expressed purpose was to make war on them, the second part was more general, to uphold the Peace, and so the Confederacy could be seen, like the Peace, as permanent, and the various treaties by which states joined it were concluded for ever.[4]

[1] Cf. Tod 133, vv. 11–14; 144, vv. 12–14.
[2] An inscription published by J. H. Oliver, 'Inscriptions from Athens', *A.J. Arch.* xl (1936), 461 ff., and discussed by Accame, *La lega ateniense*, pp. 229 ff., reveals a Theban president of the Council of Allies in 373/2.
[3] Tod 123, vv. 17–18.
[4] Cf. Tod 118, v. 37 (the alliance with Chios, which was regarded as a model for the others—cf. Tod 123, vv. 24–25), Tod 127, vv. 1–2.

IV

The Period of Athenian Leadership; the Treaty of 375 and the Two Treaties of 371

THE Athenians, the Thebans and their allies won notable successes during the following years, but by the summer of 375 the war seems to have stagnated, and both sides were ready for peace. The Spartans still controlled the Peloponnese, and thus maintained what for nearly two centuries had generally been regarded by their leaders as the essential minimum of power, and, though there were signs of discontent there,[1] these would be better dealt with in peace than in war. The Athenians too had reasserted their right to the leadership of the maritime states, which could hardly now be challenged, but they had to do rather more before they could honourably make peace. They had, they claimed, gone to war to make the Spartans respect the Peace and especially to help the Thebans, and so they needed, on the one hand, to secure a renewal in broad outlines of the King's Peace and, on the other hand, to make it impossible for the Spartans to continue to threaten Thebes.[2]

During 375 a treaty which met these requirements was concluded, the actual initiative coming from the King of Persia, whose true motive may well have been, what Diodorus says it was,[3] a need of Greek mercenary soldiers, rather than any desire to meddle in Greek affairs. The treaty presumably acknowledged the King's right to rule the Asiatic Greeks; and for the Greek homeland too it was basically a renewal of the King's Peace, a Common Peace, reaffirming the principle of autonomy, but containing also a new general clause that all cities should be free of foreign garrisons.[4]

[1] Xen. *Hell.* v. iv. 60; Plut. *Ages.* 26. 3; cf. Polyaenus II. i. 7, 18, 20, 21.
[2] On Athenian obligations to the Thebans cf. Momigliano, 'Un momento di storia greca', *Athenaeum*, N.S. xiv (1936), 12.   [3] Diod. xv. 38. 1.
[4] See Appendix II; for the new clause Diod. xv. 38. 2.

This provision was one of the definitions of autonomy written into the charter of the Athenian Confederacy, and no doubt the Athenians and their allies would have liked to see all of them included in the Common Peace agreement. But apart from this consideration, a prohibition of foreign garrisons had particular relevance for the question of Theban security. Since the failure of full-scale Spartan expeditions into Boeotia the chief danger to the Thebans lay in the presence of Spartan garrisons in some of the small cities of southern Boeotia that were hostile to the Thebans (and the Sphodrias incident had shown that they could be a danger to the Athenians also), and of a Spartan army in Phocis to the west.[1] The Spartans may have argued, what was true, that these garrisons were present with the consent of the governments of the cities, but the withdrawal of all foreign garrisons, however welcome, was made a provision of the treaty, being regarded as a prerequisite of secure peace.[2]

The Spartans subsequently withdrew their garrisons from the Boeotian cities and their army from Phocis;[3] and in fact the Thebans were the only real beneficiaries of this Peace. There may already have been some mistrust at Athens of Theban ambitions and of excessive Theban control of those Boeotian cities which before the Peace were not still garrisoned by the Spartans,[4] and it is possible that the Athenians publicly threatened to exclude the Thebans from the confederacy.[5] But

---

[1] Xen. *Hell.* VI. i. 1.

[2] Cf. the 'Cold War' agitation, esp. in the late 1950's, for the withdrawal of American bases from the countries of Western Europe.

[3] From the Boeotian cities—Isocr. xv. 110 (and there can have been no Spartans present when Tanagra, Thespiae and Plataea were coerced—cf. below); from Phocis—J. Hatzfeld, 'Jason de Phère a-t-il été l'allié d'Athènes', *Rev. d'étud. anc.* xxxvi (1934), 447 ff., and R. Sealey, '*IG* ii². 1609, and the transformation of the Second Athenian Sea-League', *Phoenix*, xi (1957), 95 ff., have argued that the Spartan army remained in Phocis throughout the next four years, until ordered to advance into Boeotia in 371 (Xen. *Hell.* VI. iv. 3), but the Thebans were evidently attacking Phocis with some success before the peace conference in 371 (Xen. *Hell.* VI. iii. 1), and a Spartan army was more probably sent over then in response to a fresh appeal. The possibility of a Spartan army being sent on two occasions is not considered in other discussions—cf. A. G. Woodhead, '*IG* ii². 43 and Jason of Pherae', *A.J. Arch.* xli (1957), 369, n. 6. If G. L. Cawkwell, 'Notes on the Peace of 375/4', *Historia*, xii (1963), 84 ff., is right in arguing that well over a year elapsed before this Peace broke down, this point should now be settled.

[4] Xen. *Hell.* VI. ii. 1; expansion of Theban power—ibid. v. iv. 63, VI. i. 1.

[5] Isocr. xiv. 37.

the Thebans certainly remained members of the confederacy[1] and the evidence of the peace terms shows that the Athenians did not desert the Thebans at the peace conference. It is clear that Diodorus' account of the exclusion of the Thebans from the treaty is an intrusion from his account of the Peace made at Sparta in 371, and that Ephorus, whom he and Nepos followed, was wrong to see in this Peace a formal division of hegemony between the Athenians and the Spartans; indeed there was not even anything in the terms that gave the two cities special responsibility for the maintenance of peace.[2]

Yet there was in a sense a division of influence, for Spartan leadership in the Peloponnese and the manner in which it was exercised were not affected by the terms of the Peace. The Athenians and their allies were not in a position to force the Spartans to bring the Peloponnesian League into line with their own interpretation of autonomy and the new clause banning foreign garrisons did not alter the Spartans' control within the Peloponnese, because there garrisons were not a normal method of imposing authority. This recognition of Spartan leadership was, however, only tacit, for it is clear that at Athens the Peace was regarded as a great triumph.[3] Victories in war had restored the Athenians to the first rank and the conclusion of this Peace was an acknowledgement, again only tacit, of this rank. The Athenian alliance had been broken up as illegal after the Common Peace of 387/386; the confederacy had been shaped to fit the principles of Common Peace, and now when another treaty was concluded neither the Spartans nor the Persians were able to raise any objection to its existence.

In this situation it was quite possible that those who wished to restore the Athenian empire of the fifth century but had been held in check by the moderates between 386 and 378 under the threat of Spartan superiority and been given only a little rein by the formation of the confederacy would see this Peace as the dawn of a new imperial era. Timotheus, whose interference in Zacynthus, according to Xenophon,[4] led to the resumption of hostilities, may have acted on a mistaken view of

[1] Cf. Xen. *Hell.* vi. iii. 2, 19; *IG* ii². 1607, vv. 49 and 155; and the inscription referred to above, p. 57, n. 2.

[2] See Appendix II.

[3] Isocr. xv. 109–10, vii. 12, xiv. 41; Philochorus ap. Didym. vii. 68.

[4] *Hell.* vi. ii. 2–3, but cf. Cawkwell, art. cit., *Historia*, xii (1963), 84 ff.

the significance of the Peace; Isocrates, who was closely associated with him,[1] probably regarded the Peace as the successful first stage of the re-establishment of Athenian hegemony, though achieved by different methods from those advocated in the *Panegyricus*. But the arguments for moderation were still strong. The Peace was a Common Peace, reaffirming the principle of autonomy; and the Athenians had prospered in the war because of their support of that principle, which had to remain the basis of any successful foreign policy. Further the initiative of the King of Persia in the peace negotiations was no sign of weakness and the terms were substantially those which he had proposed in 387 to protect his interests in the Aegean, so that there was no reason to suppose that he would not be provoked by any attempt to form a new empire. So, fear of Persian power[2] and the value of a Common Peace policy remained the chief deterrents to the imperialists.

The Peace lasted at the most for about a year and a half,[3] and then warfare was renewed by the Spartans but was confined to the north-west. The necessity of defending their distant allies, the Corcyreans, did not leave many opportunities to the advocates of expansion at Athens; and then in 373, after a summer of costly and unsuccessful effort, the moderate politicians were able to confirm their superiority. Timotheus was prosecuted by Iphicrates and Callistratus and only narrowly acquitted,[4] and also a movement to make an issue between the Athenians and the Thebans of the Theban destruction of Plataea was stifled.[5]

A part of this movement was the publication by Isocrates of his pamphlet *Plataicus*. This work purports to be the speech of a Platacan embassy seeking help at Athens. It seems unlikely that it was actually written for this purpose, but it probably was a pamphlet written by Isocrates to induce the Athenians to

---

[1] Cf. esp. Isocrates' eulogy of Timotheus in *Antidosis* (xv) 107 ff., also Plut. *Vit. X. Orat.* 837c.

[2] The recall of Chabrias from the service of the King's enemies in Egypt is placed by Diodorus (xv. 29. 2–4) in 377/376, but the date should probably be earlier —cf. H. W. Parke, *Greek Mercenary Soldiers* (Oxford, 1933), pp. 59 ff.

[3] Cf. Cawkwell, art. cit., *Historia*, xii (1963), 84 ff.

[4] Ps.-Dem. il. 9–10; date—cf. ibid. 22 (Nov. 373).

[5] For the date of the destruction of Plataea cf. Momigliano, art. cit., *Athenaeum*, N.S. xiv (1936), 27 ff.: summer 373.

help the Plataeans.[1] Its arguments are, on the whole, the statement of the Plataeans' case as it could best be stated.

It has been seen that, though the Athenians were already before the Peace of 375 showing some anxiety about the increasing power of the Thebans, they were under strong obligations to set the Thebans free from any threat of Spartan attack and had induced the Spartans to agree in the Peace to withdraw their garrisons from the cities of Boeotia and their army from Phocis. These stipulations had been carried out; but the Thebans had shortly proceeded to coerce Tanagra and Thespiae into their league and now to destroy Plataea.[2] There must now have been much stronger feeling at Athens in favour of a showdown with the Thebans.

Plataea itself held a special place in Athenian affections, a place which this particular Plataea had not altogether lost through being founded by the Spartans. Further, the moral issue was no longer so evenly balanced as before the Peace, for the Thebans could reasonably be reckoned to have forfeited their claims on Athenian loyalty by their recent aggressions. Finally, the moral issue aside, there were good grounds for arguing that the Athenians must assert their leadership by some positive action.

The principal argument on the other side was one of expediency. To break with the Thebans might produce a *rapprochement* between them and the Spartans, a notoriously dangerous combination, to fight which would be beyond the already attenuated resources of Athens; and even if the Spartans did not actually join with the Thebans, they might still simply ignore them (they had had little contact with them since the withdrawal of the garrisons) and leave the Athenians as badly off with two wars on their hands. There was also the argument that the Plataeans had assisted the Spartans, though they had not done so since the Peace of 375, which had guaranteed freedom and autonomy to all.

So in the *Plataicus* Isocrates made something of the traditional

[1] G. Mathieu, *Les Idées politiques d'Isocrate* (Paris, 1925), p. 94, thought that it was written in 371, as a background to the peace conference; criticized by W. Jaeger, *Demosthenes* (Cambridge, 1938), p. 199.

[2] Diodorus says that Thespiae was destroyed soon after Plataea and before 371 (xv. 46. 6 and 51. 3); Pausanias seems to place its destruction after Leuctra (ix. 14. 2). Xenophon (*Hell.* vi. iii. 1) links Thespiae with Plataea in the diplomacy of 371. Tanagra is mentioned with Thespiae by Isocrates (xiv. 9) as being only coerced into the Boeotian League.

friendship between Athenians and Plataeans, and tried hard to defend the Plataeans against the charge that they had assisted the Spartans.[1] He made a great deal more of the duty of the Athenians to defend freedom and autonomy and the independence guaranteed to all cities by the Peace (he clearly means that of 375), to which he made frequent reference,[2] and by the charter of the confederacy before whose council the Thebans as members should have brought their complaints before taking action against the Plataeans.[3] 'But surely,' he wrote, 'it will be the most outrageous thing if you are going to permit those cities which you thought ought not to be in servitude to the Spartans now to be destroyed by the Thebans.'[4] He presented the danger of an alliance between the Thebans and the Spartans as the only argument open to those who would abandon the Plataeans,[5] admitting that the Thebans were capable of such treachery and citing examples from past history, but suggesting that they would see the dangers for themselves of such a policy; in any case, he argued, honour demanded that the Athenians should take the risk.[6]

Prudence, however, prevailed. But it prevailed not only over the genuine champions of Plataea as a small city oppressed, but also over those who sought to use the fate of the Plataeans as a means of extending Athenian power; and so the decision, however fatal to the Plataeans, might be said to have been beneficial to other small cities that were in the path of any renascent Athenian imperialism. Timotheus, the close associate of Isocrates, was meanwhile disgraced and was not re-elected general until 366; and the Thebans remained in the confederacy.[7]

Two years later the question of relations with the Thebans again became paramount at Athens. The situation had changed in that, while the Athenians had to some extent recovered in Corcyra, they had become more than ever straitened in resources and weary of warfare. The Spartans meanwhile had again transported an army to Phocis to oppose the Thebans and there were perhaps other hints that they had not abandoned

---

[1] Isocr. xiv. 11 ff. [2] Ibid. 1, 5, 12, 14, 17, 39.
[3] Ibid. 21.   [4] Ibid. 17.   [5] Ibid. 33.
[6] Ibid. 34 ff.; on the *Plataicus* as a straightforward anti-Theban document, cf. Momigliano, art. cit., *Athenaeum*, N.S. xiv (1936), pp. 1 ff.; on Isocrates' concern with the Athenians' position as head of the confederacy, cf. Jaeger, *Demosthenes*, p. 201.   [7] Cf. above, p. 60, n. 1.

all ideas of revenge for the defeats of the early seventies.[1] There may have been talk at Athens of co-operation with the Spartans against the Thebans;[2] indeed there must have been still some of that fellow feeling for the Spartans, the other leading city, which could turn the traditional rivalry into temporary accord against an upstart. Xenophon himself probably had some feeling of this sort, but, as he observed, the Athenians as a whole were still not prepared to make war on the Thebans 'partly through shame' (he refers presumably to their claim to have freed the Thebans from the Spartans, and the Thebans were still their allies), 'partly because they did not think it advantageous.'[3] In any case, peace was the first necessity and Callistratus, who had been campaigning with Iphicrates in Corcyra, left him with the promise that he would either produce some money or make peace.[4] Money was hard to find and, if Callistratus wanted peace, then peace was likely to ensue.

At Athens it was voted that peace should be made. An embassy was first sent to the Thebans inviting them to join in an approach to the Spartans, another indication that the Athenians were not intending to discard their allies without some negotiations; and the Thebans were present at the subsequent peace conference at Sparta, which was attended also by representatives of the Spartans' allies and of the members of the Athenian confederacy.[5] The composition of the Athenian embassy itself seems to reflect the indecision at Athens about the precise sort of peace terms that were desirable.[6] There are other examples of men of divergent views being sent together to conduct negotiations for the Athenians,[7] but it is hard to understand how they could have addressed to this conference speeches

[1] Cf. above, p. 59, n. 3; the Spartans may have been worried by signs of Theban interest in the grievances of the Peloponnesian allies, among whom there had been severe, but temporary, unrest after the last Peace—Diod. xv. 40, but cf. Beloch, *Griechische Geschichte*, III. i. 174, who dates to after the battle of Leuctra.

[2] P. Cloché, *La Politique étrangère d'Athènes de 404 à 338 a.C.* (Paris, 1934), p. 85, regards this as the *only* alternative to continued association with the Thebans.

[3] *Hell.* VI. iii. 1.   [4] Ibid. 3.

[5] Ibid. 2–3; the Thebans and the Athenians' allies, ibid. 19. On Diodorus' account of Persian initiative, and on suggestions that Dionysius of Syracuse was represented see Appendix III.

[6] On the members of the embassy cf. R. Sealey, 'Callistratus of Aphidna and his Contemporaries', *Historia*, v (1956), 193, and D. J. Mosley, 'The Athenian Embassy to Sparta in 371 B.C.', *Proc. Camb. Phil. Soc.* N.S. viii (1962), 44 ff.

[7] e.g., notoriously, the embassies to Philip in 346.

which clearly expounded differing opinions, which is what Xenophon says occurred, for he includes his version of the substance of three speeches delivered by Callias, Autocles and Callistratus.

This seems to be one of the occasions on which there is no real reason but improbability (an important, but subjective consideration) to disbelieve Xenophon, but good reason to wish that he had told us more when he must have been able to.[1] There is, for instance, virtually nothing in Xenophon's account about the negotiations apart from the speeches; and it may be that the different views expressed by the three Athenians represent not the open admission of rival policies, but successive stages in cleverly handled negotiations. At any rate, whether the Athenians' disagreement was only private or whether it was made public, Xenophon's presentation of these speeches seems to show how at three stages of the peace conference the Athenian position was expounded to the other Greeks, with the final position lying somewhere between the other two and made more plausible by the previous statement of them, all three being within the general framework of the principles of Common Peace.[2]

Callias' only argument for peace which had particular relevance in the circumstances was his assertion of the common indignation of Athenians and Spartans at the Theban treatment of Thespiae and Plataea.[3] This strong hint at co-operation between the Athenians and the Spartans, and at a Common Peace treaty which would in some way condemn Theban leadership in Boeotia, must have alarmed the Thebans and those of the Spartans' allies who hoped for concessions in the treaty,[4] and also those of the Athenians' own allies who had joined the confederacy primarily to protect themselves against Spartan aggression. Autocles, on the other hand, accused the Spartans of depriving their allies of autonomy and of forcing them to fight wars that they did not want, and contrasted their stand

---

[1] Xenophon had defects as an historian, especially in his failure, as here, to present a clear picture, but he did not wilfully invent falsehoods; and in this case, being resident in the Peloponnese, he was in a good position to discover the truth (cf. Mosley, art. cit., p. 41).

[2] This interpretation is argued at greater length in Ryder, 'Athenian Foreign Policy and the Peace-conference at Sparta in 371 B.C.', *C.Q.* N.S. xiii(1963), 237 ff.

[3] Xen. *Hell.* VI. iii. 5.   [4] Cf. above, p. 64, n. 1.

on behalf of the smaller Boeotian cities at the time of the King's Peace with their later enslavement of Thebes. He professed to be trying to reconcile the Spartans with the Athenians by pointing out their faults, but he must have given the impression that the Athenians had not yet made up their minds and might still insist on a treaty which would guarantee the present position of the Thebans (whose policy in Boeotia he did not mention) while pressing for some liberalization of Spartan leadership in the Peloponnese.[1]

Callistratus' speech presented an Athenian attitude between these two extremes. Like Autocles, he censured the Spartan interpretation of autonomy with regard to Thebes and Boeotia, but he made no accusations about the Spartans' Peloponnesian allies, and said that the Athenians were dissatisfied with some of their own allies—a veiled allusion to the Thebans; and when he stressed the pacifying effect in Greece as a whole of an agreement between Athens and Sparta, he was not, like Callias, thinking of an alliance between the old-established leaders, but emphasizing the value of such a peace to Greeks in general, even if it did not wholly satisfy their separate aspirations, the emphasis on the value of peace throughout the speech being a clear hint that the Athenians were not prepared to take sides in any dispute between the Spartans and the Thebans.[2]

It was in fact now possible for the Athenians honourably, and without forfeiting their moral leadership, to do what was required by their material weakness, to take up a position of neutrality. The speech of Autocles suggests that the status of the Spartans' Peloponnesian allies could now be as much a matter for discussion at a panhellenic conference as that of the Boeotian cities; Plutarch indeed reports a violent quarrel between Epaminondas, the Theban, and Agesilaus, in which accusations and counter-accusations about infringements of autonomy were freely uttered.[3] It could be argued that neither side deserved Athenian blessing; the combined effect of the speeches of Callias and Autocles would have been to foster this belief and to make Athenian neutrality seem attractive to both sides. It should,

[1] Xen. *Hell.* VI. iii. 7–9.
[2] Ibid. 10–17; Cloché, *La Politique étrangère d'Athènes*, pp. 84 ff., not admitting the option of neutrality, considered that Callistratus was recommending a division of hegemony, and that the terms of the treaty amounted to one.
[3] Plut. *Ages.* 28. 1.

too, have seemed to those outside the quarrel who could calculate soberly unlikely that Athenian withdrawal from it would lead to drastic changes in the Greek international scene; the Spartans had been unable to penetrate Boeotia from the isthmus since 378 and, though they had an army in Phocis, they had already failed from that direction before, while it seemed beyond the bounds of possibility that the Thebans should invade the Peloponnese.[1]

The treaty which was now concluded is a measure of Callistratus' success. It was a Common Peace treaty, essentially similar to those previously concluded in 387/386 and 375,[2] with no definition of the status of Thebes and the Boeotian cities and with two minor innovations, and one of major importance. According to Xenophon, the autonomy principle was supplemented by stipulations that harmosts should be withdrawn and armies and fleets demobilized.[3] Harmosts were Spartan governors imposed on subject-allies; they had been a regular feature of the Spartan empire in the Aegean after 404, but now they can only have been in Peloponnesian cities, and, if Xenophon is right (and this is another case where there is no reason to disbelieve him, but where further information, which he must have had, would be useful), this provision marked a further Spartan concession to the definition of autonomy contained in the charter of the Athenian confederacy and one which affected, though marginally, Spartan control of the Peloponnese. It would be a matter of pure speculation to suggest why the Spartans would have made this concession; possibly the Athenians were anxious to extract something from the Spartans to offset their own impending withdrawal from the dispute over the Boeotian cities, and the Spartans felt themselves under some pressure from their own allies. The provision for the demobilization of fleets and armies looks more like an attempt to improve the chances of a Common Peace treaty becoming effective. Demobilization might well be regarded as a necessary preliminary to the ratification of a Common Peace treaty, for Greek cities did not keep substantial military or naval forces in being except for warlike purposes; and at this time the Spartans

---

[1] There was *popular* expectation of a Spartan victory at Athens and elsewhere (Xen. *Hell.* vi. iii. 20; Diod. xv. 51. 2–3).
[2] See Appendix III.   [3] *Hell.* vi. iii. 18.

had an army in Phocis, which the Athenians had to try to remove, if they were to seem to make a conscientious effort to secure peace; they had too a fleet of their own at Corcyra and a similar fleet had caused trouble after the previous treaty.

The demobilization clause also makes sense when seen in connexion with the most important innovation of this Peace, the guarantee clause which provided for the future maintenance of peace. According to Xenophon, who seems to be quoting the actual words used, it was laid down that 'if anyone acts against this agreement, those who want to may go to the help of the injured cities, *but those who do not want to are not bound by oath to do so*'.[1] It is obvious, and has been generally recognized,[2] that this clause owed much to the needs of Athenian policy; for, if war were resumed between the Spartans and the Thebans over the question of the Boeotian cities, a guarantee clause of this sort would absolve the Athenians from the obligation to defend the Peace inherent in a multilateral treaty, but not expressed in either of the Common Peace treaties already concluded, and would enable them to remain neutral. But, special circumstances apart, this new clause, a type which may be termed a *voluntary* guarantee clause, did represent the natural first step towards the creation of a system to guarantee the Peace, because it involved no extra surrender of sovereignty on the part of the signatory city; a short and feeble step perhaps, but all that the League of Nations could take when its more conscious fashioners came up against the same problem, and it would be over-cynical to assume that the intrinsic merits of the clause as a means to keep the peace were ignored. For the voluntary guarantee clause defined more clearly the obligation of a city in the event of a dispute between two other cities; and though in the absence of further definition it was presumably left to the third party to decide which seemed the injured city and which the aggressor, there seems to have been some thought given to the possible procedure to be adopted in a dispute. When subsequently the Spartans were preparing to move their army from Phocis into Boeotia, one of their leaders, Prothous, is reported by Xenophon to have objected; the Spartans, he

---

[1] *Hell.* VI. iii. 18, and see Appendix II.

[2] Cf. Underhill's note (ad loc.) and esp. Hampl, *Die griechischen Staatsverträge*, p. 105.

said, should dissolve their army (in accordance with the demobilization clause), and then call on the cities to send such contributions as they wished to Delphi, after which, if anyone refused to leave the cities autonomous, they should call together again those who wished to fight for autonomy, and lead them against its opponents.[1]

The total effect of these innovations was undoubtedly intended to be to make more difficult the sort of policy pursued under the aegis of a Common Peace treaty by the Spartans after the King's Peace; yet the Spartans were able at the oath-taking ceremony first to take the oaths on behalf of themselves and their allies, while the allies of the Athenians all swore separately, and then as presidents to force the issue over the Theban claim to represent all Boeotia. At first the Thebans were written down under their own name among the contracting cities, but on the next day asked that the name should be changed to the Boeotians. Agesilaus, who was evidently presiding, refused the request, as he had done at the time of the King's Peace, and threatened to strike the Thebans out of the Peace altogether; then the conference broke up with the name unchanged.[2]

The Spartans now rejected Prothous' advice, which has been discussed above, that they should disband their army in Phocis and allow time for the smaller cities to determine their positions in the dispute, and ordered Cleombrotus to advance from Phocis into Boeotia to see that the cities were autonomous.[3] Yet, though the Spartans were precipitately taking unilateral action, they still claimed to be acting in support of the Peace and there is no suggestion that Cleombrotus would have pressed an attack on Thebes, if he had found the cities independent.[4] The Spartans were making a last effort to enforce by arms their interpretation of the autonomy principle as precluding close federations dominated by one city, as they had done with Boeotia at the King's Peace and later with the Olynthian League,

---

[1] Xen. *Hell.* VI. iv. 2; cf. Underhill's note.
[2] Xen. *Hell.* VI. iii. 19; these events do not support the view of E. Bickermann, 'Les préliminaires de la seconde guerre de Macédoine, la Paix de Phoenicé', *Rev. de philologie*, 3rd ser. ix (1935), 64, that a city was regarded as autonomous only when it could swear its own allegiance to treaties which bound it.
[3] Xen. *Hell.* VI. iv. 3.
[4] Diodorus (xv. 51. 3) mentions an ultimatum to the Thebans.

an interpretation which they had been compelled tacitly to abandon in 375, when the re-established Theban hegemony in Boeotia was not challenged by the treaty.

The crushing defeat of Cleombrotus at Leuctra settled this particular point most emphatically. The right of the Thebans to rule Boeotia was henceforward accepted in Common Peace treaties proposed or concluded, as readily as that of the Athenians to rule Attica or of the Spartans to rule Laconia;[1] and there is no evidence that the existence of any other federal combination of city-states, such as the league of Arcadian cities founded in 370 or the Thessalian League, was questioned at any of the later panhellenic peace conferences.[2] The Spartans made another brief attempt in the fifties to win support by championing the autonomy of the Boeotian cities, but without success;[3] while Philip's action in breaking up Theban control of Boeotia after his victory at Chaeronea in 338 was his unilateral treatment of a beaten enemy, and preceded his organization of Greece through a Common Peace treaty.[4]

After the Theban victory at Leuctra the diplomatic initiative remained with the Athenians. The Spartans prepared another army, which marched to the isthmus, but no further, while the Thebans, who had readily concluded an armistice on the field of battle, made no move towards the Peloponnese, partly perhaps because the extent of their victory surprised them, certainly because they were concerned with the activities of their northern ally, Jason of Pherae, who had built up a formidable power in Thessaly;[5] it is indeed even possible that the two antagonists referred their dispute to arbitration.[6] The Athenians were still well placed to act as the only true protectors of the Peace. They had dissociated themselves from the intransigence of the Thebans over the Boeotian cities and from

---

[1] Preferring Xen. *Hell.* VII. i. 27 to Diod. xv. 70. 2 on the reasons why the Thebans rejected Philiscus' proposals in 368 (cf. below, p. 79, and Appendix V).

[2] Arcadian opposition to the proposals of Common Peace in 367 (below pp. 80 ff., and Appendix VI) seems to have been caused by the favour shown to the Eleans in the frontier dispute, rather than by any threat to break up their league—Xen. *Hell.* VII. i. 38.

[3] Dem. xvi. 6 and 25, cf. below, pp. 87, 94.

[4] Restoration of Plataea and Orchomenus—Paus. ix. 1. 8, 37. 8, &c., cf. below, p. 102.   [5] Xen. *Hell.* VI. iv. 16–26.

[6] Cf. M. Cary, 'The Alleged Achaean Arbitration after Leuctra', *C.Q.* xix (1925), 165.

the precipitate action of the Spartans, and they had done enough in the peace negotiations to present themselves as potential friends to any of the Spartans' Peloponnesian allies that might seek to ease themselves of their hegemony. Further, their leadership of the confederacy was still respectable; there had been financial stringency during the Corcyra campaign of 373–1, but the Aegean allies had not suffered excessively,[1] and there is no reason to believe in a recrudescence of Athenian imperial ambitions at this time;[2] indeed the Athenians still seem to have had a healthy fear of Persian sensitivity.[3]

In this situation and before the year was out, the Athenians summoned a new conference of Greek states at Athens, to which, according to Xenophon who is our only source for this treaty, all those cities that wanted to share in the King's Peace were invited. There the representatives agreed that they should swear adherence to 'the treaty which the King sent down and to the resolutions of the Athenians and the allies', and should undertake to go to the help of any city that might be attacked.[4]

The reference to the resolutions of the Athenians and their allies has led some to believe that this agreement represented an extension of the Athenian confederacy to include the Spartans' Peloponnesian allies, but, though Xenophon does not list the participants, it is clear from his later narrative that not only the Peloponnesian states, but also the Spartans themselves took part in the treaty, and that the treaty was a Common Peace treaty, which the Athenians claimed to be a renewal of the King's Peace, and nothing more.[5] The 'resolutions of the Athenians and the allies' are best explained as being those which at the foundation of the confederacy had defined the freedom and autonomy which it was formed to protect.[6] The

---

[1] There is no evidence of extortion in Timotheus' Aegean voyage of 373, rather of successful diplomacy (Diod. xv. 47. 2 ff., cf. A. G. Woodhead, 'The Aegean Allies 375–373 B.C.', *Phoenix*, xvi (1962), 258). Iphicrates was severe on the Athenians themselves (Xen. *Hell.* VI. ii. 14), and subjugated the Cephallenian cities (ibid. 33), extracting money (ibid. 38), but did not go into the Aegean. Sealey, art. cit., *Phoenix*, xi (1957), 95 ff., proposed to transfer *IG* ii². 1609, and therefore the cleruchy to Samos, from the late 60's to the late 70's.

[2] The recognition of the Athenian claim to Amphipolis and the Chersonese does not belong to the conference at Sparta in 371—cf. Appendix III.

[3] Cf. Xen. *Hell.* VI. iii. 12. [4] *Hell.* VI. v. 1 ff.

[5] For a discussion, see Appendix IV.

[6] As by M. Sordi, 'La pace di Atene del 370 a.C.', *Riv. di filol.* lxxix (1951), 53 ff.

general acceptance of these definitions, and especially their acceptance by the Spartans, had from then on been the ideal of the confederates, and the Spartans had been forced to make some concessions to their views in both the treaty of 375 and that recently concluded at Sparta; now they were forced to accept them unreservedly.

The undertaking to go to the help of any city that might be attacked was another development, making obligatory what in the previous treaty had been only optional. This again was in a sense a natural development, though one that undoubtedly owed much to the current need for security of the Peloponnesian states; and this *compulsory* guarantee clause, as it may be termed, remains a feature of Common Peace treaties from now onwards. Some modern commentators regard the presence of such a clause in the treaties as an indication that there was a formal alliance between the signatories and speak of a new type of agreement, the Common Peace and Alliance.[1] But it is clear that, however similar the combination of a Common Peace treaty and a compulsory guarantee clause seems to us to be to a general defensive alliance between the signatories, the Greeks regarded the two as quite different. Originally, as its derivation shows, an alliance ($\sigma\upsilon\mu\mu\alpha\chi\iota\alpha$) was concluded with the purpose of making war, and this was usually still the case in the fourth century; and the Corinthians justly observed to the Thebans in 365 that the alliance (offered to them by the Thebans) was not peace, but a change of war.[2] Moreover, an alliance on a large scale often led to imperialism, for big alliances had to have leaders and leaders were apt to be oppressive. A Common Peace treaty, on the other hand, consecrated the autonomy of all cities and was intended to produce (and did produce) an end to war, however temporary. The virtual defensive alliance which the guarantee clause of some Common Peace treaties made to appear to exist between the participants was the *result* of the state of general peace, which needed guarantee (and as likely as not against some of the participants), and not its *cause*; an ordinary defensive alliance produced peace between

---

[1] Esp. H. Berve, review cit. *Gnomon*, ix (1933), 301, and, most recently, K. Dienelt, 'Der korinthische Bund', *Jahreshefte Oesterr. Arch. Inst.* xliii (1956), 247 ff.

[2] Xen. *Hell.* vii. iv. 10, where the important phrase $\mu\epsilon\tau\alpha\lambda\lambda\alpha\gamma\dot{\eta}$ $\pi o\lambda\dot{\epsilon}\mu o\upsilon$ is wrongly translated 'change from war' in Liddell and Scott (9th ed.) s.v. $\mu\epsilon\tau\alpha\lambda\lambda\alpha\gamma\dot{\eta}$ 2; $\mu\epsilon\tau\alpha\lambda\lambda\dot{\alpha}\sigma\sigma\epsilon\iota\nu$ can take an object of the thing changed (ibid. s.v. $\mu\epsilon\tau\alpha\lambda\lambda\dot{\alpha}\sigma\sigma\omega$).

its members as a by-product of its chief purpose, which was combined action against external agression.[1] These differences and the incompatibility of some other forms of alliance with the principles of Common Peace[2] made the idea of an alliance unpopular with the supporters of Common Peace; and it is evident that, whatever similarities existed between this Common Peace treaty concluded at Athens in 371, or those of 362/361 and, later, of 338/337, and a general alliance of all the Greeks, the Greeks themselves were at pains to distinguish them from alliances.[3] But, though in a treaty with this guarantee clause a city did not see itself allied to the other signatories, it did bind itself to prompt military action on their behalf; but without further machinery a problem remained: who was to decide when action was needed and who was to direct the action?

The only other information given in Xenophon's account of this treaty is that the Eleans refused to take the oath on the grounds that they would have to leave autonomous certain border areas which they claimed were theirs. They had, as has been seen, been compelled by the Spartans to give them up in 399, and presumably the Spartans had, if necessary, reaffirmed the situation after the King's Peace and the subsequent treaties. Either the Eleans, who may have reabsorbed these areas after Leuctra, assumed that the autonomy principle would be interpreted to their disadvantage and withdrew, or there was discussion of the question, and for the first time that is known the application of the general terms of a Common Peace treaty to a particular problem was decided before the conclusion of the treaty, a procedure which becomes regular in the negotiations of the next decade. Either way the Eleans were probably looking forward to Theban intervention, which they later eagerly fostered.[4]

---

[1] So the Athenian confederacy, though itself a defensive alliance formed to protect the King's Peace, was not itself a Common Peace treaty.

[2] e.g. the Athenian alliances of the fifth century and of the Corinthian War. On 'offensive and defensive' alliances and the autonomy principle, cf. Autocles' remarks at Xen. *Hell.* vi. iii. 8.

[3] See the discussions of these treaties in Appendixes IV, VIII, X, and in particular the way in which σύμμαχος and kindred words are avoided in contemporary descriptions of the signatories—for 371, Xen. *Hell.* vi. v. 2 ('those who have sworn this oath'); for 362/1, Tod 145, v. 2 ('those who share the Common Peace'); for 338/7, Tod 177, vv. 9–10 ('those who share the Peace') and Ps.-Dem. xvii. 10, 19 ('those who share the Peace').　　　　[4] Xen. *Hell.* vi. v. 19 and 23.

The objects of the Athenian leaders in organizing this new treaty have been misinterpreted, though it is not doubted that it was the Athenian answer to the unexpected victory of the Thebans, who took no part in it. Those who see in the treaty merely an extension of the confederacy to include the Spartans' allies naturally conclude that the Athenians wanted to break up the Spartan alliance and take it over for themselves;[1] even the most persuasive champion of the case for a simple Common Peace treaty embodying the confederacy's definitions of autonomy believes that the Athenians hoped thereby to disrupt the Peloponnesian League.[2] A good number of Athenians probably had such hopes at any time, but it is hard to understand why, if this was the common aim, they refused less than a year later to give assistance to the Arcadians in their dispute with the Spartans. The inclusion in the treaty of the definitions of autonomy could well have seemed to the Athenians an object worth achieving in itself for its value to their prestige; and they may even have hoped that ready Spartan concessions to their allies would serve, like their own liberalism in the confederacy, to bind together the Peloponnesian alliance as a stable counterpoise to Theban power, but no longer a source of danger to the rest of Greece.

The Athenian calculation proved over-optimistic. The Spartans failed to respond to their lead by acknowledging with good grace the right of the Mantineans to rebuild their city.[3] The Arcadians and Mantineans for their part seemed more concerned to raise, by force if necessary, a new league against the Spartans than to allow others the autonomy that they themselves had wanted and obtained.[4] Their behaviour may have been the stated reason for the Athenian refusal to help them against the Spartans, and some Athenians may have genuinely

---

[1] e.g. Marshall, *Second Athenian Confederacy*, pp. 78 ff.; Accame, *La lega ateniense*, pp. 159 ff., is less emphatic.

[2] Sordi, art. cit., *Riv. di filol.* lxxix (1951), 56 ff., who interprets ἀκολουθεῖν at Xen. *Hell.* VI. v. 1 absolutely (the allies 'needed a leader') and prefers the reading οὕτω to οὔπω (cf. Marchant's critical note in O.C.T.) to show that the Peloponnesian states were no longer loyal to the Spartans and that the Athenians knew it. But Xenophon has already told of the strong support given by the Peloponnesian allies to Archidamus when he marched north after Leuctra (*Hell.* VI. iv. 18).

[3] Ibid. v. 3 ff.

[4] Coercion of the Heraeans—ibid. 22; and probably of the Orchomenians —ibid. 11.

believed that they had thereby forfeited any right to assistance, though others, no doubt, were primarily anxious not to weaken the Spartans any further. In any case the Arcadians and their allies turned to the Thebans and the Athenians' peaceful front in the Peloponnese was broken.[1]

The Thebans had by now been released by Jason's death from their fears of Thessalian power, and had been able to consolidate their own hold on central Greece; and their response seems to have been prompt. But there are some signs that even after Leuctra the Thebans were not united in seeking for their city a future as a great power in Greece. According to Diodorus,[2] Epaminondas persuaded them to abandon their attempt to overcome the Orchomenians by force and to enrol them, and others later, on more generous terms as more willing allies; a body of willing allies was a better basis for an extension of power than the subjugated cities which the more conservative Thebans would have preferred. The decision to intervene, though, was consistent with the interest which the Thebans seem to have shown already in the grievances of the Spartans' allies; and it is reasonable to suppose that the claim, which was certainly made later,[3] that the invasions of the Peloponnese were undertaken in the cause of freedom was openly made when the first of them was launched late in 370.

The success of the Theban invasion, which led to the devastation of Laconia and the refoundation of Messene, induced the Spartans to seek an alliance with the Athenians. Their ambassadors found the Athenians still conscious of their assumed position as protectors of the peace. The Spartan orators, Xenophon reports, indulged in such accounts of past services rendered as were a normal part of diplomatic occasions of this kind, but the principal argument that they and their allies used was that the Athenians should grant an alliance to the Spartans in accordance with their oaths to the Peace which they themselves had sponsored.[4] The question whether the Spartans or their enemies were more to blame for breaking the Peace was one of the chief topics of discussion among the

[1] Diod. xv. 62. 3; Dem. xvi. 11–12; on Athenian motives, cf. Momigliano, *Filippo il Macedone* (Florence, 1934), p. 77.   [2] Diod. xv. 57. 1.
[3] Cf. Isocr. viii. 58; Plut. *Pelop.* 31. 1; and Epaminondas' epitaph (Paus. ix. 15. 6).
[4] Xen. *Hell.* vi. v. 36–37, and see Appendix IV.

Athenians, who eventually voted for an alliance with the Spartans.[1]

It is clear that many Athenians, with, no doubt, varied motives, still regarded support of Common Peace as the keystone of the city's policy, or at least found the contention that a course of action was in accordance with the principles of the Peace a powerful argument in its favour. Support of these principles coincided with the narrow national interest, which was to thwart the Thebans.[2] To abandon the Spartans would be effectively to surrender to the Thebans; it would be an acknowledgement that the Athenians could not uphold the Peace against the city which must be regarded as the transgressor.

The failure of the Peace concluded at Athens to prevent a Theban invasion of the Peloponnese must, however, have seemed to some an indication that the usefulness of the Peace as an instrument of policy was nearly finished. At any rate it was probably thought fit now or at the time when the details of the alliance were worked out, in about May 369, to bring up the Athenians' claim to Amphipolis, a claim which was apparently recognized by the Spartans and by the allies of both cities.[3] This was the beginning of a campaign waged with arms and diplomacy intermittently over the next thirty years to recover the city, which had originally been an Athenian colonial foundation, had been lost to Brasidas in 424, awarded to the Athenians at the Peace of Nicias, but never handed over. One would suppose that the revival of the Athenians' claim would have looked like a breach of the spirit of their undertaking not to seek territory overseas (though in the letter this undertaking was limited to the land owned by their allies in the confederacy), but apparently a majority of the allies approved; perhaps Theban ambitions in Thessaly and Macedonia were already beginning to cause alarm.[4] The Athenians followed up this recognition of their claim with an expedition to the Amphipolis area under Iphicrates (probably in the spring of 368), but this was preceded by the Theban Pelopidas' first

---

[1] Xen. *Hell.* VI. v. 36, 37 and 49.

[2] The speech of Procles of Phlius (Xen. *Hell.* VI. v. 38 ff.) was designed to exploit Athenian fear of the Thebans.   [3] See Appendix III.

[4] Pelopidas' first mission to Thessaly and Macedonia was not until the summer of this year (369)—see Appendix XIII; but the Thebans had probably begun to intrigue in Thessaly after Jason's death.

mission to Thessaly and Macedonia, and seems to have been chiefly concerned with thwarting Theban plans; at any rate no attack was made on Amphipolis itself.[1]

There is in fact no evidence of a break in the Athenians' liberal policy towards their allies in the next few years. It is true that the Euboeans and the Acarnanians had left the confederacy after Leuctra, but they were persuaded by Theban strength rather than by Athenian oppression.[2] The council of the allies was still being consulted, even in such particularly Athenian matters as the decree in honour of Dionysius of Syracuse.[3] This decree was passed in the summer of 368; and some time in the same archon-year (369/368) the Athenian people voted a decree of thanks to the Mytileneans for their services in the war against the Spartans.[4] It has been suggested that, as the Athenian thanks were somewhat late, 'the Athenians were anxious to conciliate the Mytileneans, who had evidently expressed some misgivings about the real intentions of Athens'.[5] But in view of the terms of commendation the cause of anxiety is more likely to have been the Athenian alliance with the Spartans than any acts of tyranny against the allies.[6] The Athenians referred back in the decree to the time when the Spartans were attacking the Greeks contrary to the oaths and the treaty;[7] this time had passed, but, no doubt, the Mytileneans were not the only allies to view the new Athenian alignment with misgivings, though there is no reason to suppose that the council of the confederacy had not approved it. It is noteworthy too that the moderate Athenian politicians remained in the ascendancy. Callistratus was prominent in negotiating the alliance with the Spartans[8] and almost certainly was the man who

[1] Pelopidas had made Alexander of Macedon an ally of the Thebans (Diod. xv. 67. 4). After Alexander's death, Eurydice invited Iphicrates to secure the throne for her two sons by Amyntas, Philip, and Perdiccas (Aeschines ii. 27 ff.); Iphicrates put Perdiccas on the throne, but in summer 368 his regent, Ptolemy, was in turn won over by Pelopidas (Plut. *Pelop.* 27. 3). Aeschines' ἐπ' Ἀμφίπολιν (l.c.) suggests that he thought Iphicrates' mission was to take the city; Marshall, *Second Athenian Confederacy*, p. 82, concludes that this was so.

[2] Xen. *Hell.* vi. v. 23; cf. Cloché, *La Politique étrangère d'Athènes*, p. 95. The Euboeans especially may have come into the confederacy through Theban influence in 377. [3] Tod 133, vv. 11–13.

[4] Tod 131. [5] By Tod, in his commentary on this inscription.

[6] Cf. Marshall, *Second Athenian Confederacy*, pp. 84 ff., 105 ff.; the inscription is not discussed by Accame.

[7] Tod 131, vv. 44–45. [8] Ps.-Dem. lix. 27.

proposed this decree in honour of the Mytileneans;[1] he remained a powerful figure until after the loss of Oropus in 366.

All was well with the confederacy. But on the mainland the Common Peace policy had failed. The Athenian interpretation of the Peace now counted for nothing in central Greece and in most of the Peloponnese.

[1] Tod 131, v. 37 with commentary.

V

The Period of Theban Leadership and the Peace of 362/361

IT is a significant indication of the failure of the Athenians that, when in the spring of 368 Philiscus came over from Asia and organized a peace conference at Delphi, they took no prominent part in it.[1] The Thebans and their allies and the Spartans certainly took part, but the conference broke down because Philiscus supported the Spartans and proposed a Common Peace to include the return of Messene to Spartan rule[2]— the first certain instance of the application of the autonomy principle to a particular case being discussed before the Common Peace was concluded, and indeed leading to its rejection; and also the first indication of the Spartans' new attitude to Common Peace treaties, that they would accept nothing which would leave the Messenians independent. The Thebans for their part regarded the preservation of Messene as essential; but, after the failure of Epaminondas' second invasion of the Peloponnese in summer 369, he had been prosecuted and, though acquitted, had not been elected Boeotarch for 368,[3] and the Thebans now abandoned the policy of military intervention,[4] the more readily as the Arcadians were beginning to resent their leadership,[5] and relied on diplomacy to keep the Spartans down.

[1] They are not mentioned in either account (Xen. Hell. VII. i. 27 and Diod. xv. 70. 2), though Diod. is only general.

[2] See Appendix V.

[3] The expedition—Xen. Hell. VII. i. 15–22; at Pelop. 25. 1 ff. Plutarch says that Epaminondas' disgrace was after the first expedition (spring 369), but he later has him as general in summer 369 (Pelop. 26. 1); true, the other Boeotarchs had been afraid of overstaying their commands in winter 370/369 (Plut. Pelop. 24. 2), but in carrying on Epaminondas and Pelopidas were not simply being brazen; they alone had been re-elected (cf. Beloch, Griechische Geschichte, III. ii. 247 ff.).

[4] Pelopidas remained a Boeotarch, but was allowed no troops for his second expedition to Thessaly (Plut. Pelop. 27. 1). For the change in policy, cf. Momigliano, Filippo il Macedone, p. 79.   [5] Xen. Hell. VII. i. 22 ff.

Our sources, Xenophon and Diodorus,[1] appear to differ on who sent Philiscus. Xenophon says that it was Ariobarzanes, the satrap of Hellespontine Phrygia, and gives no reason; Diodorus makes Artaxerxes himself inspire his mission with the object of persuading the Greeks 'to put an end to their wars and conclude Common Peace'. The two accounts are not of course incompatible, as the satrap was the King's officer, though two years later he revolted and, if Diodorus is wrong here, could well have been pursuing some private purpose. At all events it was the first intervention from Asia in Greek affairs since the peace negotiations of 375, and only the second since the King's Peace; and it is indicative of the effect of the King's Peace on relations between the Greeks and Persia that both these interventions were efforts to restore the conditions of peace. The Persians had not used their military strength in Greek quarrels since 387, but the threat of it had remained a powerful deterrent to Athenian imperialism in the Aegean.

That the King's opposition was still feared is clearly shown by the events of 367, when all the leading Greek states sent embassies to him and evidently attached great importance to the result. The Spartans started the rush, hoping, no doubt, that Philiscus' goodwill was a sign that the King would again agree to give some more decisive backing;[2] and the Thebans followed, primarily to prevent Spartan success, but also with an eye to obtaining Persian support for themselves. Arcadians, Eleans, Argives and Athenians joined them.[3]

Pelopidas for the Thebans won the King's approval for a Common Peace treaty which included specific rulings on disputed points in favour of Theban interests: Messene was to remain independent of the Spartans, the districts around Triphylia to belong to the Eleans and not to be free to join the Arcadian League, Amphipolis to be free (and the friend and ally of the King); further, as a special application of the principle of demobilization which had been embodied in the first treaty of 371, the Athenians were to lay up their fleet.[4]

It is clear that mistrust of the Athenians, connected evidently

[1] Locc. citt., p. 79, n. 1.
[2] Plut. *Pelop.* 30. 1; Xen. *Hell.* vii. i. 33; Philiscus had left them 2,000 mercenaries (Xen. *Hell.* vii. i. 27; Diod. xv. 70. 2).
[3] Cf. Xen. *Hell.* vii. i. 33.
[4] See Appendix VI.

with their operations round Amphipolis, was again a dominant motive in Persian policy and this mistrust would go some way to explaining the preference of the Thebans over the Spartans. But, according to Plutarch,[1] the King found Pelopidas' arguments not only 'more trustworthy than those of the Athenians', but also 'simpler than those of the Spartans', and Xenophon makes Pelopidas allude to the current military superiority of the Thebans as well as to their past record of friendship with the Persians;[2] and it must be concluded that the prospect of helping the Spartans recover Messene, which must have been their chief demand, daunted the King, who preferred the Thebans to some extent simply because their proposals seemed likely to be accepted in Greece without a great effort on his own part.

With Persian support thus seemingly secured, the Thebans were well on the way to being where the Spartans had been at the time of the King's Peace, and they now summoned representatives of the Greek states to Thebes to take the oaths to ratify the new treaty.[3] The Athenians meanwhile were badly shaken and one of their ambassadors, Timagoras, who had collaborated with Pelopidas, was executed.[4] Antalcidas, who had been one of the Spartan mission, committed suicide.[5] But the Thebans found strong opposition from the Arcadians, who walked out of the gathering, which then broke up without ratifying the Peace; and when the Thebans tried to persuade individual states to take the oaths separately, they failed at the first attempt, at Corinth.[6]

The Thebans thwarted, the true position of the King now became apparent; he had already shown signs of weakness during the negotiations, when the Athenian Leon expressed dissatisfaction at Pelopidas' proposals,[7] and now he recognized the Athenian claim to Amphipolis.[8] For the first time in twenty years the Athenians felt that they had little to fear from the King.[9] In the next campaigning season (366) they began to take

---

[1] *Pelop.* 30. 3.   [2] Xen. *Hell.* VII. i. 35.   [3] Ibid. 39.
[4] Ibid. 38.   [5] Plut. *Artax.* 22. 4.
[6] Xen. *Hell.* VII. i. 39–40.   [7] Ibid. 37.
[8] Dem. xix. 137 (and probably to the Chersonese also, for here most likely belong Dem. ix. 16, xix. 253, and Ps.-Dem. vii. 29—cf. Appendix III).
[9] Perhaps now the Athenians erased vv. 12–14 of Aristoteles' decree (Tod 123, cf. above, pp. 54 ff.); these lines must have contained some reference to the

advantage of their newly realized freedom of action, first to obtain money and then to strengthen their hold on the Aegean against an expected Theban naval offensive.

First, Timotheus, who early in the year had been elected general (for 366/365) for the first time since 373,[1] entered the service of Ariobarzanes, who was on the point of rebellion against the King.[2] The Athenians did not cast aside all caution, for Timotheus was apparently instructed 'not to break the treaty with the King', and in fact left the satrap's employ as soon as his revolt became open;[3] but his mere presence would have been enough to provoke a strong reaction a few years earlier. The Athenians would presumably have asserted that he was acting in a private capacity (he may still have been a private citizen), and that he and his men were simply mercenaries; yet some years before, when the King had complained of similar activity on the part of Chabrias in Egypt, he had been instantly recalled.[4] Then Timotheus, now certainly in an official capacity, laid siege to Samos, which was being held by a protégé of the Persians contrary to the terms of the King's Peace,[5] and during his successful campaign he apparently interfered in Erythrae on the Asiatic coast.[6]

After the failure of their attempt to impose their terms on the other Greeks, the Thebans permitted Epaminondas to invade the Peloponnese again (probably late in 367), but his success in Achaea was short-lived.[7] Then about midsummer 366 Oropus on the frontier of Attica fell into the hands of the Thebans, and, after none of the Athenians' Peloponnesian allies had come to help them recover it,[8] Callistratus, the promoter of the alliance with the Spartans, the Corinthians and the rest, was prosecuted and, though acquitted, lost influence.[9] A more aggressive policy

---

King's Peace, and now for the first time since the decree was passed a renewal of the Peace had been proposed of which the Athenians disapproved.

[1] He is named as general in an inscription of December 366 (*IG* i². 108, vv. 9–10); the elections were normally in January—Aristotle, *Ath. Pol.* 44.

[2] Nepos, *Timotheus*, i. 3 ff.   [3] Dem. xv. 9.

[4] Diod. xv. 29. 1 ff.; cf. above, p. 61, n. 2.

[5] Dem. xv. 9; Isocr. xv. 111.

[6] *IG* i². 108, v. 2; the siege of Samos lasted ten months—Isocr. l.c.

[7] Xen. *Hell.* vii. i. 41–43; for the date, cf. Appendix XIII.

[8] Xen. *Hell.* vii. iv. 1.

[9] Aristotle *Rhet.* i. 1364a; Plut. *Dem.* 5. 1 ff.; cf. Sealey, art. cit., *Historia*, v (1956), 195 ff.

was now introduced on the mainland to match that in the Aegean: an alliance with the Arcadians, active enemies of the Spartans as well as of the Thebans, was followed by an abortive surprise attack on Corinth.[1] Athenian plans are no longer tempered by a careful respect for the principles of the Peace.

As for the Thebans, their breach with their Arcadian allies was thus made definite, but they did now have a chance to win the Corinthians and the other loyal allies of the Spartans in the north-east Peloponnese into their sphere of influence. Early in 365 they asked these states again to accept the terms rejected in 367 and they assented, though they refused to conclude also an alliance with the Thebans and were unable to persuade the Spartans to renounce their claim to Messene and make peace along with them.[2] The Thebans, then, won only partial success for their Common Peace policy. War between the Arcadians and the Spartans was not ended, though it seems to have languished with both sides formally allied to the Athenians, and war between the Arcadians and the Eleans flared up before the end of 365; moreover, the Athenians never acknowledged the Theban version of the Peace, and the Thebans spent 365 preparing a fleet to challenge their power in the Aegean.[3]

The Athenians seem to have lost their fear of Persian power, and to have abandoned their careful adherence to the principles of the Peace in their dealings with the other mainland

---

[1] Xen. *Hell.* VII. iv. 2 ff.; on the change in Athenian policy after the trial of Callistratus, cf. Cary, *C.A.H.* vi, 104, and Cloché, *La Politique étrangère d'Athènes*, p. 117. G. L. Cawkwell, 'The Common Peace of 366/5 B.C.', *C.Q.* N.S. xi (1961), 84, thinks that 'the affair of Oropus had discredited the opposition to a Common Peace sponsored by Thebes', and that there was a change of policy leading to Athenian participation in the Peace of 366/5 (see Appendix VII); but he seems to neglect these episodes, which must follow the loss of Oropus and do not indicate a change of attitude towards the Thebans.

[2] Xen. *Hell.* VII. iv. 6–11; Xenophon names the Corinthians and the Phliasians and adds 'those who came with them'; the Epidaurians can be added from Isocr. vi. 91. That the terms were those proposed in 367, where applicable, and for Diodorus' account (xv. 76. 3) of a Common Peace sponsored by the King in 366/365, see Appendix VII.

[3] War with Eleans—Xen. *Hell.* VII. iv. 13 ff. (for date, see Appendix XIII). Non-participation of Arcadians and Athenians in the Peace, cf. Ryder, 'The supposed Common Peace of 366/5', *C.Q.* N.S. vii (1957), 202, and Appendix VII. Theban naval preparations—Diod. xv. 78. 4 ff.; a fleet of 100 ships in 364 (for the date of the Theban naval expedition, cf. Sealey, art. cit. *Historia*, v (1956), 198, n. 150) argues a considerable effort in 365.

states. These developments were certainly such as to cause anxiety among their allies in the confederacy, but they do not seem to have been accompanied by violations of the guarantees made in its charter. A cleruchy was sent to Samos after the surrender of the Persian governor, but perhaps not until 361, and in any case Samos was not a member state.[1] Operations around Amphipolis and the Chersonese continued into 364,[2] but when the Theban fleet took to the sea that summer, and for a while controlled the Aegean, there was no widespread disaffection. Byzantium and Ceos are the only states known to have seceded; Byzantium remained independent, but the Ceans were subdued and deprived of much of their autonomy. The Theban fleet withdrew and never reappeared.[3]

Neither side could thus gain any decisive advantage in the intermittent warfare of the mid-sixties, and, even when a split in the Arcadian League enabled the Thebans to send a large army into the Peloponnese in 362, the culminating battle at Mantinea was rendered indecisive by the death of Epaminondas, and was followed by the conclusion of a new Common Peace treaty. This treaty, unlike any of its predecessors, does not seem to have been promoted by some one or two of the leading cities as a means of preserving or extending their influence, but rather to have been the result of the general state of exhaustion.[4]

This difference was reflected in a significant change in one of its general provisions. Whereas in earlier treaties and in those proposed in the last decade it had been laid down that each city should possess its own territory,[5] it was now agreed that each city should have what it held, a provision usually associated with temporary truces, which left the perennial problems still unsolved, but avoided making their solution a necessary preliminary to peace. This clause was accompanied

---

[1] Diod. xviii. 18. 9 indicates 365; Schol. Aeschines i. 53 puts a dispatch of cleruchs in 361/360, but this was probably a reinforcement (cf. Marshall, *Second Athenian Confederacy*, p. 92).

[2] Dem. xxiii. 149 ff.

[3] Diod. xv. 79. 1; Byzantium, cf. Accame, *La lega ateniense*, p. 179, n. 3; Ceos—Tod 141 and 142, with commentary, esp. pp. 125 and 131.

[4] Diod. xv. 89. 1; cf. Xen. *Hell.* vii. v. 27; and see Appendix VIII.

[5] In the King's Peace, see Appendix I; in the Peace of 375, Isocr. viii. 16; in the proposed Peace of 367, presupposed by special territorial provisions (see Appendix VI); in terms offered in 365, Xen. *Hell.* vii. iv. 10.

by a provision for immediate demobilization, and there is some evidence that the treaty made provision for arbitration on disputed territory.[1] In the case of Messene, the new clause meant that the Messenians were to remain free; the Spartans felt too strongly on this subject to accept any compromise and they refused to take part in the Peace. The Messenians, however, were free, and they and their allies, backed now by a generally accepted Common Peace treaty with a compulsory guarantee clause, were able to ignore the Spartans.

In fact, not only the Messenians but also the other Peloponnesian states had come through a turbulent decade to a position of independence which they had not enjoyed for a long time. Though the process had been fostered under the Athenian championship of the Peace and had then been speeded up by the Thebans, the Peloponnesians succeeded in becoming free of the Spartans without falling under the control of either of the other two leading states; and from now on until the Macedonian conquest, though at times susceptible to the interaction of Spartan threats and Theban influences, they avoided any sort of domination.

Another question to be examined in connexion with this Peace is the possibility that the Greeks were prepared, at the time of its conclusion or soon after, to use it as an instrument of common defence against external attack. It seems most likely, and is fairly generally accepted, that this was the Common Peace treaty referred to in the now lost inscription recording the answer given to the emissary of 'the satraps'.[2] In it 'the Greeks' assert their determination to enjoy their Common Peace and to join in resisting any attack from Persia. This terminology and the location of the inscription at Argos suggest that it did emanate from a general gathering of Greek representatives, from the actual peace conference[3] or possibly from a meeting held at a panhellenic festival;[4] though the use of the Attic dialect and the avowed connexion of the confederacy with

---

[1] For the terms see Appendix VIII. On arbitration see Accame's interpretation of Tod 145, vv. 19–20 (*La lega ateniense*, p. 175).

[2] Tod 145; on its dating see Appendix VIII.

[3] So Hampl, *Die griechischen Staatsverträge*, p. 30.

[4] The Pythian was in August/September 362, the Isthmian in 361. The Mytileneans had addressed an appeal to the Spartans and their allies at the Olympic festival of 428 (Thuc. iii. 8. 1, 15. 1).

the principles of Common Peace suggest that the Athenians and their allies, claiming to speak for all the Greeks, cannot be ruled out as its source.[1]

Whatever the truth about the provenance of this inscription, and, whether it was addressed to the satraps at this time in revolt or to those loyal to the King, the tone of its references to the King is very different from that of the charter of the confederacy and not at all consistent with the position he occupied in Greek international politics from the King's Peace to the conference of 367. While it was obviously not the intention of the Greeks to embark on a war of liberation in Asia Minor, it is safe to say that this time a formal recognition of the King's right to rule the Asiatic Greeks was not included in the treaty.[2] In this respect too the Peace of 362/361 marks the end of a chapter.

[1] It was a belief that the Athenians and their allies were the source of the reply that induced Momigliano, art. cit., *Riv. di filol.* n.s. xii (1934), 494 ff., to place it in 371–370. On the dialect question, cf. C. D. Buck, 'Interstate Use of the Greek Dialects', *Class. Phil.* viii (1913), 158 ff.

[2] That the King had no part in the negotiations see Appendix VIII, p. 144. For the fullest treatment of the panhellenic importance of the inscription cf. Taeger, *Der Friede von 362/1*, pp. 1 ff., 31 ff.; Hammond's paragraph on a Greek League, with a congress of delegates, a federal financial chest, &c. (*History of Greece*, p. 511) surely goes well beyond the evidence.

VI

The Eclipse of the Leading Powers and Rise of Macedon

THROUGHOUT the period covered by the last three chapters Common Peace was, as it were, a going concern. One at least of the three leading states, and often more, had been at any one time struggling to win the position of protector of the Peace, and there had been some loosening of the old spheres of influence to match the developments and adaptations in the treaties themselves. But, though in some respects the Peace of 362/361 was an improvement on its predecessors, since it was not concluded through the initiative of any one power or through the private compromise of any two powers to further their own policies, but apparently through general weariness, and since it was accompanied by the germs of an idea of defensive unity against external enemies, yet after it the leading states seem no longer interested in a Common Peace policy.

The Spartans remained absorbed in their feud with the Messenians, their diplomacy in Greece directed towards obtaining allies against them and their activities outside Greece towards replenishing the treasury; and when in 353 they canvassed other Greek states about substituting 'possessing their own territory' for 'having what they held' in the terms of the Peace[1] (an interesting indication that the Peace was still thought to be valid in spite of the warfare of the intervening period), their motive was clearly to find recognition and military support for their claim to Messene, and they met with no favourable response.

The Thebans made a desultory attempt in the Peloponnese to assert their own interpretation of the demobilization clause in the treaty soon after its conclusion.[2] But their energies were

---

[1] Dem. xvi. 16.   [2] Diod. xv. 94. 2.

subsequently taken up in maintaining their power in central Greece, where the struggle with the Athenians continued indirectly in Thessaly and then in Euboea. The showdown with the Phocians in 356 was a part of this struggle,[1] but it developed into a protracted and exhausting war of its own, on which Theban efforts were concentrated for a decade. There is no sign in the sources that the Thebans tried to use championship of political liberty as a propaganda weapon in this war along with their avowed support of the god of Delphi.

It is not possible to pass definite judgement on the Athenian diplomatic activity recorded on inscriptions from the years 362/361 and 361/360: the making of alliances with four Peloponnesian states, the Arcadians, Achaeans, Eleans and Phliasians, and then with the Thessalians.[2] These moves clearly were directed against the Thebans, but it is not certain that they should be seen as a return to a policy of bilateral alliances and as evidence of loss of faith in the effectiveness of the latest treaty; the treaty after all in spite of its compulsory guarantee clause provided no definite machinery for states feeling in need of protection to obtain it, and it was natural that they should seek the security of a precise contract with one more powerful, regarding it, as it were, as within the framework of the Peace. The confederacy had been formed as such an alliance, but these new allies were not enrolled into it, though the confederate states were included in both alliances as the allies of the Athenians,[3] and their council was consulted before the conclusion of the first,[4] and may well have been before that of the second also.

Whatever the truth about these alliances, there are other signs that the Athenians had abandoned their policy of respect for the principles of Common Peace. Callistratus, its most powerful advocate, was prosecuted again and this time exiled;[5] and the Athenians' attitude towards their allies seems to have become more high-handed. The practice of sending settlements of Athenian citizens to key places in and around the Aegean,

---

[1] For previous trouble with Phocians—Xen. *Hell.* VII. v. 4; Phocian exiles honoured at Athens—*IG* ii². 109 (year 363); Athenian alliance with Phocians at the beginning of the war—Diod. xvi. 27. 5 and 29. 1.

[2] Tod 144 and 147; the first came after the battle of Mantinea, see Tod's commentary, pp. 137 ff.

[3] Tod 144, vv. 18–19; 147, vv. 12–13. [4] Tod 144, vv. 12–14.

[5] Cf. Sealey, art. cit., *Historia*, v (1956), 197 ff.

which had been one of the most unpopular features of the fifth-century empire and against which the territory of the confederates had been guaranteed in the charter, had been resumed with Samos probably as early as 365; and cleruchies were now sent to the newly captured Potidaea (in 362/361) and Methone.[1] It is true that neither city is known to have been enrolled into the confederacy, and so the letter of the charter was probably not infringed, and that the settlers sent to Potidaea were invited by the pro-Athenian government,[2] but these moves were not likely to allay anxiety. Moreover, the captures of these and other cities round the north-west Aegean were episodes in the unsuccessful campaign against Amphipolis; and this was continued with some vigour even after the Peace might have been expected to put an end to the Theban threat in the area, which could have constituted an excuse for Athenian action in the sixties; and the cities, it seems, became simply dependents of Athens, though probably secured with some assistance from the allies. Efforts to secure the Chersonese also continued, and dangerous succour was sent to rebellious satraps, while the internal security of the Aegean was neglected to the extent that Alexander of Pherae was able to send out his ships on damaging piratical raids.[3]

The prestige of the Athenians was certainly on the wane, for in the summer of 357 their success in Euboea against the Thebans and the re-enrolment of the Euboean cities in the confederacy[4] could not prevent a serious movement of secession among the allies. Though this movement received the outside prompting of Mausolus, ruler of Caria, and seems to have been sparked off by coercive action from the Athenians,[5] its scale and strength suggest that it was based on a deep-seated dissatisfaction with Athenian leadership.

The secession was led by Rhodes, Chios and Cos, who were joined by the independent Byzantines, and perhaps by other cities in the Hellespontine area;[6] but in spite of the devastation

---

[1] Potidaea in 361—Tod 146; Methone—cf. D. M. Robinson, 'Inscriptions from Macedonia 1938', *Trans. Amer. Philol. Assoc.* lxix (1938), 58.

[2] Tod 146, vv. 5 ff.

[3] Amphipolis, Chersonese, and Alexander's raids, see Hammond, *History of Greece*, p. 514; aid to satraps, cf. R. P. Austin, 'Athens and the Satraps' Revolt', *J.H.S.* lxiv (1944), 98 ff. [4] Tod 153, esp. vv. 8–9.

[5] Cf. Marshall, *Second Athenian Confederacy*, pp. 109 ff. [6] Cf. ibid., l.c.

of several islands by the rebel fleet of a hundred ships[1] the movement did not spread through the Aegean. The Athenians themselves put a comparable fleet to sea and garrisoned vulnerable islands;[2] but all their efforts to defeat the rebels failed, and, when their admiral Chares put himself and his army in the service of a rebel satrap, Artabazus, to obtain sorely needed money, the Great King reacted strongly, reasserting his authority against Greek interference on the mainland of Asia for the first time in a decade, and ordered him to withdraw.[3]

Chares complied, and the Athenians now made peace with the disaffected allies and recognized their secession from the confederacy.[4] The terms and wording of this treaty are nowhere given by the orators or Diodorus, though an ancient scholiast wrote of an undertaking by the Athenians to leave *all* their allies autonomous.[5] The confederacy certainly continued to exist right down to the Macedonian conquest in 338, but its charter had included strict guarantees of autonomy and it is not impossible that there was some renewal of guarantees to the loyal allies, connected perhaps with the withdrawal of Athenian officers and garrisons sent out for protection in the war, but probably not part of the agreement with the rebels, which must have amounted to something more than a bare guarantee of autonomy.[6]

The confederacy hereafter continued in existence and the individual allies continued to be treated more or less in accordance with the terms of the charter. But the military power on which the Athenians had based their championship of the Peace between 378 and 366, and more recently their defiance of the Persians had vanished. Though there was still popular agitation for a policy of action even against the Persians, political control at Athens was in the hands of moderates headed by Eubulus, who eschewed foreign adventures and concentrated

[1] Diod. xvi. 21. 2.
[2] Andros—Tod 156, vv. 10 ff.; Amorgos—Tod 152, v. 10.
[3] Diod. xvi. 22. 1 ff.
[4] Diod. l.c., Isocr. viii. 16.   [5] Schol. Dem. iii. 28.
[6] Accame, *La lega ateniense*, pp. 192 ff., has argued that the treaty was simply a bilateral agreement between the Athenians and the rebellious allies, rejecting Schaefer's interpretation of Dem. xv. 26 and of the scholiast (*Demosthenes und seine Zeit*, i (2nd ed., Leipzig, 1885), 188 ff.). Isocr. viii. 16 would make this point certain, if there were agreement on the date of Isocrates, viii, *On Peace* (cf. p. 91, n. 2).

on the conservation of Athenian resources, which were used only to defend the Athenians' most pressing interests.[1]

Athenian policy, then, for the next few years followed a course that was passively consistent with the principles of Common Peace (the latest expression of which, the treaty of 362/361, does seem, as has been seen, to have been regarded still as the normal condition of Greek affairs in spite of recent conflicts), rather than of active support or of exploitation of them. But there were those who counselled a fresh declaration of support for the Peace and a more positive foreign policy aimed at restoring Athenian prestige and power by its protection.

One of these was Isocrates, who published his pamphlet *On Peace* soon after the treaty with the allies in 355.[2] In it his advice to the Athenians was twofold: first, to make peace not only with the rebellious allies, as had been done, but with all men, by re-establishing the King's Peace,[3] and second, to abandon the naval hegemony.[4] Put beside that part of the *Panegyricus* where the original King's Peace was denounced as being not a treaty but an ukase, Isocrates' commendation of the Peace makes strange reading. True, he seems to have in mind the treaty of 375 in particular,[5] a renewal of the King's Peace which many Athenians and probably Isocrates himself had regarded at the time as a triumph for Athens. Yet that treaty too had been concluded through the mediation of the Persians and had recognized their authority in the Asiatic cities. In the *Plataicus* Isocrates had been able to ignore the King's part in this treaty, though using the treaty itself as the basis of his case against the Thebans. Now in *On Peace* he made no bones about the King's connexion with the Peace,[6] even though it was probably open to him to argue that the King had not been concerned in the latest treaty of 362/361. The reason for Isocrates' frankness is not hard to see and demonstrates again the basic realism of his policies. Artaxerxes had recently made

---

[1] Cf. Hammond, *History of Greece*, pp. 545 ff.

[2] For the date cf. Momigliano, art. cit., *Annali di Pisa*, ser. ii, v (1936), 109 ff.; the work is placed before the end of the war by G. Mathieu, *Les Idées politiques d'Isocrate*, p. 116, F. Kleine-Piening, *Quo tempore Isocratis orationes quae περὶ εἰρήνης et Ἀρεοπαγιτικός inscribuntur compositae sint*, Diss. Münster (Paderborn, 1930), p. 42, and M. L. W. Laistner, 'Isocrates: De Pace and Philippus', *Cornell Stud. in Class. Phil.* xxii (1927), p. 17.

[3] Isocr. viii. 16.

[4] Ibid. 64.

[5] Cf. the reference to the removal of garrisons in c. 16.

[6] viii. 16.

a very real threat to intervene, and the Athenians had hurriedly given way. There was still considerable feeling against the Persians at Athens and soon after the publication of this pamphlet a popular agitation in favour of war with Persia led to a debate, in which Demosthenes spoke effectively for restraint in his speech *On the Symmories.*[1] No responsible public figure could give any encouragement to this anti-Persian hysteria.

More significant than Isocrates' newly expressed attitude to the King is the difference between the way in which he now proposed that the Athenians should support the principles of Common Peace or, as he put it, should 'behave as the common treaty commands'[2] and the way in which he had in the *Plataicus* proposed that they should support them. Then, in the *Plataicus,* the Athenians were to use the principles of Common Peace as a means of justifying the establishment, by force if necessary, of Athenian authority over the Thebans. Now he recommended the Athenians to give up their hegemony, which, he said, had been unjust, impracticable and positively dangerous to the city;[3] Athenian power and prestige should now be built up through peaceful support of the principles of Common Peace, through what might be called moral diplomacy. The best interests of Athens were still Isocrates' first concern, but now they were more akin to the best interests of other and lesser cities.[4]

A Common Peace policy of this sort was probably the only practicable alternative to the negative peace policy of Eubulus and others, but the latter prevailed. The residue of the confederacy was not dissolved, a modicum of naval power was retained, and ships continued to be built on a considerable scale.[5] Isocrates soon realized that the abandonment of the naval

---

[1] For the date of *On the Symmories*, cf. Jaeger, *Demosthenes*, p. 224, n. 6.

[2] C. 20—Isocr. here used the phrase αἱ κοιναὶ συνθῆκαι, the nearest he ever came to κοινὴ εἰρήνη; he often used 'the peace', ἡ εἰρήνη, to mean the King's Peace or a renewal of it.

[3] Isocr. viii. 66.

[4] Only Momigliano, art. cit., *Annali di Pisa*, ser. ii, v. (1936), 112 ff., has discussed *On Peace* in the context of Common Peace, showing that Isocrates was advocating a policy of support for the Peace with an eye to the greater glory of Athens. Those who believe that he was a panhellenic idealist have always found this work hard to fit in—e.g. Laistner, op. cit., *Cornell Stud. in Class. Phil.* xxii (1927), who succeeds in discerning as his real aim here the formation of a Greek alliance against Persia (p. 18).

[5] *IG* ii². 1613, a naval list for 353/352, gives 349 ships, though these were far too many for the Athenians to be able to man or pay for at sea.

hegemony was too much to ask for. A few months later he published his *Areopagiticus*,[1] a pamphlet which had as its chief theme the need for constitutional changes at Athens to restrict the power of the many, but contained some advice on foreign policy; moral diplomacy to protect the Peace was still recommended though now it was to be backed by a naval hegemony that was not oppressive.[2] At about the same time Xenophon published his short pamphlet on the *Revenues*,[3] and in it the historian who in his *Hellenica* ignored the common pattern of the Common Peace treaties recommended a similar foreign policy to that put forward by Isocrates.[4] Here again a new foreign policy was made the result of internal changes, this time economic, favouring the propertied classes. It should be remembered that for trade and agriculture peace is better than war and that diplomacy is cheaper than war and more acceptable to the taxpayers.

It is clear that Isocrates at least now came under strong attacks from his critics, for in 354 or 353 he published his *Antidosis*, the defence of his life and his beliefs; but it is reasonable to see his unpopularity as caused more by the oligarchic views expressed in the *Areopagiticus* than by his advocacy of a Common Peace foreign policy. Backing for such a policy indeed was not at this time limited entirely to those with oligarchic sympathies; the early speeches of Demosthenes show that support of the Peace was one of his principal ideas.

Shortly before Isocrates had published his *Areopagiticus*, Demosthenes had delivered his first political speech, *On the Symmories*. Hitherto he had supported the moderates in the law-courts and he now spoke against popular clamour for a war with the Persians. He was mostly concerned with showing that the King was not threatening Athens, and that to fight him would be exceedingly dangerous; and, though he denounced in principle Persian interference in Greece and hinted at the

---

[1] For the date cf. Momigliano, art. cit., *Annali di Pisa*, ser. ii, v (1936), 122 ff.; for other views cf. F. Miltner, 'Die Datierung des Areopagitikos', *Mitteil. d. Vereins klass. Philol. in Wien*, i (1924), 42 ff., and W. Jaeger, 'The date of Isocrates' *Areopagiticus* and the Athenian opposition', *Harv. Class. Stud.* Suppl. i (1940), 409 ff.   [2] Isocr. vii, esp. 80.

[3] For the date cf. Thiel's edition (Amsterdam, 1922), p. xii, and Momigliano, art. cit., *Annali di Pisa*, ser. ii, v (1936), 120.

[4] C. v. 10.

attitude he was later to take up over Rhodes,[1] he did not mention the King's Peace as the basis of relations between Athens and Persia (before this audience it would scarcely have been tactful to do so). As for relations with other Greeks, he bade the Athenians pursue a just policy and begin no unjustified wars,[2] but he did not in this context allude to freedom and autonomy or to *the* Peace. A just policy was, however, not to be one of complete isolation and non-interference; he urged a reform of the financial system not only for the defence of Athens, but also, he hinted, for the protection of others.[3]

War was prevented, but Demosthenes' practical proposals were not carried out. In 353 he spoke again on foreign affairs in favour of an alliance with the Megalopolitans against the Spartans. This alliance, he argued, would contribute towards the essential object of Athenian foreign policy, which was to keep both the Spartans and the Thebans as weak as possible,[4] because the best way to this object was to ensure that the Athenians should protect the weaker states against the strong, and be seen to be the guardians of freedom.[5] This freedom is specifically connected with the conditions of *the* Peace[6] (that of 362/361), but no such stress was laid on the Peace as to suggest that respect for its principles rather than the propaganda value of defending freedom was an influential factor in the decisions of the Athenian people. Demosthenes had also to meet the objection that the alliance made with the Spartans in 369 had never been repudiated, and was thus led into the generalization, familiar in the twentieth century, that in the pursuance of a just foreign policy there was no room for alliances which bound the city to support another, right or wrong.[7] His arguments in these ways seem to develop from the needs of the present situation into specious generalizations about the implications of a Common Peace policy, principles which were not real starting-points, but were designed to give a good moral flavour to measures of expediency.

Isocrates, by contrast, though he did commend his policy as being beneficial to the city in particular, seems more of an idealist, because he dealt only in generalizations and was

---

[1] Dem. xiv. 6.   [2] Ibid. 3, 35, 37, and 41.   [3] Ibid. 13.
[4] Ibid. xvi. 4–5.   [5] Ibid. 15 and 32.   [6] Ibid. 10.
[7] Ibid. 6.

not arguing any special problems of foreign policy. But the difference was largely superficial; to be the protectors of freedom, as Isocrates urged, the Athenians would constantly have had to declare their own position on individual issues, and in their private debates on the merits of a case could not have been silent on the true interests of their city. On this occasion Demosthenes failed to carry the day, but the policy of those in control was not altogether passive, for they had concluded an alliance with the Messenians in 355, though still themselves allied to their implacable enemies, the Spartans.[1] This move had so far prevented any outbreak of war between the two cities.

Two years later Demosthenes spoke in favour of assisting the Rhodian democrats against the royal house of Caria, who had virtually gained control of the island after the Social War, in which the Rhodians had seceded from the Athenian confederacy. Earlier he had warned the people against provoking the King, but now he claimed that the King was in the wrong, because his vassals had interfered in a city to which he had abandoned any claim 'in the treaty' (the King's Peace).[2] As in the case of the Megalopolitans, Demosthenes made the point that by supporting the Rhodians the Athenians would be defending freedom and thereby win repute.[3] But he did not proceed from there to more theorizing on the implications of a Common Peace policy, eschewing, for instance, the relevant corollary of his previous argument, that a just policy recognizes not only no permanent friends, but also no permanent enemies. Instead he chose to interpret the defence of freedom as the defence of democracy, and was prepared to say that 'I believe it would be better for you that all Hellenic peoples should be democracies and be at war with you than that they should be governed by oligarchies and be your friends'.[4] His argument is a salutary reminder that there were other views of international justice than those of Isocrates and Xenophon; that Athenians especially were likely to believe it no less important that the people within a city should be free from the domination of a few powerful men than that the city itself should be free from the domination of its more powerful neighbours.

Again Demosthenes failed to persuade the Athenians and soon

[1] Paus. iv. 28. 1 ff.; cf. Dem. xvi. 8–9. [2] Dem. xv. 27.
[3] Ibid. 3–4, 8. [4] Ibid. 18.

he was completely absorbed in his campaign against Philip of Macedon.[1] Philip's growing power had been encroaching on Athenian interests since 357, and in 352 Eubulus and his colleagues had shown energy rare for them in sending an expedition to block his passage through Thermopylae. Eventually it was their failure against Philip that turned them again to consider the possibility of another Common Peace treaty.

Soon after the fall of Olynthus to Philip in 348 Eubulus and Aeschines had directed a diplomatic campaign to bring the Peloponnesian cities into the war alongside the Athenians, but without success.[2] When a further series of embassies were sent out to these and other Greek cities in the winter of 347/346, peace negotiations with Philip had already begun[3], and the ambassadors were this time given the alternative object of bringing the other Greeks into a peace agreement with him; and, as the Greek cities to be approached were at present neutral, the idea must have been to expand any bilateral agreement with Philip into a Common Peace treaty.[4] But this possibility was clearly not something for which the Athenian leaders were in the last resort ready to sacrifice their chances of ending the war with Philip.

In the final negotiations between the Athenians and Philip's ambassadors in the spring of 346 a Common Peace treaty does seem to have been the object of the Athenians' allies in the confederacy. First they proposed that no debate should take place in the Athenian assembly on the subject of peace with Philip, until the embassies returned from the other Greek states, in order that the Greeks should be able to take part if they wanted;[5] but this proposal was overruled, and Demosthenes saw

[1] The First Philippic was delivered probably in 351, but its date is a vexed question—cf. Cawkwell, 'The Defence of Olynthus', *C.Q.* n.s. xii (1962), 122 ff.

[2] Dem. xix. 304 ff.

[3] Aeschines ii. 57, 60–61 (including quotation from the first decree of the allies), iii. 58, 65, and 68, against the denial of Demosthenes (xviii. 23). Schaefer, *Demosthenes und seine Zeit*, ii (2nd ed., Leipzig, 1886), 220, identified these embassies with those referred to in Dem. xix. 304 ff., and assigned them to the earlier period; Cawkwell, 'Aeschines and the Peace of Philocrates', *Rev. d'étud. grec.* lxxiii (1960), 418 ff., also identifies, but thinks the Demosthenes' passage refers to the winter of 347/346.

[4] The Peace alternative is clearly stated by Aesch. ii. 57; Cawkwell, art. cit., *Rev. d'étud. grec.* lxxiii (1960), 426, suggests that his statement is a reading-back from a later date and thinks that, when these embassies were sent, peace was not yet being seriously considered by Aeschines and Eubulus.

[5] Quoted by Aesch. ii. 60–61.

that the dates for the debate were fixed without reference to it.[1] Perhaps the presence of some ambassadors from some of the other Greek states (which may have been the case)[2] encouraged the allies to continue to press for some kind of a Common Peace treaty; at any rate they passed a new motion recommending that the Athenians should discuss and decide on peace terms (as was already their intention), but that any Greek city should be allowed to be included in the Peace within three months.[3]

This motion was one of two before the assembly when the debate began; the other, proposed by Philocrates, was for a bilateral peace between Philip and his allies and the Athenians and their allies with the express exclusion of Halus and of the Phocians[4] (allies of the Athenians, but not members of the confederacy), on whom Philip had fairly evident designs. The allies' motion seems to have won much favour at first,[5] but the Athenian people were chiefly concerned with the fate of Halus and the Phocians, and were provoked by Philocrates' proposal into fresh bellicosity, which Aeschines and his friends had to work hard to assuage.[6] It also became clear that Philip would accept no terms which did not leave him freedom of action over Halus and the Phocians[7] and in the end a bilateral treaty was concluded with no reference to Halus and the Phocians, a treaty which Aeschines and Eubulus, as well as Demosthenes, supported.[8]

[1] Decrees adduced by Aeschines (ii. 61, iii. 68), but not extant.

[2] Cf. Demosthenes' assertion (xix. 16).

[3] Quoted by Aesch. iii. 68 ff., but not mentioned in Aesch. ii; referred to probably by Dem. xix. 15 and 144. Schaefer, *Demosthenes und seine Zeit*, ii. 216 ff., and Accame, *La lega ateniense*, pp. 202 ff., identify this decree with that quoted in Aesch. ii. 60–61. However, that decree does not deal with the debate concerning peace as already arranged, but proposes that it should be deferred until the ambassadors return; this decree is clearly said to have been presented on the first day of the debate and deals with the nature of the Peace being discussed (cf. Cawkwell, art. cit., *Rev. d'étud. grec.* lxxiii (1960), 420, n. 1). The use of the compound προσέγραψαν in Aesch. iii. 69, cannot be regarded as a strong argument for identification. Cawkwell, art. cit., p. 435, agrees that the allies' proposal was for a Common Peace.

[4] Dem. xix. 159; for the two proposals, cf. Hammond, *History of Greece*, p. 552, and A. W. Pickard-Cambridge, *C.A.H.* vi, 236.

[5] Aesch. iii. 71.

[6] Aeschines' speech referred to by himself at ii. 74 and by Dem. xix. 16; cf. Cawkwell, art. cit., *Rev. d'étud. grec.* lxxiii (1960), 437, whose explanation of the purpose of the speech largely agrees with this.   [7] Cf. Aesch. iii. 72.

[8] Dem. xix. 159 and 278; the Peace supported by Aeschines—Aesch. ii. 79, &c.; by Eubulus—Dem. xix. 290 ff.; by Demosthenes—Aesch. ii. 68.

It is hard to be certain whether Philip's objection to the express inclusion of Halus and the Phocians in a bilateral treaty would have extended also to a Common Peace treaty, but it seems more likely that they would have. It is true that he would have had precedents (though not very auspicious) for arguing that the Phocians at any rate had put themselves outside the protection of such a treaty, but Common Peace treaties had a general stabilizing effect which he could well have thought undesirable, and were based on a general recognition of autonomy that the destroyer of Olynthus might feel would be embarrassing; and, although there were states, such as the Thebans, likely to support him rather than the Athenians, they could not be relied on, and, though he did three years later profess himself ready to accept an Athenian proposal to expand the bilateral treaty into a Common Peace treaty, he only set about organizing a Common Peace in 338, when the *status quo* was favourable to himself. Further, though he was ready to exploit inter-city rivalries, he does not seem to have indulged in that particular kind of support of autonomy, in championing small cities against larger neighbours and separatist movements within federal states, that characterized a persistent attempt to pose as the champion of peace and freedom; not, that is, until after his victory at Chaeronea, when he broke up Theban control of Boeotia and dissolved the Athenian confederacy.

As for the Athenian leaders, any intentions they may have had of pressing for a general treaty to cover all Greece were frustrated, partly by the fact that public controversy became centred on the position of Halus and the Phocians, partly by the response of the Peloponnesian cities which must have been largely, if not wholly, negative;[1] moreover, if Philip was opposed to the idea, they would certainly have been apprised of his attitude by the Macedonian ambassadors, and, even if he were not, they might well have had second thoughts about its advantages. Demosthenes at any rate, hard though he worked for peace at this juncture, seems to have despaired of the other Greeks at an early stage.[2]

---

[1] The only indication that some states responded is Demosthenes' assertion (xix. 16) that ambassadors were present at the debate in the assembly—cf. Cawkwell, art. cit., *Rev. d'étud. grec.* lxxiii (1960), 438.

[2] Dem. xviii. 23, an inaccurate statement, but one which probably represented

The short period between the conclusion of the Peace of Philocrates, which included on Philip's insistence an alliance between the two parties, and Philip's attack on the Phocians saw the publication of Isocrates' *Philippus*.[1] There in the form of an open letter to Philip Isocrates presented what might have seemed to any Athenians but those few at the top who were aware of Philip's plans—and even to some of them—a practicable and honourable alternative to a policy of continued hostility to Philip and of using the Peace as a breathing-space before renewing the struggle. He urged Philip to lead a panhellenic crusade against Persia (as a decade later he set out to do) as the leader of Greece and not as its conqueror as he was to become. He presented the Persian war as an alternative to and not as a consequence of aggrandisement in Greece, and urged Philip to use his influence and not his power to bring peace, preserving for the Athenians a special position as his most valuable allies.[2]

In the proposed pacification of Greece the importance of the four leading cities, the Argives, the Thebans, the Spartans and the Athenians, was stressed; Philip should reconcile each of them with himself and also with one another, and this reconciliation should precede any expedition against the Persians. But Isocrates nowhere went into details about the machinery of reconciliation, and it is not safe to say that he was advising Philip to bring about a new Common Peace settlement,[3] though it would by now have been regarded as the natural framework of a general pacification.

With the advantage of hindsight it can be said that at this stage there was virtually no chance of Philip accepting the role of peacemaker in Greece or of the Athenians accepting him. It is doubtful whether Philip would ever have stopped short of becoming the dominant partner in any alliance, and probable that he always intended to establish some sort of control in

his sentiments, shown also by his haste in fixing the debate before the Greeks had responded.

[1] For the date cf. cc. 7–8, which speak of the Peace as newly made.

[2] For this interpretation cf., against the general view, S. Perlman, 'Isocrates' *Philippus*—a reinterpretation', *Historia*, vi (1957), 306 ff.

[3] C. 69 in particular has been adduced by those who see Isocrates' inspiration behind the settlement of 338/337 (cf. Beloch, *Griechische Geschichte*, iii. i. 575, n. 2), but it amounts to nothing more than a general picture of Philip as the arbiter of Greek quarrels.

Greece; he was in particular already planning the intervention in Phocis which finally alienated Athenian public opinion. But it is possible that the *Philippus* did something to prepare the ground for the Common Peace settlement organized by Philip in 338/337, different though it was from the pacification envisaged by Isocrates.

Philip now marched against the Phocians, reduced them to submission, and then summoned the Amphictyonic Council to discuss their fate.[1] Diodorus' description of what followed[2] has led to the belief that the Council proclaimed a new state of Common Peace in Greece. It might have suited Philip's purpose better now than a few months earlier to have promoted a Common Peace treaty, as his immediate objectives had been secured, but his general objections to such a treaty discussed above would still have been valid, and in fact there is strong evidence against this interpretation of what is, by comparison with its appearances in Diodorus' Book XV, a vague and obscure use of the phrase κοινὴ εἰρήνη.[3] It can be said with certainty that there was no generally agreed Common Peace treaty at this time, and with probability that Philip did not, like the Thebans in 365, try to make propaganda value out of a unilateral proclamation of a state of Common Peace.

Athenian relations with Philip remained nominally peaceful. But the anti-Macedonian politicians, while they did not by any means have everything their own way,[4] had sufficient support to prevent any serious attempt to make the Peace and the alliance really work;[5] and there was, as far as is known, no move from elsewhere in Greece to avert a renewal of war that was likely to affect most of the city-states.

In 343 Philip sent an embassy to Athens to express his goodwill and to offer to amend the treaty;[6] in reply the Athenians proposed that the treaty be extended into a Common Peace to cover all Greeks.[7] Philip professed himself ready to accept this suggestion,[8] though there is no certainty that he would in fact have done so and he may still have considered a general pacification based on the autonomy principle as against his own

---

[1] Diod. xvi. 59. [2] Ibid. 60. 3. [3] See Appendix IX.
[4] e.g. the successful prosecution of Timarchus in 345 and the agitation which led to Demosthenes' Second Philippic in winter 344/343.
[5] e.g. the rejection of Philip's offer to cut a canal through the Chersonese in 345.
[6] Ps.-Dem. vii. 18. [7] Ibid. 30. [8] Ibid. 32.

interests. But in any case the Athenians, under the influence of the anti-Macedonian politicians, also proposed that the clause of the Peace of Philocrates which gave to each side 'what they held' should be replaced (presumably in the general treaty) by its alternative, that all should possess 'their own territory'.[1] As the Athenians claimed as their own Amphipolis and Potidaea, which Philip had taken over, and Cardia, his ally in the Chersonese, this proposal was totally unacceptable to him, and must have been known to be.[2]

It looks as if Philip's opponents at Athens were anxious to avoid making a Common Peace treaty with him, now that he seemed willing to agree to it, thinking perhaps that in these circumstances (maybe, in any) it would be disadvantageous to the city and damaging to their own political position. Speaking to the Athenians about these negotiations, Hegesippus, while idealizing the Athenian proposal for the extension of the Peace of Philocrates to all Greeks ('. . . thinking it just and humane not that only they and their allies and Philip and his allies should enjoy the Peace, while those who were allies of neither themselves nor Philip should be left in the middle and be at the mercy of the more powerful, but that these also should enjoy security by the Peace'),[3] was at pains to show the Athenians how Philip's practice differed from his professions now about the freedom and autonomy of the Greeks.[4]

Philip does not seem to have persisted in any attempt to make capital out of the Athenian attitude, and nothing is known of any favourable reaction to his plan elsewhere in Greece. At Athens the anti-Macedonian politicians were still not all-powerful,[5] but they carried the people with them on all vital issues directly affecting relations with Philip.[6] When they did finally succeed in forming a block against him, it was an alliance for war and it failed on the field of Chaeronea.

---

[1] Ibid. 18.

[2] The Athenians were also prepared to talk about Olynthus and the other Chalcidian cities—cf. Ps.-Dem. vii. 28.

[3] Ps.-Dem. vii. 30–31.   [4] Ibid. 32.

[5] e.g. the rejection of Persian overtures early in 343 and Aeschines' acquittal in the summer.

[6] e.g. the sending of troops to Acarnania in winter 343/342, support of Diopeithes in 341, abrogation of the Peace in 340, and subsequent rejection of Philip's overtures.

VII

Macedonian Domination; the Peace of 338/337 and After

PHILIP's victory at Chaeronea was decisive. He had defeated the combined army of the Athenians, the Thebans and their allies from central Greece and Achaea, and had forced these states to make separate treaties with him. He put garrisons in Thebes, Chalcis and Ambracia, restored the Boeotian cities that the Thebans had destroyed and freed them from Theban control, dissolved the Athenian confederacy and took over the Chersonese. He then entered the Peloponnese, put a garrison on Acrocorinth and reorganized frontiers in favour of his friends in Arcadia, Messene and Argos. The Spartans alone refused to submit. He was now militarily supreme in Greece and his supporters were in power in most of the cities.[1]

It was only at this point that he summoned the representatives of the cities to a meeting at Corinth and laid before them his new adaptation of Common Peace.[2] In organizing the Peace of 338/337, then, Philip was not trying to use the autonomy principle, as the Spartans, Athenians and Thebans had done, in the course of aggrandisement to win over other states outside his political control or to weaken his enemies by detaching their allies;[3] and he was not using it, as the Persians had done, to preserve the *status quo* of a self-cancelling balance of independent states outside his control. The Peace of 338/337 was a different sort of weapon to Philip than any previous Common Peace treaty had been in the hands of its promoters. It did not represent a settlement short of victory, for, as has been said, Philip's

---

[1] Cf. Hammond, *History of Greece*, pp. 570 ff.

[2] On the character of Philip's settlement in general—simply a Common Peace with no alliance between him and the Greeks—see Appendix X.

[3] Cf. Hampl, *Die griechischen Staatsverträge*, p. 92, on the difference between the value of this Peace to Philip and that of the King's Peace to the Spartans, who exploited it to try to win control of Greece.

victory was complete; and it was not a compromise by which he conceded any real power.

The actual provisions of the treaty show considerable developments from those of previous treaties, mostly at the expense of the sovereignty of individual cities (whom Philip was able to coerce), but likely also to increase the efficacy of the treaty as a means of preventing war.

First, in the guarantee: there was a compulsory guarantee clause of the usual sort binding all to go to the help of the injured party;[1] also a supra-national body, a synhedrion of representatives of the Greeks,[2] was for the first time set up to decide who was the injured party. These representatives were probably not answerable to the individual cities for the decisions of the synhedrion, and were not necessarily chosen by single cities; further, the decrees of the synhedrion were binding on all cities without ratification, though the entrenched clauses of the original treaty, that all cities should be free and autonomous, could not be overthrown;[3] finally, to organize and lead action taken to implement decisions of the synhedrion the office of Hegemon was created.[4] The wars subsequently conducted by Alexander against the Thebans (in 335) certainly,[5] and by his regent Antipater (in 331) probably,[6] were proclaimed as actions of the Greeks in defence of the treaty, and were the first and only punitive actions carried out in defence of a Common Peace treaty by the general body of the signatories after decisions reached by a set procedure.

Second, in the definition of autonomy: there were clauses in the treaty dealing with possible provocative action by one city against another, especially on the sea, which are known here for the first time, but may have occurred in earlier treaties;[7] the important innovation was an attempt to stop indirect interference from without in the domestic politics of a city:

---

[1] Tod 177, vv. 19–23; Ps.-Dem. xvii. 6, 8 and 19; and see Appendix X.

[2] Tod 177, vv. 19–23; Ps.-Dem. xvii. 15; and see Appendix X.

[3] See Appendix X.   [4] Tod 177, vv. 22–23; and see Appendix X.

[5] Cf. Diod. xvii. 9. 5 (Alexander's proclamation to the Thebans) and 14. 1 (his commission of their punishment to the synhedrion).

[6] Cf. Diod. xvii. 73. 5 (punishment of Spartans entrusted to the synhedrion); Aesch. iii. 254 ('those who transgress the Common Peace') probably refers to the Spartans.

[7] Tod 177, vv. 9–11; Ps.-Dem. xvii. 19; on something like this clause in the Peace of Philocrates cf. Accame, *La lega ateniense*, pp. 207 ff.

the constitution existing in each city at the time of the treaty was guaranteed, and certain types of foreign-assisted subversion were specifically prohibited;[1] this measure left few loopholes for aggression.

Though Macedonian supremacy particularly affected those powerful cities which had tended to lead or control their smaller neighbours, there does not seem to have been any new prohibition on close federations; Theban control of Boeotia and the Athenian confederacy were broken up after the battle of Chaeronea before the general settlement,[2] but there is evidence that under Alexander the Boeotian and Arcadian leagues continued to exist, and 'common meetings' of the Boeotians, the Arcadians and the Achaeans were the subject of some instructions sent by Alexander to Greece in about 324.[3]

Third, in resolving territorial disputes: thanks to Philip's supremacy, some of these had already been settled in the separate agreements which he had made with cities before the general treaty; it is known that Oropus was taken from the Thebans and given to the Athenians, and that Philip settled disputes between the Spartans and their neighbours by force in favour of the latter, perhaps through an arbitrating tribunal[4], though the Spartans would not recognize its legality and subsequently remained outside the treaty. The synhedrion now existed as a body to which other problems could be referred; an extant inscription records the arbitration at the synhedrion's request of the Argives in a quarrel between Cimolus and Melos.[5]

Seen in isolation then, this Peace was the best of the Common Peace treaties and came nearest to a formulated compromise

---

[1] Tod 177, vv. 14–15; Ps.-Dem. xvii. 10, 15–16.

[2] Boeotia—Paus. ix. 1. 8; confederacy—Paus. i. 25. 3; cf. Accame, *La lega ateniense*, pp. 222 ff.

[3] The Boeotians and the Arcadians dealt as states with Alexander in 336— Arrian i. 7. 11; Diod. xvii. 3. 4; κοινοὶ σύλλογοι of Boeotians, &c. in Hyperides, *c. Dem.* 18.

[4] Oropus—Paus. i. 34. 1; Spartans—Polyb. ix. 33. 11–12, who talks of a 'common judgement from all the Greeks'. C. Roebuck, 'The Settlements of Philip II of Macedon with the Greek States in 338 B.C.', *Class. Phil.* xliii (1948), 73 ff., takes this to mean the *de iure* confirmation in the treaty or by the synhedrion of transfers of territory carried out earlier by Philip; I. Calabi, 'Il sinedrio della lega di Corinto e le sue attribuzioni giurisdizionali', *Riv. di filol.* lxxviii (1950), 63 ff., disagrees and suggests a separate arbitrating tribunal set up by Philip before the meeting at Corinth. [5] Tod 179.

between city sovereignty and the rule of law. But it had been imposed by a conqueror, and indeed it seemed in many ways to consolidate his supremacy. The reaffirmation of the autonomy principle did not affect the position of Philip's garrisons in Thebes, Chalcis, Corinth and Ambracia or the other arrangements that he had made after Chaeronea; but, administered by the carefully constituted synhedrion, it was likely to diminish still further the power of the larger cities, who were his chief potential enemies, and to win him further support in the smaller cities, who would see in the treaty a protection from the encroachments of the larger. The guarantee of existing constitutions favoured his friends, who had come to power in many cities on the flood-tide of his success. Moreover, the prospect of peace throughout Greece would please those who for one reason or another cared more for stability and quiet than for national independence, while the whole tendency of making the settlement in the now customary Common Peace form, which had been the basis of Greek international relations for most of the past fifty years, was to disguise the supremacy which Philip in fact held. Finally, apart from these intrinsic advantages which the Common Peace arrangement gave to Philip, he received in the treaty, and by immediately subsequent actions of the synhedrion, special guarantees and special powers; the Greeks were made to swear to respect and defend the rule of Philip and his successors in Macedonia,[1] and he was then elected to the office of Hegemon of the Greeks[2] and appointed commanding-general of a war against the Persians.[3]

Whatever the theoretical merits of the Peace of 338/337, there is no escaping the fact that the Common Peace treaty form, which had emerged originally from the principle of city-state independence, had now become the instrument of domination of all city-states by an external power. It might be thought that this was to be the final failure of the Common Peace experiments.

But Common Peace was not finished. The city-state system was enslaved, but not broken up; the wraith of Common Peace, the treaty of 338/337, saw to that, if to nothing else. If Greece became really free again, Common Peace could still be revived; and, if Macedonian rule continued and Philip's

---

[1] Tod 177, vv. 4-5.   [2] See Appendix X.   [3] Diod. xvi. 89. 3, &c.

successors proved to be more severe, the reinstitution of the settlement of 338/337 remained a price that the Greeks could expect for their valuable co-operation with a master whose position was less sure than that of Philip. Philip had set up his adaptation of the Common Peace treaty form as a standard of liberality for the governing of relations between the Greeks and their Macedonian rulers.

The treaty of 338/337 had been concluded for ever and guaranteed the kingdom of both Philip and his descendants. On Philip's death in 336 the Greeks were inclined to feel that Macedonian power had died too, and Alexander had to move quickly to assert his position. He evidently regarded the office of Hegemon as his rightful inheritance, and his possession of it was recognized severally by the Greek cities; only the command against the Persians, which had been voted to Philip personally, was voted to Alexander at the meeting of the synhedrion which he summoned at Corinth. Philip's settlement was left unaltered.[1]

At first at any rate Alexander, though in no way compromising his supreme power, tried to observe the letter of the treaty. When in 335 the Thebans on his rumoured death laid siege to the Macedonian garrison and tried to rouse the rest of Greece,[2] he made the punitive war an action of the synhedrion, and it was that body which fixed the fatal sentence, when the Thebans surrendered;[3] and it was that body to which he demanded the surrender of ten Athenian orators who had proposed abrogation of the treaty.[4] The fact that he dropped this demand shows where the real decisions were made.

When he crossed to Asia in 334, Alexander had to delegate his powers as Hegemon to Antipater, whom he left as regent of Macedonia; whether this move was formally approved by the synhedrion is not known. As he advanced into Asia, Alexander left the Greek cities autonomous, though it is not clear whether they were enrolled into the Common Peace treaty and sent representatives to the synhedrion;[5] later, when the Chians

[1] Diod. xvii. 4; Arr. i. 1. 2; cf. Larsen, 'Representative Government in the Panhellenic Leagues', *Class. Phil.* xx (1925), 316, n. 3. [2] Diod. xvii. 8. 3 ff.
[3] Diod. xvii. 9. 5 and 14. 1 ff. [4] Aesch. iii. 161.
[5] This very vexed question seems to allow no probable solution; cf., for instance, F. Miltner, 'Die staatsrechtliche Entwicklung des Alexanderreiches', *Klio*, xxvi (1933), 39 ff.; E. Bickermann, 'Alexandre le grand et les villes d'Asie', *Rev. d'étud. grec.* xlii (1934), 346 ff.; V. Ehrenberg, *Alexander and the Greeks* (Oxford,

rebelled in 332 and assisted the Persians, it is likely that he handed over their ringleaders for judgement to the synhedrion, who passed the decision back to him.[1] In Greece in 331 Antipater was faced with a war against the Spartans, who were supported by some of the other Peloponnesian states, and he probably made this too an action of the synhedrion; certainly he was helped by some of the Greek cities, and at the end referred the fate of the Spartans to the synhedrion, who again passed the decision on to Alexander.[2] But, while such actions as these were formally correct, it is fairly clear that in the Greek cities the oligarchic governments installed under Macedonian protection were being less than just to their political opponents, many of whom were driven into exile.[3]

It was probably the problem created by the vast number of these exiles, of whom many had become skilful soldiers in Alexander's mercenary army, that he tried to solve by his so-called Exiles Decree,[4] which has been widely interpreted as a flagrant violation of the treaty.

The literary sources say only that Alexander sent Nicanor to read out at the Olympic festival a proclamation that all exiles save the Thebans and those guilty of sacrilege should return to their own cities, and that Antipater had already been ordered to coerce any city unwilling to co-operate.[5] It is clear, though, from a Tegeate decree regulating the return of exiles that Alexander had sent a *diagramma* containing detailed instructions,[6] perhaps direct to individual cities, though there is no evidence that the synhedrion was ignored. But, if he did act through the synhedrion, he was using it only as a means of publicity and as an inferior executive; the proclamation at Olympia came from him and so, it seems, did the instructions to

1938), pp. 1 ff.; T. Lenschau, 'Alexander der grosse und Chios', *Klio*, xxxiii (1940), 201 ff.; W. W. Tarn, *Alexander the Great*, ii (Cambridge, 1948), 199 ff. Ehrenberg also denied the inclusion of many islands in the League, but did not convince Lenschau or Tarn.

[1] Tod 192, vv. 14–16 (Alexander's proclaimed intention to send wrongdoers to the synhedrion) and Arr. iii. 2. 5 ff. (his own judgement of them) could be interpreted otherwise; cf. Ehrenberg, *Alexander and the Greeks*, pp. 23 ff.; Lenschau, art. cit., *Klio*, xxxiii (1940), 204 ff., and Tod's commentary on 192.

[2] Diod. xvii. 62. 6 ff., 73. 5.

[3] Cf. E. Badian, 'Harpalus', *J.H.S.* lxxxi (1961), 28.

[4] Cf. Badian, art. cit., pp. 28 ff.

[5] Diod. xvii. 109. 1, xviii. 8. 2 ff.; Hyper, *c. Dem.* 18; Dinarchus, *c. Dem.* 81 ff.; Plut. *Moralia*, 221A; Justin xiii. 5. 2; Curtius x. 2. 4 ff.   [6] Tod 202.

Antipater.[1] Moreover, whatever the method, the forcible return of exiles, however just it might be said to be, was something against which the cities had been guaranteed in the treaty.[2]

Even so, it would not be safe to say that Alexander had consciously decided to do away with the treaty of 338/337 as the basis of his relations with the Greeks.[3] His distance from Greece and his autocratic position in the East would naturally make him think less of constitutional niceties and it could, no doubt, have been argued that the Exiles Decree was a justified exception, because it respected a transcendent justice.[4] His alleged request for deification in the Greek cities makes the position no clearer; there is no agreement even that the request was made, let alone about what, if any, political significance it had.[5]

Alexander's last important action that concerned the Greeks was his decision, not carried out, to substitute Craterus for Antipater as regent of Macedonia and Hegemon of Greece.[6] This move may have been intended to meet Greek grievances, but it is evident that opposition to Macedonian rule, especially at Athens, was more fundamental than mere discontent with the way in which the settlement of 338/337 had been carried out by Antipater. Many Greeks were far from convinced by the battle of Chaeronea that their special form of political existence had been extinguished. In the theoretical field Aristotle continued to think only in terms of the city-state; and in practice at Athens (the only city, as often, about which much is known at this period) the anti-Macedonian politicians, especially Lycurgus, worked hard to renovate strength for another war. When Lycurgus said that Greek liberty was buried with the dead of Chaeronea,[7] he did not mean that it could never be resurrected, but that phantoms appearing in Macedonian guise should be known for what they were. To cherish hopes of true freedom was

---

[1] Cf. Heuss, art. cit., *Hermes*, lxxiii (1938), 135 ff., for the strongest condemnation. On possible role of the synhedrion cf. H. Bengtson, *Die Strategie in der hellenistischen Zeit*, i (Munich, 1937), 46 ff.

[2] Ps.-Dem. xvii. 16. [3] As Heuss, l.c., implies.

[4] Exile 'contrary to the cities' established laws' was also prohibited in the treaty—Ps.-Dem. xvii. 15.

[5] The story is found to be false by J. P. V. D. Balsdon, 'The "Divinity" of Alexander', *Historia*, ii (1950), 383 ff.; on possible political implications contrast esp. Tarn, *C.A.H.* vi. 419, and Balsdon, art. cit., pp. 386 ff.

[6] Arr. vii. 12. 4. [7] c. Leocr. 50.

not folly. Athens had not been taken; Philip indeed must have been glad to avoid the necessity of a siege. Alexander had hesitated to extract the ten orators by force. When Alexander crossed to Asia, the Persians became for a few years possible allies; then, as he pushed further and further eastwards, it must have seemed increasingly probable that he would be killed or his empire fall to pieces behind him.[1] In 324 Harpalus nearly succeeded in detaching the Athenians from loyalty to Alexander;[2] they and the Aetolians, it is said, had special reasons for being displeased with the Exiles Decree,[3] while the assistance given to the Spartans in 331 is evidence of unrest in the Peloponnese.[4]

The news of Alexander's death in 323 was the signal for a widespread and confident uprising. The Athenians and the Aetolians formed an alliance of Greek cities, which overthrew the treaty, and began to expel Macedonian garrisons, though they did not succeed in winning universal support.[5] Antipater, who was legally regent of the young king, Philip Arrhidaeus, suppressed this movement, but he could hardly have punished the offending cities through the synhedrion—as Alexander had punished the Thebans, and as he himself had been willing to punish the Spartans—for they were too numerous. Indeed, though he did not, as far as is known, formally dissolve the settlement of 338/337, he did not reconstitute the synhedrion and took what measures he thought fit to prevent further trouble.

At Athens, for instance, he altered the constitution from democracy to timocracy, and installed a governor and a garrison.[6] This treatment was, according to Diodorus, much milder than the Athenians expected. Moreover, although the city was thus denied its freedom and autonomy, as defined in the treaty of 338/337, and reduced to the same sort of position that the subjects of Athens and Sparta had held in the fifth and early fourth centuries, it remained a separate entity.[7] Antipater made no

---

[1] On all this cf. A. W. Gomme, 'The End of the City-State', *Essays in Greek History and Literature* (Oxford, 1937), pp. 204 ff.; Ps.-Dem. xvii gives a fair idea of the attitude of the anti-Macedonian politicians to the treaty.

[2] Cf. Badian, art. cit., *J.H.S.* lxxxi (1961), 31 ff.

[3] Diod. xviii. 8. 6; Justin xiii. 5. 1 and 6.   [4] Diod. xvii. 62. 7.

[5] The extent of the alliance is given by Diod. xviii. 11. 1 ff.; the battle-cry was Greek freedom—cf. ibid. 9. 5 and 10. 2–3.

[6] Diod. xviii. 18.

[7] Cf. Gomme, *Essays in Greek History and Literature*, p. 213.

attempt to absorb into Macedonian territory Athens or any other Greek city which he similarly controlled. Freedom could be restored merely by the expulsion of the garrisons and governors and the restoration of the governments suppressed by Antipater. Antipater was no doctrinaire; he had put down the democracy at Athens, for example, not because he favoured a timocracy as such, but because in this particular case a timocracy favoured his supporters.

After Antipater's death in 319 Polyperchon was appointed regent on his recommendation;[1] but Antipater's son, Cassander, seemed likely to inherit most of his power—and of his unpopularity—in Greece. He also had the support of Antigonus and Ptolemy, who had both gained control over large areas of Alexander's empire.[2] Embassies from the Greek cities waited on Polyperchon,[3] sensing an opportunity to employ the differences in the Macedonian hierarchy to their own advantage.

Polyperchon now drafted a proclamation in the name of the King, which he bade the Greek envoys publish in their cities. In this proclamation[4] the King declared that he wanted to continue the goodwill which Philip and Alexander had shown to the Greeks, and reiterated the pledge that he had given on his accession, that he would observe 'the Peace and the constitutions which Philip had set up'. Some of the Greeks, he said, had wrongfully decided to make war on him, but the severity of their punishment was the responsibility of his generals (i.e. Antipater). He himself intended to maintain the position under Philip and Alexander and to uphold their *diagrammata* (including presumably the Exiles Decree, for he went on to declare that all those who had been exiled since Alexander's crossing to Asia should return, with specific exceptions). The Athenians were to receive back Samos and Oropus, which they had held at the time of the treaty of 338/337 and only since lost. Finally he proclaimed that 'all Greeks should pass a decree' that no one should make an expedition against the King or do anything hostile to him.

In this way the young King, or rather his regent Polyperchon, undertook to renew the treaty of 338/337 and the Common Peace settlement. The last sentence of the proclamation seems to

---

[1] Diod. xviii. 48. 4.   [2] Ibid. 55. 2.
[3] Ibid. 4.   [4] Ibid. 56.

show that the synhedrion set up by that treaty was to be reconstituted to pass decrees in the name of the Greeks.[1] The proclamation stressed the overthrow of existing constitutions as the way in which the treaty had been infringed by the King's representatives, and hostility to the King as the principal transgression of the Greeks. But Polyperchon invoked the Common Peace settlement not to settle Greece, as Philip had done, but to win support for himself in a war against Cassander in Greece. Greek freedom now became the battle-cry of the Successors in their efforts to win Greek support. That support was something which they all to a greater or lesser degree came to feel to be essential to the maintenance and extension of their power. The Greeks provided the brains of their world, and so were much in demand as generals and administrators.

Polyperchon achieved some success in Greece after this proclamation, but his liberations of cities were limited and insecure. Athens was freed and a democratic government restored,[2] but Cassander's troops held the Piraeus. There was really scarcely any opportunity of testing the sincerity of Polyperchon's promises; the full organization of the League could not be restored, though some sort of meeting of Peloponnesian cities was held to co-ordinate their alliance with him.[3] Garrisons remained in some of the liberated cities, but this practice had been allowed in special cases in the treaty of 338/337 and was doubtless necessary to defend them against Cassander.

Megalopolis, however, resisted all Polyperchon's attempts to win her over by persuasion or by siege. This setback was apparently enough to make most of the cities abandon him and go over to Cassander.[4] The Athenians made an agreement with Cassander by which he could retain Munychia and nominate a 'guardian of the city'—he chose Demetrius of Phaleron—and by which they were to be his friends and allies.[5] Diodorus observes that the Greeks were more impressed by Cassander's

---

[1] Recognized by Wilcken, 'Beiträge zur Geschichte des korinthischen Bundes', *Sitzb. München*, 1917, iii, abh. x. 32, as a declaration of a renewal of the treaty of 338/337; connected with Common Peace by Bengtson, *Die Strategie in der hellenistischen Zeit*, i, 84. Heuss, art. cit., *Hermes*, lxxiii (1938), 143 ff., saw no offer to renew the treaty; he took δόγμα (Diod. xviii. 56. 7) to refer to decrees of the separate cities (but why in the singular?), and considered the Peloponnesian alliance of Diod. xviii. 69. 3 to have been only a working arrangement for the war.

[2] Diod. xviii. 65. 6.   [3] Ibid. 69. 3 ff.

[4] Ibid. 74. 1.   [5] Ibid. 3.

activity than by Polyperchon's words and were satisfied with the former's moderation.[1] Polyperchon's liberations had been by no means bloodless.

In 315 both Seleucus (East Asia) and Ptolemy (Egypt) on the one side and Antigonus (Asia Minor) on the other sent embassies to Cassander and Lysimachus (Hellespontine region) to secure their alliance. Antigonus was unsuccessful and subsequently refused the demands of his four rivals for an equal division of Alexander's empire. He at once prepared to defend himself and among other measures sent Aristodemus of Miletus to the Peloponnese with a thousand talents to win support from Polyperchon and his friends. Aristodemus was able to raise a mercenary force at Sparta and to make agreements with Polyperchon, who was designated 'General of the Peloponnese', and with his lieutenant, Alexander.[2]

Shortly afterwards Antigonus published his freedom decree. He had summoned a meeting of the Macedonian army, before which he accused Cassander of plotting against Roxane and the King. The meeting voted Cassander an enemy, unless he destroyed the cities of Thebes and Olynthus, which he had restored, gave back Roxane and the King to the Macedonians and handed over the kingdom to Antigonus; it was also agreed that the Greeks should be autonomous, free and without garrisons.[3] This freedom decree also was an obvious attempt to win support in Greece,[4] and deeds rather than words will provide evidence of its sincerity. Though Antigonus had at first supported Cassander, he had shown signs of philhellenism even before Polyperchon's proclamation.[5] It is true that he condemned Cassander for refounding cities, but Olynthus had been destroyed years before the treaty of 338/337 and Thebes as the result of a vote of the Council of the League, sitting in judgement over a breach of the treaty.

Polyperchon and Alexander soon deserted Antigonus, but in 313 he sent out Telesphorus with orders to liberate the cities. He freed all the cities which were occupied by Alexander's garrisons, except Sicyon and Corinth.[6] Meanwhile in Asia

---

[1] Diod. xviii. 75. 2; for Cassander's policy of separate alliances and garrisons cf. Bengtson, *Die Strategie in der hellenistischen Zeit*, i, 133.

[2] Diod. xix. 56 ff.   [3] Ibid. 61. 1–3.   [4] Ibid. 4.

[5] Diod. xviii. 52. 1 ff.; cf. Heuss, art. cit., *Hermes*, lxxiii (1938), 143.

[6] Diod. xix. 74. 1 ff.

Antigonus granted the satrap of Caria peace on condition that he left the Greek cities in his district autonomous.[1] At about the same time he entered into negotiations with Cassander about a local peace in the Hellespont, but without result;[2] he later claimed that the talks broke down through his insistence that the Greek cities should be autonomous.[3]

In 312 Antigonus sent Ptolemaeus to join Telesphorus with the same instructions and a larger fleet. After some failures he took Chalcis and left it ungarrisoned; then with Cassander occupied in Macedonia, he won control of central Greece and apparently was able to leave the cities without garrisons there also.[4] Almost at once Telesphorus, who was in the Peloponnese, deserted Antigonus, but was defeated at Elis by Ptolemaeus, who left the city free.[5]

Antigonus' commanders were thus in control of most of Greece south of Thermopylae, but not Athens, when he concluded a general peace treaty in 311 with Cassander, Lysimachus and Ptolemy. One of the conditions of this Peace was that the Greeks should be autonomous, and Antigonus sent letters to the Greek cities claiming the credit for this clause and telling them that it had been agreed that all cities should swear to aid one another in preserving freedom and autonomy. Thus, though there was no separate treaty for the Greeks, the autonomy clause of the general treaty and the Greek oath virtually constituted a renewal of the Common Peace.[6]

It has been suggested that by his championship of Greek autonomy Antigonus made the best propaganda out of an unfavourable Peace.[7] But in fact the Peace seems to have left him free to deal with Seleucus in eastern Asia,[8] and in Greece he had not fared too badly, suffering more from the disloyalty of his generals than from any strong ill feeling among the Greeks. Yet he could not afford to lose their goodwill;[9] to that extent the freedom of the Greeks was only a weapon. If he

---

[1] Ibid. 75. 1 ff.   [2] Ibid. 6.

[3] Vv. 5 ff. of the letter to Scepsis (C. B. Welles, *Royal Correspondence in the Hellenistic Period* (New Haven–Prague, 1934), no. 1); cf. R. H. Simpson, 'The Historical Circumstances of the Peace of 311', *J.H.S.* lxxiv (1954), 27 ff.

[4] Diod. xix. 77 ff.   [5] Ibid. 87.   [6] See Appendix XI.

[7] Cf. Welles, *Royal Correspondence*, no. 1, commentary.

[8] Cf. Simpson, art. cit., *J.H.S.* lxxiv (1954), 25 ff.

[9] On the importance attached by Antigonus to his being seen to liberate cities cf. Diod. xix. 74. 1, 78. 2.

succeeded in re-establishing Alexander's empire, he could restore the treaty of 338/337 in conditions of stable peace; but, if warfare continued between the great rulers without decision, Greece could obtain and preserve full freedom only with a guaranteed neutrality. However scrupulously Antigonus observed the freedom of the cities, his ambitions made him a continuing menace to Greek neutrality; if war broke out between him and Cassander or any other of the great rulers, the Greeks would have to join in.[1]

As it was, the Peace was not fully implemented and Cassander's garrisons remained in such Greek cities as he still held. In 307 war broke out again, and now Antigonus sent his son, Demetrius, to Greece to organize the Greek cities into a league[2] —as an effective weapon of war. Though Demetrius liberated Athens in that same year,[3] it was not until 302 that he was able to reassemble the synhedrion of the Greeks and formally constitute the League.[4] This League was based not on a Common Peace treaty, but on an alliance between Antigonus and Demetrius and the Greeks. It differed from the organization set up by Philip in that it was formed to fight a war with Cassander that was already in progress; Philip's machinery had been set up to preserve the Peace, and, though he used it in order to obtain the support of the Greeks against Persia, he did not form a League to fight the Persians in Greece.[5]

In the next year Antigonus was defeated and killed at Ipsus by a combination of his rivals, a defeat which meant that no one man would regain control over Alexander's empire. In so far as the conditions of war permitted, Antigonus seems to have kept his promises to the Greeks;[6] in his lifetime he certainly acquired a better reputation as a liberator than those of his

---

[1] Cf. the case of Rhodes, which Demetrius tried to coerce into a war with Ptolemy—Diod. xx. 46. 6.

[2] Diod. xx. 46. 5.   [3] Ibid. 45. 1 ff.

[4] Plut. *Demetrius* 25.

[5] Knowledge of the organization of this League is derived from the Epidaurus inscription, *S.E.G.* i. 75; cf. Wilcken, 'Zu der epidaurischen Bundesstelle vom J. 302 v. Chr.', *Sitzb. Berlin*, 1927, pp. 277 ff.; Larsen, art. cit., *Class. Phil.* xx (1925), 313 ff., xxi (1926), 52 ff.; Hampl, *Die griechischen Staatsverträge*, pp. 113 ff.

[6] e.g. at Athens after 307—cf. Gomme, *Essays in Greek History and Literature*, p. 216; the tyrannical nature of his well-known letters to Teos (Welles, *Royal Correspondence*, nos. 3 and 4) is often exaggerated. On Antigonus' freedom policy generally, cf. Heuss, art. cit., *Hermes*, lxxiii (1938), 147 ff.

rivals who attempted to imitate his policy.[1] But after his defeat at Ipsus the League of Greeks collapsed about the ears of Demetrius,[2] even though he had again secured from his enemies a general recognition of Greek freedom.[3] For all his goodwill Antigonus had not succeeded in creating any loyalty to himself in Greece. The policy of freedom for the Greek cities had been put to a good test and had failed. The Greeks were not prepared to support an overlord, however benevolent, and, if a rival appeared, many saw in him hopes of a fuller freedom or one more suited to their factional interests. They showed a marked inclination to prefer the devil they did not know to the devil they did know in the usually fanciful belief that he might be very much better. It is not surprising that, when Demetrius returned to Greece, he adopted the practice of garrisoning the cities which he held[4] and that the system of free states in Greece was not tried by any of the Hellenistic rulers for over seventy-five years.

[1] Soon after Antigonus' freedom decree of 315, Ptolemy also declared support for Greek liberty (Diod. xix. 62. 1), though allied to Cassander. He persisted with this policy against Antigonus in Asia when the war broke out again after 311 (Diod. xx. 19. 3), but the tradition records few liberations (ibid. 4–5). Eventually he rejoined Cassander, agreeing that each should 'control the cities they held' ($\kappa\upsilon\rho\iota\epsilon\acute{\upsilon}\epsilon\iota\nu$ —ibid. 37. 2), soon after he had toyed with the idea of establishing a League of free Greek cities, but had met with an unfavourable response from the Peloponnesians (ibid.). Cf. Bengtson, *Die Strategie in der hellenistischen Zeit.* i, 144; Heuss, art. cit., *Hermes*, lxxiii (1938), 150; Simpson, art. cit., *J.H.S.* lxxiv (1954), 30 ff.
[2] Plut. *Demetrius* 30–31. [3] Diod. xx. 111. 2.
[4] Cf. P. Treves, 'Dopo Ipso', *Riv. di filol.* n.s. ix (1931), 76 ff.

VIII

Common Peace and the Greek Political Theorists of the Fourth Century

THE fourth century was the golden age of Greek political thought, and it might be expected that the Common Peace treaties would have found some place in these discussions. Yet neither of the two great writers on political theory, Plato and Aristotle, mentions in his extant works either the treaties or the principle of autonomy. This silence has, of course, less significance in view of the fact that both almost entirely confined their deep interest in politics to the study of the behaviour of men within a state and ignored the question of the behaviour of a state towards other states.

Even so, this obsession with the internal workings of the city-state is the more disappointing, in that on the few occasions other than in the enigmatic *Menexenus* when external affairs enter the conversation in Plato's dialogues, Plato can be seen putting forward views, through the character of Socrates, which might be thought to indicate a mind likely to be interested in any system which would prevent imperialism and war. There is, for instance, criticism of the policy of the Athenian leaders of the fifth century in the *Gorgias*,[1] which was written well before the King's Peace; and in the fifth book of the *Republic*[2] Socrates observes that, while the struggles of Greeks with barbarians are rightly called war, those between Greeks and Greeks are a disease of Greece and are civil war.

But in the *Gorgias* passage Plato describes only the evil effects of the policies of the fifth century on the Athenians themselves, just as at the beginning of the Seventh Letter[3] and in the third book of the *Laws*[4] it is the internal working of the Athenian state which he condemns; and in the *Republic* he goes no further than sentiments which had been voiced already but more

---

[1] 518E–519B.   [2] 469B–471B.   [3] 324B ff.   [4] 698A ff.

briefly in the *Menexenus*[1] and in Lysias' *Funeral Oration*,[2] and he does not discuss the right principles of inter-state relations.

Aristotle too is a critic of empire, but his interest in international politics appears no greater than Plato's. The criticisms that are made in the *Politics*[3] are again in general terms, and included only indirectly in discussions of the purposes for which various city-state constitutions had been formulated.

[1] 242E. [2] C. 21. [3] VII. ii. 7 ff. and xiii. 11 ff.

IX

Conclusion

IN the Introduction it was emphasized that the way in which the phrase κοινὴ εἰρήνη is used in the extant works of Greek writers indicates a close connexion between what the Greeks meant by Common Peace and the firm realities of the Common Peace treaties. Now at the conclusion it must be admitted that the sources reveal no great idealistic support at any time for the concept of general peace in Greece and that none of the great politicians or writers of the fourth century can be linked with Common Peace in the way that Woodrow Wilson and others are linked with the League of Nations. A version of his 'Peace without Victory' appears, it is true, in Andocides, and his condemnation of entangling alliances in Demosthenes, but one may question the sincerity of speakers who had a special case to argue, and, if something is sought like Wilson's advocacy of a 'Community of Power' as opposed to a balance of power, it cannot be found.

In any case, whatever individual speakers said about the treaties they were not designed, at least until the period of Macedonian supremacy, as instruments of collective security, like the charter of the League of Nations (or that of the United Nations), to produce a settled peaceful order among a plurality of independent states; but they were the result of a combination of political motives and circumstances that made general peace on the basis of autonomy fairly generally acceptable.

None the less the treaties that were concluded in 387/386, in 375, twice in 371, in 362/361 and in 338/337, and those that were discussed at panhellenic conferences in 392, 391, 368 and 367, and on other occasions in 346 and 343 were in form nearer to the ideals which Wilson enunciated in 1917 than were the treaties that brought a formal end to the First World War and set up the League of Nations. The Common Peace treaties were all applicable to all states, irrespective of the alignment of states in the wars that they concluded, and they were based on a single general principle of freedom and autonomy for all. The Pact of Paris of 1928 (the Briand–Kellogg Pact) alone approached this expression of an equally applicable principle, and it was not generally adopted. Similarly in the Common Peace treaties of 371 at Athens, of 362/361 and of 338/337 guarantee clauses were included and were sworn to by the participants such as were never generally accepted between 1919 and 1930; only the Draft Treaty of Mutual Assistance and the Geneva Protocol rendered military sanctions obligatory, but these agreements too were never accepted.

Yet this perfection may appear little more than an exercise in hopeful generalization, for, though the Common Peace treaties were in theory a solution of the problem of Greek international life, producing peace through a universal guarantee of independence, in practice they had at first obvious weaknesses which contributed to their failure to produce lasting peace; the independence which was guaranteed was not defined, and the guarantee was not made explicit. But as time went on the Greeks introduced into the treaties qualifications of autonomy and developed the guarantee clause binding all cities to go to the help of the injured party, improvements which, though usually to be related to particular situations and having their origins in power-politics, were still improvements and perhaps to some extent recognized to be so. But the central problem of the practical working of the guarantee remained intractable, until it was solved by the formation through the imposed Peace of 338/337 of the synhedrion of the Greeks, by which some sort of compromise was achieved between the duties and the privileges of an independent state; but the circumstances of the synhedrion's foundation made it appear to many to deny in practice the premise of the Common Peace treaties, that all states should be free and autonomous.

Though, as has been said, Common Peace does not seem ever to have been a widely held ideal, it must have become a very strong habit of thought. The conclusion of each Common Peace treaty marked its participants' reaffirmation that the legal condition of Greece was one in which all cities, large and small, were independent. The number of times that these principles of Common Peace were either reconstituted after a new war by a new treaty or proposed as the basis of a pacification shows how ready the Greeks were to admit, for whatever motives, that such was the legal condition of Greece. The early years of the sixties in particular show the leading cities each having to put the principles of the Peace as the foundation of their varying policies, and indeed the assumption was sometimes made that the terms of the Peace were still valid at times when a particular treaty might be said to have broken down. Xenophon obscures the true nature of the Common Peace treaties in his *Hellenica*; they were in conflict often with the purely national outlook of Isocrates and Demosthenes. Yet all three speak in the fifties as if it were generally admitted that the principles of Common Peace were right and had to be the starting-point of any foreign policy.

Further, it has been shown how the Athenians, the Spartans and the Thebans all at various times expected and obtained important support from the smaller cities by proclaiming themselves the defenders of Common Peace. Agesipolis and his friends in Sparta in the years after the King's Peace advocated, and the moderate Athenian leaders between 386 and 366 and again between 355 and 346 brought into effect, policies both passive and active which may be judged to have been in accordance with the principles of the Peace. These principles had sufficient support for Philip of Macedon to use a Common Peace treaty as the basis of his settlement of conquered Greece and for his successors to regard that settlement as the true legal expression of a liberal policy towards Greece; but they were not popular enough of themselves to reconcile the Greeks to the rule of Philip and Alexander or to win them without question to the side of any of the Successors who proposed to re-establish the treaty.

The treaties failed to prevent imperialism and war, but they at least assisted the smaller cities to keep more free of both. In the fifth century the Athenians and the Spartans, acting in opposition or in concert, had dominated the smaller cities, and the growth of their two systems had greatly increased the scope of war. At the beginning of the fourth century a greater division of power had produced the conditions in which the Common Peace treaties became possible. The enshrinement of the principle of autonomy in the treaties increased the power of the smaller cities to protect themselves; a state which blatantly transgressed the treaty had broken its oaths, and was open to attack from other participants. The association of the King of Persia with the treaties gave the Greeks of the Aegean the advantage of his support without the disadvantages of his active interference. Though the Spartans, the Athenians and the Thebans all sponsored treaties for their own interests, none of them succeeded in using the treaties to gain control of Greece or permanently to subject any part of it; the Peace of 362/361 was not the product of any particular one of the leading states, and in the following decades Greece was less dominated by them than at any time in the previous 200 years. Even under Macedonian domination the smaller cities were perhaps, through the settlement of 338/337, more free than in the golden age of Greek liberty.

It is true that the treaties consecrated the division of Greece into small political units and made the task of the panhellenists harder. But during the century concessions had to be made in the strict interpretation of the autonomy principle in favour of the federal state (for example, in Boeotia and Arcadia). It would certainly be wrong to say that the treaties led to subservience to Persia, for it was the Persians' decisive influence that prompted the original proposals which led to the King's Peace; or that they led to Philip's domination, for, though the independent Peloponnesian states, for instance, used their newly won freedom of action to do nothing to oppose him, they were not being entirely irresponsible, and the treaty of 338/337 was the result, not the cause, of Macedonian conquest.

APPENDIX I

The King's Peace

(a) *'Possessing their own territory'* ($\H{\epsilon}\chi o\nu\tau\epsilon s$ $\tau\grave{\eta}\nu$ $\dot{\epsilon}av\tau\hat{\omega}\nu$)

Martin first suggested that this phrase was added,[1] though it is not mentioned by Xenophon or Diodorus. He referred to Justin's notice of this Peace (vi. 6. 1 ff.: 'civitatibus libertatem *suaque omnia* restituit'), and to Andocides' statement (iii. 19) that in 392/391 the Spartans were ready to make peace $\tau\grave{\eta}\nu$ $\dot{\epsilon}av\tau\hat{\omega}\nu$ $\H{\epsilon}\chi o\nu\tau\epsilon s$. There are these other considerations:

(i) This formula was already in use in connexion with autonomy in official documents, such as the guarantee to the Plataeans in 479 (Thuc. ii. 71. 2), and the alliance between the Spartans and the Argives in 418 (Thuc. v. 79. 1).

(ii) In Aristoteles' decree (of 377) the Athenians proclaim that the object of their confederacy is to make 'the Spartans leave the Greeks free, autonomous and at peace in secure possession of all their own land' (Tod 123, vv. 11–12), but reserve their other definitions of autonomy until later in the decree. This arrangement suggests that $\H{\epsilon}\chi o\nu\tau\epsilon s$ $\tau\grave{\eta}\nu$ $\dot{\epsilon}av\tau\hat{\omega}\nu$ was regarded as closely linked with $\dot{\epsilon}\lambda\epsilon\acute{v}\theta\epsilon\rho o\iota$ $\kappa a\grave{\iota}$ $a\vec{v}\tau\acute{o}\nu o\mu o\iota$ in the King's Peace.

(iii) Isocrates' reference in *On Peace* viii. 16, to a King's Peace which laid down that the Greeks should be autonomous, that garrisons should depart from foreign cities and that each city should possess its own territory seems to be to the treaty of 375, when the second clause was almost certainly a novelty, but there is no reason to suppose that the third clause was also new on that occasion.

It is hard to evaluate another passage of Isocrates which appears to have some bearing on this question. In *Panegyricus* iv. 177 he said that those who negotiated the King's Peace 'ought to have decided either that each city should possess its own territory or that they should enjoy the conquests of war or that they should hold that which they happened to have at the time of the Peace, and to have fixed one of these and made it a general principle'. Isocrates was criticizing the autonomy clause as too vague, because it played into the hands of the Persians and shackled the traditional leaders of Greece. The fact that he suggested 'possessing their own territory' as a better alternative does not

[1] Art. cit., *Museum Helveticum*, i (1944), 26.

necessarily mean that the Peace itself did not include these words as a subsidiary to the main autonomy principle.

(b) The 'definitions' of autonomy

It has been argued in the previous section that the balance of evidence leads to the conclusion that the clause there discussed was included in the King's Peace, although neither Xenophon nor Diodorus mentions it. In this case also silence in Xenophon and Diodorus proves nothing; Xenophon records no definitions of autonomy and Diodorus none in his account of the Peace, while his statement (xv. 5. 1) that under the Peace all the cities had removed their garrisons and inherited autonomy by agreement need mean nothing more than that any cities which had foreign garrisons before the treaty did not have them after it (which must have been the case). The most cogent evidence that the definitions were not included in the treaty is the wording of Aristoteles' decree (referred to above) which seems to put the definitions (πολιτευομένῳ πολιτείαν ἣν ἂν βούληται . . . κ.τ.λ.— vv. 20–25) in a different category to the actual terms of the Peace (vv. 10–12). Other arguments are from silence, viz. (i) that none of these definitions has hitherto been associated in treaties with freedom and autonomy, (ii) that there is no recorded complaint from the period that the Spartans were incontrovertibly transgressing the *letter* of the treaty by, for instance, interfering in the internal political balance of Phlius and Thebes and stationing garrisons in these cities, (iii) that the clause in the Peace of 375 which provided that all cities be free of foreign garrisons is readily explicable there as an innovation related to the political situation (cf. above p. 59). These arguments are not overwhelmingly strong, but the burden of proof here rests with those who would believe that definitions of autonomy were included in the Peace, and that burden is one which in the present state of the evidence they cannot sustain.

APPENDIX II

The Peace of 375

XENOPHON (*Hell.* VI. ii. I) gives neither the terms of this Peace nor the states that took part in it besides the Athenians and the Spartans. Diodorus (xv. 38) supplies more details. Artaxerxes, he says, wanted Greek mercenaries for his war in Egypt, and so decided to try to secure a pacification in Greece. Accordingly he sent ambassadors to the Greek cities calling upon them to make a Common Peace;[1] they readily heeded him, and all made peace on condition that all cities should be autonomous and free of foreign garrisons. The Thebans would not accept these terms, because they aimed at the control of all Boeotia; the Athenians objected and, after a bitter argument between Epaminondas and Callistratus, the Thebans were excluded. The Spartans and the Athenians then divided the hegemony.

Diodorus' account here is very similar to his account (xv. 50) of the Peace of 371 at Sparta, in which he again tells of the intervention of the King, the conclusion of a Common Peace and the opposition and exclusion of the Thebans. It is well known that in 371 the Thebans were excluded from the Peace, and it is clear that they were included in the Peace of 375, since they remained active members of the Athenian confederacy after it (cf. above, p. 60), and since Isocrates takes it for granted in the *Plataicus* that they and the Plataeans had been parties to a Peace which guaranteed autonomy to all after the refoundation of Plataea and after the liberation of Thebes from the Spartans in 379; Isocrates' evidence indeed makes it plain that the Peace of 375 was a Common Peace, for he can refer to no other treaty (cf. esp. ss. 1, 5, 10 and 14).

Diodorus' account of the exclusion of the Thebans in 375 must be a doublet drawn by him or by his source from the account of the treaty of 371, the factual basis of the misinterpretation being an Athenian threat to remove the Thebans from the confederacy, which is mentioned by Isocrates (*Plataicus* 37).[2]

---

[1] . . . τοὺς παρακαλέσοντας τὰς πόλεις κοινὴν εἰρήνην συνθέσθαι.

[2] A. Roos, 'The Peace of Sparta of 374 B.C.', *Mnemosyne*, N.S. ii (1949), 265 ff., defends Diodorus against accusations of negligence and error in confusing the two treaties; he points out that Diodorus evidently knew that his accounts were similar, and blames a pro-Theban source for the story of Theban opposition in 375/374. Cf. also S. Lauffer, 'Die Diodordublette xv 38 = 50 über die Friedensschlüsse zu Sparta', *Historia*, viii (1959), 315 ff.

Further evidence that this Peace was a renewal of the King's Peace is the initiative of the King. On this subject also Diodorus repeats himself in his account of the Peace of 371 at Sparta, but here, if there is a doublet, it seems to be the latter, since in 371 the King probably did not take the initiative (cf. the next appendix) and the King's motive in 375, his need of mercenaries, is more convincing than that given for 371, that he observed that Greece was again disturbed. Moreover, Didymus, quoting (col. vii. 62 ff.) a passage from Philochorus about the erection of an altar to Peace and other festivities at Athens which are known from Isocrates (xv. 109) to have followed this Peace, connects it with a 'Peace from the King'.[1]

The statements of Diodorus (referred to above) and of Cornelius Nepos (*Timotheus* 2) that the Athenians and the Spartans now divided the hegemony led Hampl[2] to suppose that there was a compulsory guarantee clause to this treaty by which all the signatories were pledged to attack a transgressor under the leadership of the Athenians by sea and of the Spartans on land. But this suggestion is improbable. There is, for instance, no mention of any guarantee clause to this Peace in Isocrates' *Plataicus*, which purports to be the appeal of the Plataeans at Athens for help against Theban aggression.[3] In support of his theory Hampl argued that the voluntary guarantee clause of the treaty of 371 at Sparta which laid down that 'if anyone acts against this agreement, those who want to may go to the help of the wronged cities, but those who do not want to are not bound by oath to do so' (Xen. *Hell.* vi. iii. 18) necessarily presupposes a clause in the previous treaty by which all were bound by oath to such action. But even in the absence of a formal guarantee clause participants in a Common Peace could be felt to be under some obligation to defend it, and this clause in the 371 treaty was, as Hampl himself saw,[4] to a great extent the result of the Athenians wishing to stand aside from any war between the Spartans and the Thebans, while at the same time preserving their position as respected leaders of a confederacy dedicated to the defence of the Peace and of autonomy; and the voluntary clause seems also to be the more natural first step in fixing a guarantee clause for a Common Peace treaty, as it involved no extra surrender of sovereignty (cf. above, p. 68).

It has been argued above (p. 60) that the Peace did represent a mutual recognition by the Spartans and the Athenians of their respective alliances, and, when the Peace broke down almost at once after a quarrel between the Spartans and the Athenians, the impression

---

[1] Isocr. *Plataicus* 41 does not mean that the King had nothing to do with this Peace, but that he kept out of Greek affairs while Athenian naval power was being rebuilt—cf. Roos, art. cit., p. 276.   [2] *Die griechischen Staatsverträge*, p. 17.
[3] Cf. Roos, art. cit., p. 281.   [4] Op. cit., p. 105.

might easily have been created that the main meaning of the Peace had been a *rapprochement* between the two cities. Hence Xenophon in his very brief account only mentions them,[1] and Diodorus and Nepos (or their common source) exaggerated the mutual recognition of alliances into an explicit division of hegemony such as was proposed in 369 (Xen. *Hell.* VII. i. 2; Diod. xv. 67).[2]

[1] Cf. Sordi's defence of Xenophon in 'I carattori dell'opera storiografica di Senofonte nelle Elleniche: II. Le Elleniche come opera storica', *Athenaeum*, xxix (1951), 323 ff.

[2] For the clause about the withdrawal of garrisons, see above, pp. 58–59. This treaty is generally interpreted as a Common Peace (or as a general peace by those who do not use the term Common Peace); for a list of dissentients cf. Lauffer, art. cit., *Historia*, viii (1959), 336, n. 73.

APPENDIX III

The Peace of 371 at Sparta

(a) The conference

Xenophon's account makes it clear that the conference was attended by ambassadors from the Thebans and from the other allies of the Athenians and by representatives of the allies of the Spartans (Xen. *Hell.* VI. iii. 3 and 19).

The part played by the King of Persia is more controversial. Diodorus (XV. 50. 4) says that he promoted the conference; but his account of the conclusion of this Peace is closely similar to that of the conclusion of the Peace of 375, and he (or his source) has already been shown to have read the exclusion of the Thebans back from this Peace to that of 375. So, as his account of Persian intervention in 375 seems authentic, his account of it here is open to suspicion.

There is nothing in Xenophon to suggest that the King initiated this Peace. True, there was nothing either about his part in the Peace of 375, but this narrative is a good deal more detailed. The references in his account of the conference at Athens later in 371 (*Hell.* VI. v. 1, 2) to 'the Peace which the King sent down' probably refers to the original King's Peace; and there is one passage which strongly suggests that the Persians had not promoted the conference at Sparta. Callistratus is made (at Xen. *Hell.* VI. iii. 12) to answer allegations that the Athenians wanted peace only because they were afraid that Antalcidas would bring back some help for the Spartans from the King. It is clear first that, if Antalcidas had gone to Persia, he had not returned (and, if he had not returned, he was still negotiating); second that, if the King had promoted the peace negotiations and was through a representative directing them, allegations that the Athenians were afraid of possible Persian interference make nonsense. This second point is still valid, even if, as Momigliano suggested,[1] Callistratus did not mean that Antalcidas was in Persia, but that the situation of 387 might recur. It must be concluded that the King had no part in this conference.[2]

---

[1] Art. cit., *Riv. di filol.* lxii (1934), 486.

[2] Diodorus' version is accepted by, among others, Heuss, art. cit., *Hermes*, lxxiii (1938), 164; Taeger, *Der Friede von 362/1*, p. 27; Momigliano, loc. cit.; and Bengtson, *Griechische Geschichte*, p. 257; against them cf. Underhill, *Xenophon's Hellenica*, p. 239; Accame, *La lega ateniense*, p. 152; and Lauffer, art. cit., *Historia*, viii (1959), 321 ff. The statement of Dionysius of Halicarnassus (*Lys.* 12) that the King actually swore to the treaty is clearly wrong.

There is also no reason to suppose that Dionysius of Syracuse was represented. It is true that he had sent some assistance to the Spartans during the past few years, but the passage in the decree passed in his honour at Athens in 368 (Tod 133, vv. 23 ff.) which has been adduced[1] to prove that he was represented at this conference could refer to the later Peace concluded at Athens, and in any case need not necessarily mean that he had had a share in the conclusion of the Peace rather than that he had merely helped in its maintenance.

(b) *The terms*

The autonomy clause is mentioned by Xenophon (*Hell.* vi. iii. 18) and Diodorus (xv. 50. 4), who refers to the Peace as Common Peace, and is assumed by Plutarch (*Ages.* 27. 3 and 28. 1–2). The stipulation that harmosts should be withdrawn and armies and fleets demobilized, and the guarantee clause are only in Xenophon's account.

It has been held[2] that at this peace conference the Athenian claim to Amphipolis and the Chersonese was recognized. The evidence for this belief consists of four passages from the orators written during the late forties of this century. Demosthenes in 343 (xix. 253) referred to 'Amphipolis, which the King and the Greeks decided was yours' and in 341 (ix. 16) described the Chersonese in similar terms; Hegesippus in 343 (Ps.-Dem. vii. 29) called Amphipolis 'the place which the Greeks and the King voted and decided was yours', while Aeschines in 343 (ii. 32) said that 'after a meeting of the Spartans and other Greeks, Amyntas, the father of Philip, being one of them and sending a representative and being fully in control of his own vote, voted with the other Greeks to assist the Athenians to recover Amphipolis' and that he himself provided evidence for this statement from the public records by producing 'the common decree of the Greeks' and the list of those who voted.

It was argued above that the King had nothing to do with the Peace of 371 at Sparta. But the decision of the Greeks at least could still have been made at this conference, since, as Accame pointed out,[3] these passages do not necessarily mean that the decisions of the King and of the Greeks were simultaneous. Accame rightly maintained that the decision of the King about Amphipolis can only be the recognition of the Athenian claim which he certainly made after the rejection of Pelopidas' peace proposals in 367 (Dem. xix. 137); those proposals included provision for the independence of Amphipolis and the King, who had approved them, declared Amphipolis his friend and ally.

---

[1] e.g. by Momigliano, loc. cit.

[2] e.g. by Heuss, Taeger and Bengtson, locc. citt.

[3] *La lega ateniense*, p. 155.

Were it not for the Aeschines passage, it would then be reasonable, taking account of oratorical exaggeration, to see the Greek recognition of the Athenians' claims in the refusal of the Greeks in general to accept Pelopidas' proposals at the conference at Thebes (Xen. *Hell.* vii. 1. 39).

But Aeschines unequivocally states that the Athenian claim was recognized by the Greeks at a time when Amyntas was King of Macedonia or at latest very soon after his death (before midsummer 369).[1] Aeschines' expressions '. . . of the Spartans and the other Greeks', 'with the other Greeks' and 'common decree of the Greeks' suggest a panhellenic conference leading to a Common Peace, but his choice of the word 'alliance' ($\sigma\upsilon\mu\mu\alpha\chi\iota\alpha$) to describe it seems strange. The assertion of Hampl[2] and Accame[3] that this 'common decree' could hardly have been the vote of the conference at Sparta in 371, because the Peace there concluded contained only a voluntary guarantee clause, is not cogent, for action voted by all the Greeks was presumably voluntary. More cogently Papastavrou[4] argued that Aeschines' claim that he could substantiate his statements from the public records shows that the conference was at Athens, and must have been the peace conference later in 371. Hampl, though, pointed out that an Athenian would hardly have referred to the Peace then concluded as an alliance of the Spartans and the other Greeks; all agree that the Athenians were the leaders at this conference and Hampl's arguments[5] that it resulted in a Common Peace treaty and not in any extension or conversion of the Athenian confederacy have been greatly strengthened by Sordi's study[6] (see the next appendix). Hampl suggested the Peace of 375, but, though it should not be ruled out, as Accame ought, on the grounds that Hampl's belief in a compulsory guarantee clause there is mistaken, this date is far too soon after the foundation of the confederacy. There remains the possibility, suggested by Accame,[7] that Aeschines was exaggerating the scope of the conference at which the Spartans and their allies sought an alliance

---

[1] Diod. xv. 60. 3 puts Amyntas' death in 370/369 'about the same time' as the deaths of Jason of Pherae and Agesipolis of Sparta, who had then reigned a year (since Leuctra in July 371); but Diodorus' information probably came from a chronographic source which simply put the three deaths in the same Attic year. The different, but not necessarily more reliable, source followed by the Parian Marble puts Amyntas' death in 371/370 (Tod 205, s. 72).

[2] *Die griechischen Staatsverträge*, p. 18.

[3] *La lega ateniense*, p. 156.

[4] τὸ ἐν Ἀθήναις συνέδριον τῶν συμμάχων τὸ κατὰ τὸ ἔτος 370 π.Χ., *Hellenika*, x (1937–8), 53 ff.

[5] Op. cit., pp. 19 ff.   [6] Art. cit., *Riv. di filol.* lxxix (1951), 34 ff.

[7] Loc. cit.; supported by Cawkwell, 'The Common Peace of 366/5 B.C.', *C.Q.* N.S. xi (1961), 80 ff., who points out that Athenian operations around Amphipolis began soon after the conclusion of this alliance.

with the Athenians in the winter of 370/369 (Xen. *Hell.* vi. v. 33 ff.), the details of which were worked out in May 369 (ibid. vii. i. 1 ff. and cf. Appendix XIII for the date). Amyntas was perhaps a member of the Athenian confederacy, certainly an ally of the Athenians (cf. Tod 129), and the representative ($\sigma\acute{v}v\epsilon\delta\rho o\varsigma$) to which Aeschines refers could well have been his representative on the Council of the Allies. An assertion by the Athenians of their claim to Amphipolis at this moment, when their attempts to restrict the Thebans without war by means of a Common Peace treaty appeared to have failed, would be more in accord with their policy than at any time during the previous few years. There can be no certainty in the interpretation of these four vexed passages, but the last date (370/369) is here preferred for the recognition by the Greeks of the claim to Amphipolis at least.

APPENDIX IV

The Peace of 371 at Athens

ONLY Xenophon gives an account of this Peace. He tells how after the defeat of Cleombrotus and the withdrawal of the second Spartan army from the Isthmus the Athenians decided to call on 'those cities that wanted to share in the Peace which the King had sent down' to send representatives to Athens (*Hell*. VI. v. 1). 'When they came together they decided to swear with those who wanted to share with them this oath: "I will abide by the treaty which the King sent down and by the decrees of the Athenians and their allies. If anyone attacks any city of those that have sworn this oath, I will help them with all my power." All the others rejoiced in the oath, but the Eleans opposed it, since they must not leave autonomous the Marganeans, the Scilluntians and the Triphylians; for these cities belonged, they said, to them. The Athenians and the others, having voted, as the King had written, that the cities great and small alike should be autonomous, dispatched officers to administer the oath and bade the supreme authorities in each city swear it; and all swore except the Eleans' (*Hell*. VI. v. 2).

This account leaves little doubt that the King's Peace and the autonomy principle were reaffirmed by the oaths of a substantial number of the Greek states and that this was another Common Peace treaty, different in detail from that preceding. There are, however, two points of considerable importance which are hard to determine: first, the role of the Spartans, and second, the significance of the 'decrees of the Athenians and their allies' in the oath.

(i) Xenophon does not say exactly who swore to the Peace, merely that all those who sent representatives to Athens swore to it, except the Eleans. The Thebans were obviously not represented; and Xenophon's silence about the Spartans has led some modern commentators to suppose that they too had nothing to do with the affair.[1]

Sordi[2] has shown that Xenophon's narrative of subsequent events makes it clear that the Spartans were a party to this Peace. Directly

---

[1] e.g. H. Swoboda, 'Der hellenische Bund des Jahres 371 v. Chr.', *Rh. Mus* xlix (1894), 329 ff.; Marshall, *Second Athenian Confederacy*, p. 80; Taeger, *Der Friede von 362/1*, p. 28; Accame, *La lega ateniense*, p. 162.

[2] Art. cit., *Riv. di filol.* lxxix (1951), 34 ff.

after his account of the Peace Xenophon tells how the Mantineans decided to assert their autonomy by rebuilding their city, which the Spartans had destroyed in 384. The Spartans objected because they had not been consulted, and were rebuffed; but 'it did not seem possible to attack them, as the Peace had been made on the basis of autonomy' (*Hell.* VI. v. 5). It would be strange if this reference was not to the Peace which Xenophon has just recorded; and, while this passage is not decisive, the other passages cited by Sordi seem to afford certain proof.

After the revolution in Tegea which was effected with Mantinean assistance it seemed to the Spartans that 'they should help according to their oaths . . . and so they attacked the Mantineans on the grounds that contrary to the oaths they had come with armed force against the Tegeates' (ibid. 10). These must be the same oaths as those referred to by the Spartan ambassadors at Athens in winter 370/369, when, Xenophon says (ibid. 36), 'the greatest part of their argument was that it was their duty to help them according to the oaths';[1] the Spartans asserted that 'it was they who had gone to the help of the Tegeates, because the Mantineans had attacked them contrary to the oaths' (ibid.). These oaths were those to the later Peace of 371, that at Athens, for at this same debate at Athens in winter 370/369 Cleiteles, the Corinthian, referring to these same oaths ('How then, if you do not help us who are obviously being wronged, will you not act contrary to the oaths?'), calls them 'those oaths which you yourselves took care that all of us (the Spartans' loyal allies) should swear to all of you (the Athenians and their allies)' (ibid. 37); whereas at the peace conference at Sparta the Spartans had sworn for themselves *and* their allies (*Hell.* VI. iii. 19). Moreover, it was only by the oath sworn to the Peace at Athens in 371 that anyone could feel obliged to help a city that was wronged; the Peace at Sparta had specifically freed its participants from such an obligation. One of the Athenians' chief concerns in this debate in 370/369 was the legality of the Spartans' intervention in Tegea (*Hell.* VI. v. 36–37); but it would appear from the terms of the oath that, if the Mantineans had been in the Peace and the Spartans had not, the Athenians would rather have been obliged to help the Mantineans.

(ii) There is in the reference in the oath to the decrees of the Athenians and their allies a similarity to the usual oath taken by a new member of the Athenian confederacy; and this similarity has

---

[1] Swoboda (art. cit., p. 331) takes ὁ πλεῖστος λόγος to be not the main Spartan argument but the main topic of discussion among the Athenians; but those with no historical axes to grind disagree (cf. Underhill's Commentary, ad. loc., and Hatzfeld's translation in the Budé edition).

led some to believe that the adherents to this Peace were in fact enrolled into the confederacy.[1]

If, as has been argued, the Spartans took part in the Peace, it cannot have been merely an instrument for extending the confederacy to include all willing to take the oath. Not only is Spartan membership of the confederacy improbable in itself, but it would also have made unnecessary perhaps not the alliance between the Spartans and the Athenians of winter 370/369 (for the Athenians were having to choose in theory between two adherents of the Peace), but certainly the later discussions about the leadership of combined Spartan and Athenian forces (Xen. *Hell.* VII. i. 1 ff.).

Similarly, that the Spartans were a party to a Common Peace agreement as a result of which their Peloponnesian allies joined the confederacy, while they themselves did not, is both in itself improbable and shown to be impossible by other passages in Xenophon; the basic assumption of the speech of Procles, the Phliasian, at Athens is that the Spartans' loyal allies (those that were not now supporting the Thebans) owe allegiance solely to them (*Hell.* VI. v. 38–48, esp. 44), and they are referred to as 'the allies still left to them' (ibid. 33).

It is, moreover, clear that those who framed the oath did not think of those who were to take it as the allies of one another; they are referred to in the oath itself by the clumsy periphrasis 'those who have sworn this oath'.

What then of 'the decrees of the Athenians and their allies'? Hampl suggested that the allies were those who might at some future time fight together in defence of the Peace,[2] but the phrase comes before the undertaking to fight. Sordi's interpretation seems better: she pointed to the close connexion in the wording of the oath between the Peace which the King sent down and the decrees of the Athenians and their allies, and suggested that these decrees were those by which the Athenian confederacy was formed and Aristoteles' decree by which the Greeks were invited to join it. These decrees, as was shown above (pp. 55–56) defined more accurately the autonomy guaranteed by them and by the King's Peace; so now the cities swore to abide by the King's Peace, as interpreted by the Athenians and their allies.

---

[1] e.g. Swoboda, art. cit., pp. 324 ff.; Marshall, op. cit., p. 79; Momigliano, art. cit., *Riv. di filol.* N.S. xii (1934), 487 ff.; Accame, loc. cit.; and Cloché, *La Politique étrangère d'Athènes*, p. 96 (who is guarded about the position of the Spartans).

[2] *Die griechischen Staatsverträge*, p. 23.

APPENDIX V

Philiscus' Peace Proposals

(a) The conference

Diodorus (xv. 70. 2) does not mention a conference and is vague about whom Philiscus approached ('the Greeks'), and about who responded favourably (all but the Thebans). Xenophon (*Hell.* VII. i. 27) specifies Delphi as the venue, and mentions the Thebans and their allies and the Spartans as attending; the Athenians were probably represented, as their absence would surely have been noticed.

It has been suggested that the passage in the decree in honour of Dionysius of Syracuse (Tod 133), passed at Athens in early summer 368, which praises him and his sons for helping the King's Peace refers to the intervention of Dionysius at this conference;[1] but the reference in the decree is to the King's Peace which the Athenians, the Spartans and the other Greeks concluded (vv. 23 ff.), presumably that made at Athens in 371, and Dionysius' assistance consisted of the expeditionary forces he sent to fight the Thebans, the second of which arrived directly after Philiscus' failure to secure peace (Xen. *Hell.* VII. i. 28).

(b) The proposals

Diodorus says that Common Peace was proposed,[2] but gives no details, except that the Thebans were to be excluded because they had brought the whole of Boeotia into one federation. Xenophon agrees that the Thebans were the cause of Philiscus' failure, but says that they were unwilling to put Messene back under Spartan control.

Messene had been refounded in the winter of 370/369 by the Thebans and their Peloponnesian allies. The Spartans refused to recognize her independence, and rather than do so declined peace with the Thebans in 365 (Xen. *Hell.* VII. iv. 9) and stood out of the Common Peace treaty of 362/361 (Diod. xv. 89. 1, &c.). Philiscus evidently was well disposed towards the Spartans, for after his failure to make peace he

---

[1] By U. Köhler, 'Die griechische Politik Dionysius des älteren', *Ath. Mitt.* I. xv (1876), 1 ff., followed by Underhill's Commentary, ad. loc.

[2] παρακαλῶν . . . κοινὴν εἰρήνην συνθέσθαι . . . ἀπογνωσθείσης δὲ τῆς κοινῆς εἰρήνης; accepted as a Common Peace proposal by Heuss, art. cit., *Hermes*, lxxiii (1938), 166, n. 1.

left them a mercenary army (Diod. xv. 70. 2).[1] It seems likely, then, that a proposal to return Messene to the Spartans, however unrealistic it appears now, was the point over which the negotiations broke down and not a proposal concerning the autonomy of the Boeotian cities, which would have been, since Leuctra, equally unrealistic.[2]

[1] E. von Stern, *Geschichte der spartanischen und thebanischen Hegemonie vom Königsfrieden bis zur Schlacht bei Mantineia* (Dorpat, 1884), p. 191, suggested that the Spartans were behind the whole affair.

[2] Momigliano, *Filippo il Macedone*, p. 80, regards the proposals as thoroughly idealistic and acceptable to neither Thebans nor Spartans, but there is no evidence that the Spartans rejected them (because they were required to recognize Messene).

APPENDIX VI

Pelopidas' Peace Proposals

THE terms of peace which the Thebans unsuccessfully put before the Greeks at the conference at Thebes in 367 were those proposed by Pelopidas for the approval of the King of Persia at the gathering of ambassadors from the Greek cities at his court a short time before (Xen. *Hell.* VII. i. 33–40). The fact that the King approved them and that they were submitted to a general conference of the Greeks suggests that the terms embodied another Common Peace treaty; what is known of the terms bears out this suggestion.

Diodorus does not mention these proposals except for a retrospective reference in his appreciation of Pelopidas to his mission to Persia, recording only his success and his provision for the autonomy of Messene (xv. 81. 3). Plutarch, however, says that the terms provided for the autonomy of all the Greeks (*Pelop.* 30. 7 and 31. 1). Xenophon mentions only detailed rulings on controversial points: Messene to be free of the Spartans, the Athenian fleet to be laid up (*Hell.* VII. i. 36), and (included by Xenophon as an afterthought) the disputed districts round Triphylia to belong to the Eleans (ibid. 38, taken with VI. v. 2, VII. i. 26 and iv. 12 ff.); it also seems likely that the autonomy of Amphipolis was specifically recognized, as Demosthenes (xix. 137) definitely refers the King's acceptance of this city as a friend and ally to the time of the Athenian Timagoras' embassy to Persia. But these provisions are clearly only details of a general plan providing not only for general autonomy (a Common Peace treaty), but also that every city should possess its own territory (three out of four of the detailed rulings are on territorial disputes), and probably that there should be general demobilization (specifically stated to include the Athenian fleet).[1]

---

[1] Accepted as proposals of Common Peace by Heuss, art. cit., *Hermes*, lxxiii (1938), 166, n. 1.

APPENDIX VII

The Peace of 366/365

THE problems of this Peace have already been dealt with in an article published in the *Classical Quarterly*, N.S. vii (1957), 199 ff., and its arguments are summarized here.

The sources present two contrasting versions of Greek events in the period 366–365. As has been seen, Diodorus describes neither the peace negotiations in Persia nor the subsequent conference at Thebes, which were the subject of the last appendix, though he does refer very briefly in retrospect to Pelopidas' mission to Persia and its success (xv. 81. 3). Diodorus also ignores the Theban invasion of Achaea which comes next in Xenophon's account (VII. i. 41–43). Both historians mention the capture of Oropus, Diodorus under 366/365 (Xen. *Hell.* VII. iv. 1; Diod. xv. 76. 2), but, whereas Xenophon goes on to tell how an alliance was concluded between the Arcadians and the Athenians, how the Athenians failed to seize Corinth, how the Corinthians fought on for a while against both the Thebans and the Athenians, and how they finally made a separate peace with the Thebans in which some of the Spartans' allies in the north-east Peloponnese but not the Spartans themselves took part (*Hell.* VII. iv. 2–11), Diodorus has none of these details and says simply that the King of Persia sent ambassadors to Greece and persuaded the Greeks to put an end to their wars and to conclude Common Peace (xv. 76. 3).

It is clear enough from the chronology that here Diodorus and Xenophon are in fact referring to the same treaty. Prima facie there is good reason to believe Diodorus when in Book xv he records a Common Peace treaty; Xenophon's details, on the other hand, are a good deal more convincing than Diodorus' vagueness. On further examination it seems highly likely that, in addition to the Spartans, both the Arcadians and the Athenians and their allies were excluded from any treaty with the Thebans in 366/365, and so the treaty can hardly count as a Common Peace. On the other hand, there is evidence to suggest that the Thebans may simply have re-offered to the Corinthians, &c., the same terms (of a Common Peace) as were rejected in 367, in so far as they were applicable. If that was the case, it is possible to see how Diodorus might have been misled into thinking that there was a Common Peace treaty in 366/365, especially since, as far as is known, there was very little fighting in the summer of 365. It is possible, though not likely, that Diodorus was following not Ephorus, but a pro-Theban source who some years later invented a Common Peace here; more probable that the Thebans proclaimed at the time that this was a Common Peace treaty, even if most of their enemies boycotted it.

Since that article appeared, G. L. Cawkwell ('The Common Peace of 366/365 B.C.', *C.Q.*N.S. xi (1961), 80 ff.) has advanced further considerations in favour of Diodorus' version:

(i) That the occasion when, according to Demosthenes (ix. 16), the King and all the Greeks recognized the Athenian claim to the Chersonese was most probably a Common Peace congress and one very shortly before the Athenians began operations in the Chersonese in 365; and that the King's recognition of the Athenian claim to Amphipolis, which he had rejected in 367 (Dem. xix. 137), could well have been contained in a rescript which was the basis of a Common Peace in 366/365.

(ii) That a passage (ss. 26 ff.) in Isocrates' Archidamus (the dramatic setting of which is the debate at Sparta in 366/365 on the Theban offer of peace described by Xenophon, *Hell.* VII. iv. 7–11) indicates that the Peace being discussed included a clause recognizing the King's rule of the Asiatic Greeks; and that references in the speech to the Athenians do not indicate that the Athenians were not involved in the proposed Peace, but on the contrary the argument of Archidamus' opponents about the hopelessness of the Spartans' position could hardly have been put forward, if the Athenians were standing out of the Peace.

(iii) That the prosecution of Callistratus, the supporter of concord with the Spartans, after the failure to recover Oropus in 366 led to a change of policy and a readiness to accept a Common Peace sponsored by the Thebans.

As to (iii), the fact that Callistratus' accuser was Leodamas, a member of the pro-Boeotian group, does not mean that Athenian policy was now to be pro-Boeotian. Timotheus' re-election to the generalship in 366 and the new approach in the Peloponnese (the alliance with the Arcadians and the attempt to seize Corinth, which are not mentioned by Cawkwell) seem to show that the Athenians were pursuing a more chauvinistic and 'tougher' policy, and were now less likely than before to accept the Theban terms.

As to (ii), the references to the King's right to rule the Asiatic Greeks make as good sense, if, as was suggested above, the Thebans were now reoffering to a limited number of cities the terms proposed in 367, where applicable; Archidamus could make this point, even if the Thebans were not now including this clause. As to the Athenians, the Spartans might well have felt that the recent alliance of the Athenians with the Arcadians had made their own alliance with the Athenians of no value.

As to (i), it is not necessary to have a royal rescript leading to a general treaty as the occasion of the King's recognition of the Athenian claim to Amphipolis; as Cawkwell says, the King had in 367 left the door open to further negotiations between himself and the Athenians, and the failure of the Thebans to impose the terms could well have led him to make some separate conciliatory approach to the Athenians. The argument from the recognition by 'all the Greeks' is neat and logical, but the Demosthenes passage was composed twenty-five years later, and is it safe to put much reliance on an orator's 'all the Greeks'?[1]

[1] For a bibliography of discussions of and judgements on this Peace see Ryder, art. cit., *C.Q.* N.S. vii (1957), 201, nn. 4, 5, 6, and 202, n. 3.

APPENDIX VIII

The Peace of 362/361 and Tod 145

IT has not been disputed that the Peace concluded by the Greek belligerents after the indecisive battle of Mantinea in 362 was a Common Peace treaty. Though Xenophon ends his narrative here with the statement that after the battle there was even greater indecision and disturbance than before it, Diodorus (xv. 89. 1), Plutarch (*Ages.* 35. 3–4) and Polybius (iv. 33. 8–9) all agree that the treaty was concluded by all the Greeks except the Spartans; Diodorus calls it Common Peace,[1] Plutarch 'common pacifications' (s. 5—κοιναὶ διαλύσεις), and the dispute over the inclusion of the Messenians, described by all three authors, suggests strongly the restatement of the principle of autonomy.

There are some indications of two subsidiary clauses besides the guarantee, of which one was an innovation in Common Peace treaties:

(i) In his account of a subsequent dispute over Megalopolis Diodorus (xv. 94. 1) says that it was laid down 'in the oaths' (he means the Common Peace treaty which he has mentioned in the previous sentence) that 'everyone should return to his own territory after the battle'. Diodorus goes on to say that certain of the Arcadians who had made up the population of Megalopolis took this clause to mean that they should return to their original lands and invoked it to obtain assistance from the Mantineans and others, while the view of their opponents in Megalopolis was supported by the Thebans. Even at the time, then, there was doubt about the interpretation of this clause. The phrase 'after the battle' is strange, and perhaps Diodorus is reading a demobilization clause similar to that which Xenophon records for the Peace of 371 at Sparta (*Hell.* vi. iii. 18); at any rate such a clause would not be unexpected in this Peace.

(ii) Though there is no mention of it in Diodorus, Plutarch or Polybius, it seems that on this occasion the formula 'possessing what they held' (ἔχοντες ἃ εἶχον) was used instead of the usual 'possessing their own territory'. In his speech *For the Megalopolitans* delivered in 353, Demosthenes refers in section 16 to a Spartan proposal that all should possess their own territory—'now the Spartans say

---

[1] διελύσαντο πρὸς ἀλλήλους, συνθέμενοι δὲ κοινὴν εἰρήνην καὶ συμμαχίαν κατέταττον ἐν τῇ συμμαχίᾳ καὶ τοὺς Μεσσηνίους. Cf. xv. 94. 1: . . . γενομένης εἰρήνης κοινῆς μετὰ τὴν ἐν Μαντινείᾳ μάχην.

that the Eleans should recover part of Triphylia, the Phliasians Tricaranum and some others of the Arcadians their own territory, and that we should recover Oropus, not to see each of us possessing our own, far from it . . .'; the real motive he explains is to win allies in their own endeavour to recover Messene. The Spartans are proposing some change in the existing recognized order, which must have been that regulated by this Peace of 362/361 (albeit Sparta had stood out of it), for in spite of various wars in the interval the terms of the Peace were evidently still regarded as valid (cf. this same speech, s. 10); and the alternative to 'possessing their own territory' (the Spartan proposal) was 'possessing what they held', the formula used in truces (as in the truce of Laches, Thuc. iv. 118. 4), but equally appropriate in cases where, as in 362/361, the emphasis was on stopping war rather than on a permanent solution of differences (as in the Peace of Gela in 424, Thuc. iv. 65. 1). Messene was free *de facto* and under this formula remained so.

The guarantee clause is a source of controversy. In his account Diodorus links with the Common Peace an alliance between the signatories. Polybius says that the Megalopolitans and other Arcadians who shared their alliance saw to it that the Messenians were received 'by the allies' and shared in the oaths and the end of hostilities. These 'allies' seem to be the whole body of signatories, though Polybius' wording is obscure, and he may mean simply the members of the Megalopolitan alliance, the only one previously mentioned in his account. A passage is also adduced from the inscription Tod 145 (cf. below) which is restored to read '[ἀμυνοῦμεν κοινῇ πάντε]ς . . .' and must in the context contain some such threat of combined action on the part of the Greeks who have recently concluded Common Peace. Momigliano[1] accepted Diodorus and Polybius as adequate evidence of a formal alliance. Taeger[2] used the passage in the inscription to prove the existence of an alliance and to support the climax of his argument, that the Greeks were now near to concerted action against an outside enemy.[3]

The arguments against an alliance are either circumstantial or *ex silentio*, and are therefore dangerous. De Sanctis[4] pointed out that Xenophon says nothing about it, but to play with Xenophon's omissions and inclusions, particularly at the very end of his work, is to play with fire. He says also that there is no mention of the alliance in

---

[1] Art. cit., *Riv. di filol.* lxii (1934), 494 ff.
[2] *Der Friede von 362/1*, pp. 1 ff. and 31 ff.
[3] An alliance is also accepted by Berve, art. cit., *Gnomon*, ix (1933), 301 ff.; Larsen, review of Hampl, 'Die griechischen Staatsverträge', *Class. Phil.* xxxiv (1939), 375 ff.; and Dienelt, art. cit., *Jahreshefte Oesterr. Arch. Inst.* xliii (1956), 265 ff.   [4] 'La pace del 362/1', *Riv. di filol.* lxiii (1934), 149 ff.

subsequent history and no record of it being invoked. This argument is perhaps stronger than Momigliano will allow, for the Peace is later mentioned without an alliance (cf. Dem. iii. 28, xvi. 10).

Both the previous Common Peace treaty (that of Athens in 371) and the next one (that of 338/337) included a guarantee clause which bound their signatories to go to the help of the injured party, but, it is argued in this work,[1] no formal alliance between the signatories. A compulsory guarantee clause of this sort did not constitute of itself what the Greeks called an alliance. Nevertheless some modern scholars have believed the contrary,[2] and it is eminently possible that Diodorus, when confronted with a source that quoted such a guarantee clause in full would, in the interests of brevity, have summarized it as an alliance; and this is the only Common Peace treaty with such a guarantee that Diodorus does record (he leaves out the Peace at Athens in 371 altogether, and his account of the conclusion of the Peace of 338/337 is missing). One could equally find excuses for Polybius, if he really did mean that the Messenians were received by a body of allies who were all the signatories. It is not, for example, certain that Polybius knew what Common Peace meant;[3] moreover the arrangement of 338/337 which the Greeks knew as a Common Peace treaty with a compulsory guarantee clause was not very different in practice from that which in 224 was known as a Common Alliance and which was much more familiar to Polybius. It is not then wholly necessary to believe that Diodorus' source or Polybius' source recorded a formal alliance of all the Greeks, and of course the threat of common action in defence of the Peace made in the inscription certainly required no more than a compulsory guarantee clause as its foundation.

The inscription Tod 145 is important for two particular reasons to the study of Common Peace; it includes the first known epigraphical reference to Common Peace and two of the seven certain fourth-century uses of the phrase, and it provides valuable evidence of the hostile attitude of the Greeks to the King of Persia soon after the conclusion of a Common Peace treaty.

The inscription, which was found at Argos (and copied but then lost) but is in the Attic dialect, can only be dated circumstantially. It contains part of the reply to 'the emissary from the Satraps'. In this extract it is first pointed out that 'the Greeks by sending embassies to

---

[1] Cf. the Appendixes on those treaties (IV and X).

[2] e.g. Dienelt, art. cit.

[3] Cf. the different interpretations of Polybius' own use of the phrase at iv. 3. 8 by F. W. Walbank, *A Historical Commentary on Polybius*, vol. i. (Oxford, 1957), ad loc., and E. Bickermann, 'Les préliminaires de la seconde guerre de Macédoine, la paix de Phoenicé', *Revue de philologie*, 3rd ser., ix (1935), 71 ff.

one another have settled their differences, and attained Common Peace (vv. 4–5),[1] in order that all of them being rid of internal warfare may make their own cities prosperous and as great as possible, and may remain strong and useful to their friends' (vv. 6–8). The emissary is then informed that the Greeks have no quarrel with the King and that, if he keeps quiet and does not embroil the Greeks nor try by any means to destroy the Peace which has just been concluded, the Greeks will in turn conduct themselves peacefully towards him; but if he makes war against any of the participants in the treaty or troubles any of them with the intention of destroying the Peace either by direct action on his own part against the Greeks who made the Peace or through someone else starting from his territory, all the Greeks will defend themselves in common in a manner worthy of the Peace that has just been concluded and of their past deeds (vv. 9–18, cf. Tod's summary).

The inscription was first assigned to the immediate aftermath of this Peace by Wilhelm, who has been followed by most scholars.[2] In view of the Greeks' expressed attitude to the King, the inscription can scarcely refer to the Peaces of 387/386 or 375/374, which were negotiated under his auspices (cf. Appendix II), or to that of 371 at Sparta, which was concluded while Antalcidas was in Persia on behalf of the Spartans, and the Athenians were busy emphasizing their correct attitude towards the King (Xen. *Hell.* VI. iii. 12, cf. Appendix III). This attitude had not changed when, later in the year, the Athenians organized a second Common Peace treaty, which they called a King's Peace (Xen. *Hell.* VI. v. 1, 2), and both they and the Spartans continued to hope for Persian help down to 367, while the Thebans were excluded from both treaties in 371. There was no Common Peace in 366/365 (cf. Appendix VII), and those who think there was do so because they accept Diodorus' account of a Peace sent down that year by the King.[3] Those who believe, wrongly, in a Common Peace in 346 themselves reject a connexion of the inscription with a Persian approach to the Athenians in 344.[4] Finally, in 338/337 the conclusion of a Common

---

[1] δίοτ⟨ι⟩ οἱ [Ἕλληνες πρεσβεύσ]αντες πρὸς ἀλλήλους διαλέλυνται τὰ ⟨δ⟩ιάφορα πρὸς κ]οινὴν εἰρήνην.

[2] Wilhelm, 'Ein Friedensbund der Hellenen', *Jahreshefte Oesterr. Arch. Inst.* iii (1900), 145 ff.; followed by Taeger, Berve and De Sanctis, locc. citt.; Hampl, *Die griechischen Staatsverträge*, pp. 26 ff. and 103 ff.; Heuss, art. cit., *Hermes*, lxxiii (1938), 166; Accame, *La lega ateniense*, pp. 172 ff. and 245 ff.; Tod, commentary on 145; Bengtson, *Griechische Geschichte*, pp. 265 ff.; and Hammond, *History of Greece*, p. 511.

[3] So De Sanctis, loc. cit., against Meyer, *Geschichte des Altertums* (Stuttgart–Berlin, 1921), v, 961.

[4] Suggested by Beloch, *Griechische Geschichte*, III. i. 535, n. 1, rejected by De Sanctis and Momigliano, locc. citt.

Peace treaty was followed very closely by the decision of the Greeks to take part in a general war with Philip of Macedon against the Persians; and it would have been hard for Greeks at this time, however well disposed towards Philip, to have spoken of themselves as having settled their differences by sending embassies to one another.

In the years before 362, on the other hand, Persian interest had been flouted (cf. above, pp. 81 ff.), and there is no evidence that the Persians had any part in concluding the treaty in 362/361. Diodorus' statement (xv. 90. 2) that the Spartans were annoyed with Artaxerxes, because he had included the Messenians in the Common Peace, has been cited to prove that the King had taken part in this settlement. But, as far as the Spartans were concerned, the Peace was an application of the terms sent down by the King through Pelopidas in 367, and the recognition of Messene in 362/361 might well be laid at the King's door.[1] Diodorus' actual account of the making of the Peace strongly suggests that it was concluded solely by Greek action, and he is not one to pass over Persian intervention (cf. his accounts of the treaties of 375, 371 at Sparta and 366/365). The Greeks, then, had achieved peace by their own efforts and, if they had not removed the sources of friction between cities, they had succeeded in putting an end to ten years of war in which certain local differences had earlier prevented a pacification (cf. above Chapter V).

---

[1] Cf. Accame, op. cit., p. 172; the passage is referred back to the supposed Peace of 366/365 by De Sanctis, art. cit., p. 152.

APPENDIX IX

The Peace of Philocrates and the so-called Common Peace of 346

THE Peace of Philocrates, which in 346 concluded the war between Philip of Macedon and the Athenians, was not a Common Peace treaty. It was formally made between the Athenians and their allies (the confederacy) on the one side and Philip and his allies on the other (Dem. xix. 159 and 278). There had been efforts, notably on the part of the council of the allies, to make the treaty into a Common Peace or a virtual Common Peace, first by deferring the debates at Athens about peace until the return of a series of Athenian embassies from the other cities in Greece, and then by proposing that any other Greek city should be permitted to join in the peace within three months. These efforts had failed and it was one of Aeschines' chief accusations in his attacks on Demosthenes that Demosthenes had caused their failure (cf. above, pp. 96 ff.).

A few weeks after the conclusion of this peace Philip advanced through Thermopylae and compelled the Phocians to surrender. According to Diodorus Philip handed over the decision on the fate of the Phocians to the Amphictyonic Council: the Amphictyons then laid down terms and 'following that they made arrangements about the care of the oracle and about everything else connected with piety and common peace and concord among the Greeks' (xvi. 60. 3).[1]

The mere occurrence of the phrase κοινὴ εἰρήνη seems to have been enough to persuade Taeger,[2] De Sanctis[3] and Momigliano[4] that a Common Peace agreement was now concluded. Hampl,[5] however, pointed out that the phrase might have been used in a non-technical sense, being connected here with εὐσεβεία and ὁμονοία and introduced by the rather vague 'τὰ πρὸς . . . ἀνήκοντα'. Wüst, in his answer to Hampl's arguments,[6] ignored this one; but Griffith[7] showed that it is

---

[1] . . . καὶ τἆλλα πάντα τὰ πρὸς εὐσεβείαν καὶ κοινὴν εἰρήνην καὶ ὁμονοίαν τοῖς Ἕλλησιν ἀνήκοντα.
[2] Der Friede von 362/1, p. 59.
[3] Art. cit. Riv. di filol. lxii (1934), 150.
[4] Ibid., 493 ff.
[5] Die griechischen Staatsverträge, pp. 64 ff.
[6] Philip II von Makedonien und Griechenland (Munich, 1938), pp. 20 ff. and 177 ff.
[7] 'The so-called κοινὴ εἰρήνη of 346 B.C.', J.H.S. lix (1939), 73.

important, for, whenever Diodorus means that a proper Common Peace treaty was concluded, he says so quite clearly, associating with the phrase κοινὴ εἰρήνη some part of the verb συντίθεμαι.[1] It is Griffith's view that Diodorus creates an assumption that there was *no* Common Peace treaty. It could perhaps be argued that, as Diodorus is no longer following Ephorus, he might not describe the conclusion of a Common Peace treaty with the same clarity in Book xvi as in Book xv; on the other hand, Diodorus' change of source should make us more careful of accepting terminology used in the previous book at its face value.

Hampl argued further that the Amphictyonic Council was not a body competent to establish a Common Peace;[2] Wüst admitted that legally they could not do so, but claimed that in fact they did, and cited Hampl's own statement that Common Peace and the Amphictyony were of the same *Vertragstypus*.[3] Wüst went on to assert a 'certain connexion' (*gewisse Beziehungen*) between the Amphictyony and the Peace of 338/337, basing his views on Momigliano's identification of 'the synhedrion of the Greeks' of Aeschines iii. 254 with the Amphictyonic Council.[4] This connexion was refuted by Kaerst many years before; a later section will summarize his arguments and add some confirmatory indications.[5]

Hampl pointed out in the third place that, if there was a Common Peace agreement in 346, there ought to be mention of it in Demosthenes, Aeschines &c., but there is not. Wüst, in reply, produced several passages which he claimed referred to this peace.[6] Three of these concern an attempt by Artaxerxes Ochus to obtain help in Greece for his campaign against Egypt. Diodorus (xvi. 44. 1) says that 'the Athenians and the Spartans replied that they adhered to their friendship with the King, but refused to send any assistance': Didymus (viii. 5) quotes Philochorus as saying that in Lyciscus' archonship (344/343) the King sent ambassadors to the Athenians and asked them to preserve their traditional friendship with him, but they replied that their friendship would continue if he did not attack any Greek cities. Writing later to the Athenians Philip (Ps.-Dem. xii. 6) reminded them that they had voted that, if the King used forcible measures in any way, they would summon him, Philip, and the other Greeks against him.

Wüst rightly concluded that all these three passages referred to the same affair. He pointed out that the similarity of the Athenian answer

---

[1] xv. 38. 1 (375), 50. 4 (371), 70. 2 (Philiscus), 76. 3 (366/5), 89. 1 (362/1).
[2] Loc. cit.
[3] Wüst, op. cit., p. 25; cf. Hampl, op. cit., pp. 64 ff.
[4] Wüst, loc. cit., citing Momigliano, loc. cit.
[5] Kaerst, 'Der korinthische Bund', *Rh. Mus.* lii (1897), 524 ff.; cf. below, pp. 161 ff.   [6] Op. cit., pp. 28 ff.

here to that contained in the 'Reply to the emissary of the satraps' (the inscription, Tod 145)[1] was such that Beloch[2] erroneously connected the latter with this affair. He concluded that the Athenians in like manner rested their reply in 344/343 on the Common Peace, and pointed to Demosthenes' assertion (x. 33) that the King was the common enemy of all. But defence of Greeks against the Persians had, since the PersianWars, been a favourite theme of Athenian politicians; it would be natural for the Athenians to declare themselves against any Persian encroachment in Greek cities and, though they may have gained confidence from the sort of defensive panhellenism in Greece generally which can be seen in the 'Reply to the emissary of the satraps' and which is described by Demosthenes in his speech *On the Symmories* (xiv. 31–33), there is no reason to suppose that they needed a newly concluded Common Peace as a basis for their firm answer. The Athenians, as Philip observed (Ps.-Dem. xii. 6), evidently saw themselves as the leaders in any defensive war against Persia, which could hardly have been the case in action taken under a Common Peace decreed and organized by the Amphictyons. Shortly afterwards, when the Athenians themselves sought an alliance with Persia, Philip in his letter described their conduct as $\pi\alpha\rho\alpha\nuo\mu\iota\alpha$ and $\delta\upsilon\sigma\mu\epsilon\nu\epsilon\iota\alpha$ (ibid.); that is, says Wüst,[3] he accused them of a breach of the Common Peace. But if $\pi\alpha\rho\alpha\nuo\mu\iota\alpha$ does mean breach of a treaty, the treaty in question could as well be the Peace of Philocrates, by which the Athenians had concluded their war with Philip and become his allies: to incite the Persians to attack Philip would constitute a breach of any treaty between Athens and Philip.[4]

Wüst's examples being thus insufficient, Hampl's *argumentum ex silentio* is strengthened. Its confirmation was furnished by Griffith's examination of Demosthenes' speech *On the Peace*;[5] if the Common Peace of 346 did exist, this speech was composed within a very short time of its conclusion, and in that case the Peace concerned in the speech would be that Common Peace.

The speech represents Demosthenes' advice to the Athenians at the time when they received a demand from the Amphictyonic Council that Athens should formally subscribe to Philip's recent election to the Council into the two votes formerly held by Phocis ($\upsilon\pi o\theta$. to Dem. v; Dem. xix. 111). The Athenians had sent no representative to the

---

[1] Cf. Appendix VIII. [2] *Griechische Geschichte*, III. i. 535, n. 1.
[3] Op. cit., p. 32: 'Einen solchen Vorwurf kann aber Philipp nur mit Bezug auf die $\kappa o\iota\nu\dot\eta$ $\epsilon\iota\rho\dot\eta\nu\eta$ erheben, die Athen also Mitglieder der Amphiktione ebenso wie die übrigen Beschlüsse der Amphiktione anerkannt hatte.'
[4] Ps.-Dem. xii. 6: $\pi\epsilon\iota\sigma o\nu\tau\alpha\varsigma$ $\alpha\upsilon\tau o\nu$ (the King) $\epsilon\mu o\iota$ (Philip) $\pi o\lambda\epsilon\mu\epsilon\iota\nu$. So Hampl, 'Zur angeblichen $\kappa o\iota\nu\dot\eta$ $\epsilon\iota\rho\dot\eta\nu\eta$ des 346 und zum philokrateischen Frieden', *Klio*, xxxi (1938), 37. [5] Art. cit., pp. 73 ff.

meeting (if they had, there would have been no need for an envoy to bring the request), and it was at that meeting that according to Wüst's reading of Diodorus a Common Peace was concluded. In that case the demand from the Amphictyons would surely refer to the Peace also, but there is no mention of that in this speech or elsewhere.[1]

Demosthenes admits that the peace is, for the Athenians, a bad peace (esp. Dem. v. 13); though he himself had supported the Peace of Philocrates, he was speedily convinced, and openly declared, that the procrastination of his colleagues on the embassy sent to obtain its ratification had ruined any of the favourable prospects which it had offered to Athens (ibid. 10). Demosthenes says that above all the Athenians must not court a general war (ibid. 14 and 19); but this advice is not concerned with a Common Peace agreement, for at the same time he makes no objection to the Athenians fighting a purely local war, for instance with the Thebans, over the disputed frontier region of Oropus (ibid. 16). Griffith rightly concludes that there can have been no Common Peace treaty in force with a sanction clause binding all participants to come to the help of a victim of aggression or with a limited sanction clause like that in the Peace of 371 at Sparta.[2] Demosthenes makes it clear that the general war he fears is a Sacred War proclaimed by the Amphictyons; such a war could be proclaimed if Athens ignored the decrees of the Amphictyons concerning a subject which was very much within their own competence —namely the composition of the Amphictyonic council.

Hampl finally argued[3] that remarks made by Hegesippus in 343 exclude the possibility of a Common Peace already in existence. Hegesippus says that the Athenians had proposed to amend 'the Peace' so that all the rest of the Greeks, who had no part in it, should be recognized as free and autonomous, and that, if anyone attacked them, the cities participating in the Peace should come to their assistance. The Athenians, he says, did this thinking it just and humane not that only they and their allies and Philip and his allies should have the Peace, while those who were allies of neither Athens nor Philip were left in the middle to be destroyed by the stronger, but that these too should have security through this Peace with Philip (Ps.-Dem. vii. 30–31). From this passage it is clear that the Peace which the Athenians wanted to amend is the Peace of Philocrates, which was concluded between Athens and her allies on one side and Philip and his allies on the other. This is further demonstrated by the other

---

[1] e.g. at Dem. xix. 132 or 181; cf. Griffith, loc. cit.

[2] Art. cit., pp. 75 ff.

[3] *Die griechischen Staatsverträge*, pp. 64 ff.; cf. Griffith, art. cit., p. 72, n. 8: 'this Hampl recognises as a decisive argument against there being a K.E. already in existence.'

Athenian proposal that each of the two sides (ἑκατέρους, *not* ἑκάστους each of many) should 'possess their own territory' (ibid. 18). None the less Wüst supposes that there had been a Common Peace in 346 under Philip's auspices, and that now the Athenians were proposing a different Common Peace under their own leadership.[1] But if he is right the whole of the orator's argument about the misfortune of those states that were not allies of Athens or Philip must be dismissed as an irrelevant sophistry, and the whole Athenian proposal, which ignores any Common Peace organized by Philip and his friends since the Peace of Philocrates, appears as ridiculously naïve.

Wüst does not say in what way the Common Peace proposed by Athens in 343 differed from that which he says was already in operation, as it must have differed if it was to be under Athenian leadership and not under Philip's. Wüst's Common Peace of 346 was under the protection of the Amphictyons, whom Philip controlled, but it would have remained so only as long as Philip and the Amphictyons possessed the power and the prestige necessary to enforce it. The adoption of the guarantee clause proposed by Athens in 343, that, if anyone attacked any of the states in the Peace, the rest of the participants should come to the assistance of the injured party (Ps.-Dem. vii. 30), even if it is supposed to be a new element, would make no difference to the actual political situation. If Philip and the Amphictyons had been strong enough to uphold a Common Peace before the adoption of this clause, they would still be strong enough after it.

It must be concluded that Wüst is mistaken. Hampl's arguments, greatly strengthened by Griffith's study, show that there was no Common Peace treaty in 346.[2]

[1] Op. cit., p. 77.
[2] Accame, *La lega ateniense*, p. 209, is wholly convinced by Griffith, but Bengtson, *Griechische Geschichte*, p. 296, merely notes his article as a contrary view.

APPENDIX X

The Peace of 338/337 and the so-called League of Corinth

AFTER Philip had defeated his Greek enemies at Chaeronea in 338, he made peace with them one by one and then summoned a meeting of representatives of all the Greeks at Corinth. There within the next few months he settled the affairs of the Greeks to his own satisfaction. The manner in which he did so has been the subject of much controversy; it is agreed that he set up an international Greek organization—usually called the League of Corinth—but it has been variously argued that the letter of his settlement was one treaty of Common Peace,[1] one treaty of alliance between him and all the Greeks,[2] one treaty of Common Peace and alliance[3] or two treaties, one of Common Peace and one of alliance.[4] There is again agreement that after his settlement of Greek affairs Philip was elected commander-in-chief of a Greek war against Persia.

Philip died before he could begin the invasion of Persia on any scale and was succeeded as King of the Macedonians by his son, Alexander. Alexander had to march into Greece to make his influence secure, but it is clear that he regarded any arrangements that his father had made with the Greeks as still binding, for, when he summoned a meeting of their representatives at Corinth, he only had himself re-elected commander-in-chief against Persia. He may have reaffirmed Philip's settlement and have received fresh oaths from the Greeks, but he changed no part of the treaty (or treaties).[5]

It is then legitimate to use as evidence for the legal position of the Greeks in Philip's settlement things done and written by the Greeks or by Alexander about their legal position in his reign. Thus the speech *About the treaty with Alexander*, which is no. xvii in the Demos-

---

[1] H. Schwahn, 'Heeresmatrikel und Landfriede Philipps von Makedonien', *Klio*, Beiheft xxi (1930), 36 ff.; Hampl, *Die griechischen Staatsverträge*, pp. 34 ff.; Heuss, art. cit., *Hermes*, lxxiii (1938), 171 ff.

[2] H. Raue, *Untersuchungen zur Geschichte des korinthischen Bundes* (Diss. Marburg, 1937).

[3] Momigliano, art. cit., *Riv. di filol.* lxii (1934), 498 ff.; Wilcken, art. cit., *Sitzb. Berlin*, 1929, pp. 300 ff.; Taeger, *Der Friede von 362/1*, pp. 60 ff.; Berve, review cit., *Gnomon*, ix (1933), 309 ff.; and most recently Dienelt, art. cit., *Jahreshefte Oesterr. Arch. Inst.* xliii (1956), 247 ff.

[4] F. Schehl, 'Zum korinthischen Bund vom Jahr 338/7 v. Chr.', *Jahreshefte Oesterr. Arch. Inst.* xxvii (1932), 115 ff.

[5] Diod. xvii. 2. 2, 4. 1 ff.; Arrian i. 1. 1 ff.; and cf. below, pp. 155 ff.

thenic Corpus, but is probably not genuine, can be used as evidence for the treaty (or treaties) between Philip and the Greeks, even though Philip is never mentioned in it and it is directed against Alexander. The title of the speech ($\pi\epsilon\rho\grave{\iota}$ $\tau\hat{\omega}\nu$ $\pi\rho\grave{o}s$ $A\lambda\acute{\epsilon}\xi\alpha\nu\delta\rho\rho\nu$ $\sigma\upsilon\nu\theta\eta\kappa\hat{\omega}\nu$)[1] does not invalidate the argument of the last paragraph, for it need only mean that the treaty was in force between Alexander and the Greeks, and not necessarily that it was concluded for the first time between them.

(a) The Common Peace treaty and the foundation of the synhedrion

The speech leaves no doubt that there was a treaty which consisted only of a Common Peace agreement, that the Common Peace was not just one clause in a larger treaty. The speaker refers to 'the very treaty and the oaths concerning the Common Peace' (s. 2),[2] and to 'the oaths and the treaty that was written in the Common Peace' (s. 4).[3] There is no mention of an alliance, of allies or of a second treaty, but there are frequent references to the peace and those who share in the peace. From the speech we learn that the treaty laid down that all the Greeks should be free and autonomous (s. 8); that they should be governed according to the constitutions existing in the cities when they swore to the peace (s. 10), unless they were ruled by tyrants (s. 7); and that the internal security of the cities was guaranteed against the arbitrary execution or banishment of citizens, against revolutionary land-reform or liberation of slaves and against the interference of another city in support of exiles (ss. 15–16). The freedom of the seas was also assured (s. 19).

It can also be deduced that the treaty included a provision for common action against a transgressor state. Such a state would be declared 'the enemy of all those who share in the peace' (ss. 10, 19), who would then 'make a general expedition' against her (s. 6). In one passage the speaker seems to indicate that this process is to be begun by individual action on the part of the Athenians, who should take up arms and make an expedition against those who have broken the treaty (are they the Messenian tyrants or Alexander himself?) 'together with those who are willing' (s. 8). But this passage is more of an emotional appeal, taking the standard compulsory guarantee clause at its face value, for later the speaker mentions that the internal security of the cities is in the hands of 'the members of the synhedrion (council) of the Greeks and of those who have been appointed for the common protection'. This duty, he says, was assigned to them 'in the treaty' (s. 15). The synhedrion, then, was either already constituted or envisaged in the Common Peace treaty.

---

[1] $\alpha\dot{\iota}$ $\sigma\upsilon\nu\theta\hat{\eta}\kappa\alpha\iota$ is usually, but not always, *one* treaty.

[2] $\dot{\epsilon}\xi$ $\alpha\dot{\upsilon}\tau\hat{\omega}\nu$ $\tau\hat{\omega}\nu$ $\sigma\upsilon\nu\theta\eta\kappa\hat{\omega}\nu$ $\kappa\alpha\grave{\iota}$ $\tau\hat{\omega}\nu$ $\ddot{o}\rho\kappa\omega\nu$ $\tau\hat{\omega}\nu$ $\pi\epsilon\rho\grave{\iota}$ $\tau\hat{\eta}s$ $\kappa\upsilon\iota\nu\hat{\eta}s$ $\epsilon\dot{\iota}\rho\dot{\eta}\nu\eta s$.

[3] $\pi\alpha\rho\grave{\alpha}$ $\tau\upsilon\grave{\upsilon}s$ $\ddot{o}\rho\kappa\upsilon\upsilon s$ $\kappa\alpha\grave{\iota}$ $\tau\grave{\alpha}s$ $\sigma\upsilon\nu\theta\dot{\eta}\kappa\alpha s$ $\tau\grave{\alpha}s$ $\dot{\epsilon}\nu$ $\tau\hat{\eta}$ $\kappa\upsilon\iota\nu\hat{\eta}$ $\epsilon\dot{\iota}\rho\dot{\eta}\nu\eta$ $\gamma\epsilon\gamma\rho\alpha\mu\mu\acute{\epsilon}\nu\alpha s$.

An examination of the inscription which is no. 177 in Tod's collection shows without much doubt that it concerns the same treaty to which the author of Ps.-Demosthenes xvii refers. The inscription contains the greater part of the oath sworn by the Athenians[1] at the ratification of a treaty with Philip and the rest of the Greeks, and naturally does not contain all the terms of the treaty. Again there is no reference to allies or to an alliance, only to the peace and to the states participating in the peace.[2] The oath pledges its takers to abstain from occupying any city, fortress or harbour belonging to any state participating in the peace (vv. 9–11) and from any attempt to overthrow 'the constitutions existing in each city, when they swore the oaths concerning the peace'[3] (here the wording is the same as in Ps.-Dem. xvii. 10).

The oath also contains a provision for common action against a transgressor: 'If anyone does anything contrary to the treaty, I will help the injured party according to their demands and I will fight against anyone who breaks the Common Peace in accordance with the decision of the common synhedrion and the Hegemon' (vv. 19–23). The first part is the standard compulsory guarantee clause, the second shows the new machinery set up to supervise it, the two parts corresponding to the two revealed in Ps.-Dem. xvii.

That this oath may also refer to the treaty as 'the treaty with Philip of Macedon' does not mean that the treaty was not a Common Peace,[4] for the speech *About the treaty with Alexander* discussed a Common Peace agreement. But, on the other hand, the conjunction in the oath of a guarantee of the kingdom of Philip and his successors with the guarantee of existing constitutions in the cities (the same verb $\kappa\alpha\tau\alpha\lambda\dot{\upsilon}\sigma\omega$ covers both) does not mean that Philip was one of the participants of the Common Peace. Philip by this guarantee included the rule of his house among the existing constitutions, and his position as

---

[1] The inscription was found at Athens, but there is nothing in it which makes its contents applicable only to the Athenians.

[2] $\tau\hat{\eta}\iota\ \sigma\upsilon\mu\mu\alpha\chi\dot{\iota}\alpha\iota$ was restored by Wilcken in vv. 3–4, but $\dot{\epsilon}\nu\ \tau\hat{\eta}\iota\ \epsilon\dot{\iota}\rho\dot{\eta}\nu\eta\iota$ (Schwahn, followed by Tod) is better in view of the later references to $\epsilon\dot{\iota}\rho\dot{\eta}\nu\eta$ in v. 15, and the impossibility of restoring $\sigma\upsilon\mu\mu\dot{\alpha}\chi\omega\nu$ in v. 11 or $\sigma\upsilon\mu\mu\alpha\chi\dot{\iota}\alpha\nu$ in v. 21.

[3] The tense of $\ddot{\omega}\mu\nu\upsilon\upsilon\nu$ here does not mean, as Schehl thought, that the oaths have been taken already.

[4] vv. 5–6: $\kappa\alpha\dot{\iota}\ o\dot{\upsilon}\ \lambda\dot{\upsilon}\sigma\omega\ \tau\dot{\alpha}\varsigma\ \sigma]\upsilon\nu\theta\dot{\eta}\kappa\alpha\varsigma\ \tau\dot{\alpha}[\varsigma\ \pi\rho\dot{o}\varsigma\ \Phi\dot{\iota}\lambda\iota\pi\pi\upsilon\nu\ M\alpha\kappa\dot{\epsilon}\delta\upsilon\alpha \ldots]. \ldots$ The restoration is generally accepted and referred to the treaty which is the subject of this oath; Schehl used the passage in support of his theory that the Common Peace treaty had already been concluded and that this was the oath to the alliance. If treaties with Philip were referred to, they could well have been the separate agreements which various states, including the Athenians, had made with Philip after Chaeronea; these treaties were not invalidated by the general settlement, for restrictions on autonomy imposed by them, e.g. the garrisons at Thebes, &c., were not withdrawn.

far as the Common Peace was concerned was much the same as that held by the King of Persia in 386. Then the King attached to the Common Peace treaty a clause providing for recognition of his rule in Asia. The King also took an oath to the peace of 386; Philip too must have sworn to observe the conditions of international and internal peace which he had imposed, and the author of Ps.-Dem. xvii regarded Alexander as being bound by the treaty. In fact he obtained, as will be shown, further legal powers in Greece, which were at this stage not formally conceded to him.

The inscription then envisages a situation where there is a Common Peace treaty being ratified and a synhedrion and Hegemon (of some kind) charged with the maintenance of the peace. There is no mention of the war against Persia and no indication that the synhedrion has actually met or been constituted or that a Hegemon has been appointed. It is indeed inconceivable that the first meeting at Corinth at which Philip presented his settlement could have been that of the synhedrion as permanently constituted.[1] It is fairly certain that the synhedrion consisted of representatives of the cities in proportion to their size (i.e. military strength), and that by no means every city sent a synhedros solely from itself.[2] Such a council could not have been elected without some preliminary meeting of all the Greeks to settle the proportions, and it is surely much more reasonable to see in the first meeting at Corinth the arrival of the representatives of the cities (probably some from each) to hear Philip's plans.[3] These representatives would then have reported back to their several cities with the proposals for a Common Peace and for a synhedrion to support it; the cities then took oaths on the pattern of that contained in Tod 177 and in some way appointed the synhedrion in the way laid down by the treaty, the numbers having been assessed and agreed at the first meeting.

This order of events is confirmed by Justin's narrative (ix. 5). First Philip ordered 'omnium civitatum legatos' to be summoned to Corinth: then 'ibi pacis legem universam Graeciae pro meritis singularum civitatum statuit' (Common Peace) 'consiliumque omnium veluti unum senatum ex omnibus legit' (synhedrion). 'Auxilia deinde singularum civitatum describuntur, sive adiuvandus ea manu res oppugnante aliquo foret seu duce illo bellum inferendum. Neque enim dubium erat imperium Persarum his apparatibus peti.' A synhedrion once agreed in principle, military quotas were fixed—both as a basis

---

[1] Cf., for instance, Plut. *Phocion*, 16.4, where the Athenians are pressed to accept both the Common Peace and the synhedrion.

[2] Cf. Tod 177, vv. 26 ff. and below, p. 160.

[3] Cf. the distinction in Diodorus' account (xvii. 4. 9) of the meeting summoned by Alexander: τάς τε πρεσβείας καὶ τοὺς συνέδρους.

for the appointment of synhedroi and for supply in the case of war—but nothing official was said about a war with Persia. Philip, however, appears to hold some office in relation to the Greeks: he is described as 'dux', the translation of $\dot{\eta}\gamma\epsilon\mu\dot{\omega}\nu$, and it has been seen how in the inscription a Hegemon is mentioned though not named.

Diodorus' narrative is very brief and makes no mention of Common Peace or of any other treaty. Philip, he said in xvi. 89. 2, 'made it known publicly and privately to the cities that he wished to discuss the affairs of Greece'. 'Therefore (s. 3), when the common council ($\kappa o\iota\nu\dot{o}\nu$ $\sigma\upsilon\nu\acute{\epsilon}\delta\rho\iota o\nu$) had gathered at Corinth, he discussed with it the war against the Persians and instilling in the councillors high hopes persuaded them into war.' Finally the Greeks elected him commanding general ($\sigma\tau\rho\alpha\tau\eta\gamma\dot{o}s$ $\alpha\dot{\upsilon}\tau o\kappa\rho\acute{\alpha}\tau\omega\rho$), and he fixed the amount of their contributions to the war.

Diodorus thus appears to bring in the synhedrion as already constituted without describing its creation. This inconsistency and the omission of any reference to a settlement of Greece led Wilcken[1] to suppose that a passage had dropped out between sections 2 and 3 and that there were two sittings of the synhedrion, one at which it was constituted, and one at which war with Persia was discussed. Heuss,[2] however, pointed out that $\kappa o\iota\nu\dot{o}\nu$ $\sigma\upsilon\nu\acute{\epsilon}\delta\rho\iota o\nu$ does not always mean a formally constituted council and adduced instances of its use for an *ad hoc* meeting; he argued further from Diodorus' conscious use of $\delta\iota\acute{o}\pi\epsilon\rho$ that the sense does run on from section 2 to section 3. But if nothing has dropped out of Diodorus' narrative here, Diodorus himself is guilty of over-compression and of concentrating too much on the war with Persia. There was a Common Peace treaty—as Diodorus himself later indicates (xvii. 9. 5)—and there was a situation when there was a synhedrion and a Hegemon (even if the first had not met and the second had not been appointed) but when there had been no official word of a Persian War.

(b) Philip as Hegemon of the Peace

Heuss argues that because Philip is not named as the Hegemon in the inscription (Tod 177) he did not hold that office.[3] Now it is possible that it was intended that there should be no permanent Hegemon but that, whenever a joint military enterprise in support of the Common Peace was to be undertaken, a Hegemon should then be appointed for it. If this was the case, it would be clear to the Greeks that Philip would be appointed in any serious crisis. But it is also possible, as

---

[1] *Sitzb. Munich*, 1917, iii, Abh. x. 4 ff.; followed by Schwahn, Momigliano and Hampl.

[2] Art. cit., p. 178.

[3] Art. cit., p. 180.

Justin's narrative suggests, that Philip was made permanent Hegemon of the peace, but was not elected until the first meeting of the synhedrion after the ratification of the treaty by the oath in Tod 177.

Heuss explained all Diodorus' references to Philip (and Alexander) as Hegemon, and to his (and Alexander's) *hegemonia* as either in the non-technical sense of the control of Greece or in the technical sense of the special command against Persia.[1] He agreed with Scheele[2] in seeing no difference between the titles Hegemon and Strategus Autocrator, except where the former is used loosely of the control of Greece. Scheele concluded that Strategus Autocrator was not a genuine title and that in his narrative here Diodorus was using two traditions which used the two terms to mean the same thing. Hammond,[3] however, has shown that it was Diodorus' normal custom not to use more than one source at once but to follow whichever seemed to him the best for each subject. Whether Heuss or Wilcken is right about Diodorus' narrative of the events of 338/337, Diodorus' sources almost certainly covered the conclusion of the peace treaty and the creation of the Hegemon, the period when Philip was, if ever, appointed Hegemon of the peace, as distinct from Hegemon or Strategus Autocrator against Persia.

Of Diodorus' uses of $\dot{\eta}\gamma\epsilon\mu\dot{\omega}\nu$, $\dot{\eta}\gamma\epsilon\mu o\nu\dot{\iota}a$ about Philip in book xvi (down to Philip's death) those in 1. 4, 84. 1, 89. 1, 91. 6, 95. 2 (the two last are not mentioned by Heuss) are clearly to be interpreted in the non-technical sense. But 64. 3—'he was appointed [$\dot{a}\pi\epsilon\delta\epsilon\dot{\iota}\chi\theta\eta$—Liddell and Scott (9th ed.) s.v. $\dot{a}\pi o\delta\epsilon\dot{\iota}\kappa\nu\upsilon\mu\iota$ ii] Hegemon of all Greece'—seems to indicate an appointment and does not mention the Persian War. In 91. 1 Philip is said to be in the position 'having been set up [$\kappa a\theta\epsilon\sigma\tau a\mu\dot{\epsilon}\nu o s$] as Hegemon by the Greeks and having begun the war against the Persians'; here Diodorus is perhaps resuming in the participle phrases the two stages that have been passed—first, Hegemon of the Common Peace; second, war with Persia.

In book xvi Diodorus' use of $\dot{\eta}\gamma\epsilon\mu\dot{\omega}\nu$, $\dot{\eta}\gamma\epsilon\mu o\nu\dot{\iota}a$ can prove little, but in his account at the beginning of book xvii of the Greek reaction to Philip's death and of Alexander's march into Greece his use of the words is more revealing. On Philip's death the Athenians refused 'to abandon the leadership of the Greeks to the Macedonians' (xvii. 3. 2), too vague an expression for any close interpretation. The Thebans voted not to concede to Alexander 'the hegemony of the Greeks' (ibid. 4); if Diodorus reflects the actual words of the decree, the informal mastery of Greece would be an unusual subject for an official motion. The Arcadians, he goes on, alone of the Greeks did not concede Philip the hegemony nor did they give way to Alexander (ibid.);

---

[1] Art. cit., pp. 179 ff.

[2] $\sigma\tau\rho a\tau\eta\gamma\dot{o}s$ $a\dot{\upsilon}\tau o\kappa\rho\dot{a}\tau\omega\rho$ (Diss. Leipzig, 1932), pp. 12 ff.

[3] The sources of Diodorus Siculus XVI, *C.Q.* xxxi (1937), 79 ff.

the sources only tell of the Spartans' refusal to accept the terms of the treaty (Justin ix. 5. 3—'soli Lacedaemonii . . .') ; the Arcadians almost certainly agreed to them, and it is possible that they expressed the disagreement recorded here by Diodorus by not voting for Philip's appointment to the office of Hegemon.

When Alexander advanced into Greece he persuaded the Thessalians to vote him 'his inherited hegemony of Greece' (Diod. xvii. 4. 1). If, as Rühl thought,[1] $\tau\hat{\eta}s$ Ἑλλάδος is to be omitted, this hegemony could merely be the headship of Thessaly, which Philip had held for many years, but the omission is arbitrary.[2] Then the Amphictyons voted him 'the hegemony of the Greeks' (ibid. 2), and the Athenians craved his pardon for their tardiness in agreeing to his hegemony (ibid. 6). Finally Alexander called together the delegations and the synhedroi and persuaded them with specious arguments (ἐπιείκεσι λόγοις) to elect him Strategus Autocrator for the war against Persia (ibid. 9).[3] This is the first mention of the war against Persia, and the fact that Alexander had to persuade the Greeks with the honeyed word also suggests that what they (or most of them) had readily conceded to him during his progress down Greece was something different from the command against Persia. But it was something that could be conceded and the formal position that had been for disposal, when Philip already was informally the master of Greece, was the Hegemony of the Peace.

Having asserted and argued at length, though unsuccessfully, that Philip was not Hegemon of the Peace, Heuss had to conclude that the office of Hegemon was only conferred in the event of war.[4] He had then to show that the body which the author of Ps.-Dem. xvii described as 'those who have been appointed for the common protection' (ἐπὶ τῇ κοινῇ φυλακῇ—s. 15) had no connexion with the Hegemon, for they are clearly permanent. These men, says the author of Ps.-Dem. xvii, were with the synhedrion entrusted with the maintenance of internal peace in the cities. There is no mention of them in the inscription Tod 177, but they may still have been included in the treaty document, if not in the oath, for another inscription, Tod 183, concerning some agreement between Alexander and the synhedrion refers to this body

---

[1] F. Rühl, 'Vermischte Bemerkungen', *Neues Jahrbuch für Philologie und Pädagogik*, i (Leipzig, 1888), 114.

[2] Cf. Wilcken, 'Alexander der grosse und der korinthische Bund', *Sitzb. Berlin*, 1922, p. 99.

[3] Cf. Arrian i. 1. 2 ; Larsen, art. cit., *Class. Phil.* xx (1925), 316, n. 3, made the point that this meeting was concerned only with the war against Persia as an additional argument to those used by Wilcken, art. cit., *Sitzb. Berlin*, 1922, pp. 97 ff., to distinguish between ἡγεμών and στρατηγὸς αὐτοκράτωρ. Arrian's use of ἡγεμών, &c., suggests that he did not trouble with Greek technical terms—cf. i. 1. 2, ii. 14. 4 and vii. 9. 5. [4] Art. cit., p. 180.

by a phrase which only varies in word order from that used in Ps.-Dem. xvii.

In the Epidaurus inscription (*S.E.G.* i. 75) referring to the league of Antigonus and Demetrius there is mention of 'the synhedroi and the general left behind by the kings for the common protection' (ἐπὶ τῆς κοινῆς φυλακῆς), and later of 'the kings or the general designated by the kings' (col. ii, vv. 13–14, 17–18). Here then, in wording which recalls the phrases of Tod 183 and of Ps.-Dem. xvii, the King's generals are found filling the post 'for the common protection'. They occur in the peace-time regulations for the new league, which, since war was in progress and the kings wanted to win over the Greeks by their organization of the league, would be likely to contain some window-dressing. It is thus unlikely that innovations were included in the proposed organization of the new league for peace-time which would give the kings more theoretical power then than Philip and Alexander had at first enjoyed. It must be concluded that those who were appointed for the common protection were the body that acted for the Hegemon in his absence;[1] that the Hegemon was permanent, and that therefore he was Philip.

No treaty of alliance between Philip and the Greeks

It remains necessary to examine those passages which the supporters of a full alliance between Philip and the Greeks adduce as positive evidence for their belief. As has been shown, neither Ps.-Dem. xvii nor the inscription Tod 177 affords any evidence for such an alliance, which, if it ever existed, must have been concluded at a later meeting.[2] But there is but one later meeting of the Greeks with Philip recorded in our sources, that at which Philip was probably appointed Hegemon and at which a general war against the Persians under Philip's leadership was approved. When Philip was already Hegemon of the Peace and commanding-general of the war against Persia, he scarcely needed to secure a further connexion with the Greeks by compelling them to 'have the same friends and enemies as himself': similarly, if he was already Hegemon of the Peace and had bound the Greeks to him in an offensive and defensive alliance, he would not have had to make the Greeks vote for a war against Persia under his leadership, as he undoubtedly did.

[1] So Kaerst, art. cit., *Rh. Mus.* lii (1897), 531 ff., and others, but Schwahn, art. cit., pp. 47 ff., and Tod in his commentary on no. 183 suggest that the body included representatives of both the king and the synhedrion.

[2] Wilcken and Momigliano saw in Justin's account ample proof of the existence of one treaty of peace and alliance, but the evidence of Ps.-Dem. xvii and Tod 177 really leaves no doubt that the Common Peace treaty was complete in itself; Dienelt of course (cf. above, p. 72) takes the existence of a provision for common action in the inscription as sufficient proof of an alliance.

In fact Philip's and Alexander's position as Hegemon of the Peace and commanding-general of the Greeks against Persia explains most of the uses of σύμμαχοι, συμμαχία &c., in the history of subsequent events. Alexander fought with the Greeks against Persia; they were therefore literally, and for the war against Persia formally, his σύμμαχοι, and it is natural that Arrian, writing a history of Alexander, should refer to them as such (as at i. 24. 3, iii. 19. 5).

Arrian iii. 24. 5 has been regarded by some as strong evidence of a full alliance between Philip (or Alexander) and the Greeks.[1] There Alexander liberates all Greek prisoners provided they entered Persian service 'before the peace and the alliance which was made with the Macedonians'. It might be expected that this expression would refer to one point of time, but Schwahn pointed out that the repetition of the article (τῆς) goes against the view that there was one treaty of peace and alliance; Schehl used the passage in support of his theory of two treaties. There is no reason why it should not refer to the alliance against Persia. Hampl went further and cast doubts on the verbal accuracy of Arrian in all matters relating to the treaty and league of Corinth.[2]

Diodorus (xvii. 63. 1) tells how Antipater fighting against the Spartans in 330 collected reinforcements παρὰ τῶν συμμαχούντων Ἑλλήνων. This phrase means no more than that in the present war some of the Greeks were fighting on Antipater's side; the legal basis of this military co-operation was probably the Common Peace treaty of 338/337, and it is hard to see what states fighting together in support of it could be called except συμμαχοῦντες.[3] Diodorus does not even use the word σύμμαχοι as Arrian does (i. 9. 9) to describe a similar collection of Greek states fighting with Alexander against the Thebans, whose fate, as transgressors of the Common Peace, was submitted, like that of the Spartans, to the synhedrion for judgement (Diod. xvii. 14. 1). It is worth noting that in a surviving official document from the war against the Persians, the edict of Alexander about the Chians in 332, the Greek states are referred to not as the allies but as 'those that share in the Peace' (Tod 192, vv. 13, 14).

Larsen claimed that a reference in a second-century arbitration (Ditt. *Syll.* 665, vv. 19–20) to an earlier decision 'among the Greeks and allies' on a dispute between the Spartans and the Megalopolitans is proof of the existence of a formal alliance of Greeks at this time.[4] Larsen reasonably connected this reference with that in Polybius ix.

---

[1] By Schehl, art. cit., p. 139; Wilcken, art. cit., *Sitzb. Berlin*, 1929, p. 301; against them Schwahn, art. cit., p. 53.　　　　　　　　　　[2] Op. cit., p. 50.

[3] Cf. Xen. *Hell.* vi. iii. 18: συμμαχεῖν τοῖς ἀδικουμένοις (Peace of 371 at Sparta, where there was certainly no alliance).

[4] *Class. Phil.* xxxiv (1939), 378; xxxix (1944), 160.

33. 11-12, where Philip is said to have entrusted similar disputes concerning the Spartans to a 'common judgement from the Greeks'. But the connexion does not prove that Philip's settlement constituted an alliance of the Greeks, because the judgement described by Polybius could have been made at a special tribunal set up directly after Philip's campaign in the Peloponnese in 338[1] or at the meeting of Greek representatives summoned to hear Philip's proposed settlement (indeed the latter is the most likely occasion of it, for the rejection of the Spartans' claims would then constitute a special reason for their refusal to accept the treaty). It might be argued that there was all the same an alliance which in the second century was read back to cover events a few months before its conclusion; but it is also possible to explain the reference in the inscription as a recollection of the much more recent 'common alliance' of Antigonus Doson and later of Philip V of Macedon with the Greek states, an arrangement which on a broad view must have seemed very similar to that made by Philip II and observed by Alexander. There are altogether too many gaps in our knowledge for this inscription to weigh heavily in any balance.

Relation of the synhedrion to individual states

It has already been shown that Alexander did not alter the treaty or the synhedrion which Philip had devised to settle and to keep settled the affairs of Greece. It is not even certain that Alexander formally renewed the treaty, for it had been concluded by the Greeks with Philip and his descendants, and he himself claimed the hegemony of Greece as an inheritance; that hegemony was belatedly acknowledged by the Greeks severally, and only his appointment to the command against Persia, which Philip had personally held, was voted to him by the synhedrion (cf. above, pp. 155 ff.). The powers of the synhedrion under Alexander, then, should not be different from those fixed by Philip.

It has also been pointed out that it is reasonable to use as evidence for the organization of the Greeks under Philip and Alexander information in the Epidaurus inscription (*S.E.G.* i. 75) about the constitution of the league organized by Antigonus and Demetrius. But it is not safe to say that any general clause in the constitution of the latter *must* have existed in the treaty which originally constituted the synhedrion; the argument is only one of probability and, in spite of his careful justification of his method, Larsen[2] perhaps attached too much weight to the evidence of the Epidaurus inscription in his discussion of the league under Philip and Alexander.

---

[1] Cf. Roebuck, art. cit., *Class. Phil.* xliii (1948), 73 ff.

[2] Art. cit., *Class. Phil.* xx (1925), 314 ff.

Nevertheless Larsen's conclusions about the relation of the synhedrion to the individual cities are generally sound. He states that the three most important aspects of this relation were:

(a) that the member states were represented in proportion to their size, and that each did not have one vote as in the Second Athenian Confederacy;

(b) that their representatives had full powers to act without reference to the home government;

(c) that outside the Hegemon the synhedrion was the highest authority for everything (p. 319).

Point (a) is, as Larsen showed, adequately demonstrated by the second part of the inscription Tod 177. It is said to contain either a list of the number of representatives from each city or group of cities (as Wilhelm, 'Attische Urkunden', *Sitzb. Wien*, 1911, vi. 1 ff.) or, what amounts to the same thing, a list of votes cast in unanimous approval of the war against Persia (as is ascribed to Hiller von Gärtringen by Wilcken, *Sitzb. München*, 1917, iii abh. x, 36–37). The latter explanation is less likely as the first part of the inscription is the oath to the treaty of 338/337, which was concluded and ratified before the idea of a war with Persia was officially brought forward.

Larsen pointed out (p. 321) that many of the names in this list are not those of city-states, but those of ethnic groups. He suggested that any group of more than one city-state was called an ἔθνος, and that some of these ἔθνη may have been organized as κοινά.[1] Larsen went no further than to say that in Philip's league such ethnic groups seem to be favoured; Hampl saw here evidence that Philip was attempting to set up not a council representative of the states, but 'eine beschlußfähige, repräsentative Vertretung der Ἑλλήνων als solcher'.[2] The new synhedrion was, as had earlier been noticed, in many ways similar to the college of Boeotarchs described in the *Oxyrhyncus Hellenica* (xi. 2 ff.), and Hampl here detects the influence on Philip of his early years at Thebes. But there is slender evidence of any intention to divide the Greeks into artificial groups; it is true that ἔθνη predominate in this list, but the list only covers areas of northern and central Greece, where the political units had never been as a rule concentrated citystates, but looser organizations such as the Phocians, the Locrians, the Acarnanians and the Aetolians.

Point (b) can be proved conclusively only from the Epidaurus inscription, where it is laid down (*S.E.G.* i. 75, col. iii, v. 20) that it should not be lawful for the cities to hold those who have been sent as synhedroi to account for decisions reached in the synhedrion. The

[1] L. adduces Hyperides, c. Dem. 18—κοινοὶ σύλλογοι of Achaeans, Arcadians, Boeotians under Alexander; cf. Kaerst, art. cit., *Rh. Mus.* lii (1897), 537.

[2] Op. cit., p. 46.

argument from probability, that the league of the two kings was based on Philip's settlement, is particularly strong for those conditions in it which curbed the power of the individual states; Antigonus and Demetrius were in a much weaker position in Greece than Philip had been. It must also have been the case that, since the principle of 'one city, one vote' had been discarded, the control of the cities over the representatives was in many cases weakened.

As to point (c), the Epidaurus inscription says plainly that in the new league the decrees of the synhedrion are binding (col. ii, vv. 18–19). It is clear enough from the oath taken by new members of the Athenian confederacy (Tod 127, vv. 33–34) that there the Athenian people and the council of Allies acting in agreement had full powers to make decrees that were binding; the allies' synhedroi could indeed be briefed by their cities, but there is no evidence that decrees approved by the Athenian people and the council of Allies ever required ratification. The subjects, however, on which the two bodies could pass decrees were limited, essentially, as the oath shows, to matters of war and peace; the sovereignty of the allied states as defined in the foundation-charter of the confederacy (Tod 123, vv. 19 ff.) was guaranteed against any encroachment.

Similarly the oath to the treaty of 338/337 bound the participants to do whatever the synhedrion decided in fighting any state which might break the treaty. Again the scope of the common council's power to pass decrees binding on all participants is limited to matters concerning a breach of the treaty; and again the guarantees of autonomy, &c., made in the treaty must have been regarded as inviolable. Of the decisions of the synhedrion known from the sources all but one are concerned either with alleged breaches of the treaty (the Thebans in 335—Diod. xvii. 14. 1 ff.; the Spartans in 331—ibid. 73. 5; the ten Athenian orators demanded for trial in 335 were said to have advised the abrogation of the treaty—ibid. 15. 1 ff.; Aeschines iii. 161) or with the war against the Persians (the probable decree about Greek mercenaries in Persian service—Arr. i. 16. 6; the Chians—Tod 192, vv. 14–16; the war itself—Diod. xvi. 89. 3, xvii. 4. 9; Arr. i. 1. 2), which was represented as a punitive action for wrongs done to Greece. The one exception is the decree committing the dispute between Melos and Cimolus to Argive arbitration (cf. Tod 179, vv. 3–5); the synhedrion may have been empowered in the treaty to arrange arbitrations, but perhaps the disputants appealed voluntarily to it (cf. Tod's commentary on p. 235).

The synhedrion and the Amphictyonic Council

Schaefer (*Demosthenes und seine Zeit*, iii, 57) argued that at the foundation of the so-called League of Corinth the 'Bundesgericht'

C 2607 M

(League's court) was handed over to the Amphictyonic Council. The three passages that were adduced in support of this belief were ably dealt with by Kaerst (art. cit., *Rh. Mus.* lii (1897), 524 ff.). Since then Pickard-Cambridge (*C.A.H.* vi. 267), Momigliano (art. cit., *Riv. di filol.* N.S. xii (1934), 493 ff. and *Filippo il Macedone*, p. 164) and Wüst (*Philipp II und Griechenland*, pp. 23 ff., 177) have persisted in seeing connexions of one sort or another between the synhedrion and the Amphictyonic Council. Kaerst's arguments are here summarized with some additional observations. The passages are:

(i) Dem. xviii. 322: ὁρᾶτε δέ. οὐκ ἐξαιτούμενος, οὐκ εἰς Ἀμφικτύονας δίκας ἐπαγόντων, οὐκ ἀπειλούντων, οὐκ ἐπαγγελλομένων . . . προδέδωκα τὴν εἰς ὑμᾶς εὔνοιαν. This is all taken by Schaefer, &c., to refer to Alexander's demand in 335 for the surrender of Demosthenes and nine other orators for trial 'in the synhedrion of the Greeks' (Aeschines iii. 161). Kaerst suggested that this episode is covered by ἐξαιτούμενος only (ἐξαιτεῖν would appear to be the right word to describe Alexander's action—cf. Diod. xvii. 15. 1, Plut. *Phocion* 17. 2), and that the following words refer to another occasion when the pro-Macedonian party at Athens wanted to hand Demosthenes over to the Amphictyons. There is no mention of the Amphictyonic Council in Aeschines or in Diodorus' account of the punishment of the Thebans (xvii. 14. 1 ff.).

(ii) Pausanias vii. 10. 10: 'not even Philip . . . and Alexander forced those of the Greeks who opposed them to be sent to Macedonia, but allowed them to plead their case before the Amphictyons.' Kaerst argued that Pausanias' evidence would not by itself be sufficient; that moreover C. Wachsmuth ('Eine Hauptquelle für die Geschichte des achäischen Bundes', *Leipziger Studien*, x. 288 ff.) had thought Pausanias particularly untrustworthy in this whole section vii. 10. 7–12.

(iii) Aeschines iii. 254: 'a few days hence the Pythian games are to be celebrated, and the synhedrion of the Greeks assembled.' There is good reason to suppose that the synhedrion did meet at the panhellenic festivals (cf. originally J. G. Droysen, *Geschichte des Hellenismus*, i (2nd ed., Gotha, 1877), 162, n. 1, followed by Kaerst and then by Larsen, art. cit., *Class. Phil.* xxi (1926), 59; Berve, *Das Alexanderreich*, i. 250; Busolt–Swoboda, *Griechische Staatskunde*, ii. 1394, n. 1). Since Kaerst wrote, it has been made clear from the Epidaurus inscription that this was certainly the case in the league organized by Antigonus and Demetrius (*S.E.G.* i. 75, col. ii, vv. 13–14, 17–18).

APPENDIX XI

The Peace of 311

In 311 the struggle between Antigonus and Cassander, Lysimachus and Ptolemy for the control of Alexander's empire was brought to a temporary halt by a general peace. By its terms the four generals agreed on a division of territory, and that the Greeks should be autonomous.

Diodorus (xix. 105. 1, cf. xx. 19. 3) supplies no more than this bare fact. But a letter from Antigonus to the Greek city of Scepsis in Asia Minor, preserved in an inscription (*OGIS* 5; Welles, *Royal Correspondence in the Hellenistic Period*, no. 1), shows that there was more to this recognition of Greek freedom than a simple declaration by the generals; it had been agreed also that the Greeks should themselves swear to aid one another in preserving autonomy (vv. 53 ff.).

Heuss[1] concludes that there was a separate treaty for the Greeks, a Common Peace. It is true, as he said, that Antigonus explained this idea of Greek participation in the oaths as a precaution for the future— so that after his death the Greeks could help one another protect their independence—and so claimed to be returning to Philip's settlement, though there is no indication that the reconstitution of the synhedrion was proposed. But Antigonus' words do not make clear whether what the Greeks were to swear to was simply a declaration that all cities were autonomous and should remain so (which, even if not formally constituted and described as a separate treaty ($\sigma \nu \nu \theta \hat{\eta} \kappa \alpha \iota$), would amount to a virtual renewal of the Common Peace treaty of 338/337) or whether it was the whole treaty between him and the other generals; though even in this latter case the oath would not be far different from that to the treaty of 338/337 which included a pledge to safeguard Philip's rule in Macedonia. The proposed Greek oath, then, was at least a reinvocation of the Common Peace idea.[2]

It seems likely that the Common Peace arrangement was limited to the European Greeks and the islanders; for the reply of the people of Scepsis (*OGIS* 6) seems to refer to the Greeks as a body not including themselves. But it remains possible that when Diodorus later speaks of the Rhodians, asked by Demetrius in 307 to abandon their profitable

---

[1] Art. cit., *Hermes*, lxxiii (1938), 156 ff.
[2] Cf. Ehrenberg, *Alexander and the Greeks*, p. 43.

neutrality, 'preferring to keep Common Peace with everyone' (xx. 46. 6),[1] he is using the phrase here to mean the general condition of peace legally based on the Common Peace oaths in the treaty of 311.

[1] κοινὴν εἰρήνην αἱρουμένων ἄγειν πρὸς ἅπαντας. This is the only use of the phrase Common Peace in the three books (xviii–xx) where Diodorus' principal source is Hieronymus of Cardia.

APPENDIX XII

The Chronology of the First Part of the Corinthian War

THE chronology of the first part of the Corinthian War is an old problem, but it is necessary for the purpose of this work to determine, as surely as possible, whether or not the peace negotiations in Asia preceded those at Sparta. The most recent studies of the problem are those by Judeich ('Die Zeit der Friedensrede des Andokides', *Philologus* (1926), 141 ff.) and Momigliano (art. cit., *Annali di Pisa*, II. v (1936), 98 ff.), who put the discussions at Sparta first, and by Treves ('Note sulla guerra corinzia', *Riv. di filol.* lxv (1937), 113 ff.) and Accame (*Ricerche intorno alla guerra corinzia*, pp. 103 ff.), who took the opposite view. Judeich and Momigliano found that their interpretations of Xen. *Hell.* IV. viii. 12 ff. (on the discussions in Asia) and of Andocides *Or.* iii (on those at Sparta) were in accord with their conclusions on the chronology; so also did Treves and Accame. The only full study of the chronological problem in English is that of Underhill in his introduction to the *Hellenica* (pp. xlv ff., published in 1900); his conclusions are similar to those of Treves and Accame.

The difficulty in fixing the chronological order of the two peace conferences lies in the fact that Xenophon's narrative of land fighting in the first part of the war is separate from his narrative of naval operations, and the two are nowhere explicitly related chronologically, except at one point near the beginning; and, while his account of the conference in Asia belongs to the latter, the points of contact with what Andocides says about the conference at Sparta lie in the former.

There are two events described by Xenophon of which the dates can be fixed from firm external evidence. First, he says at IV. iii. 10 that the battle of Cnidus took place shortly before, and the battle of Coronea shortly after, an eclipse of the sun which is known to have occurred on 14 August 394. Second, he tells in IV. v. 1 ff. how Agesilaus' campaign round Corinth which achieved temporary success with the capture of Piraeum and the Heraeum, but was brought to swift failure by Iphicrates' destruction of a Spartan *mora* near Sicyon, began at the time of the Isthmian Games; and the Isthmian Games were held at the end of May and the beginning of June in even years.

The first of these dates enables the conference in Asia to be dated with fair certainty. The events of the naval war in IV. viii. 1–6 clearly belong to the rest of 394 after the battle of Cnidus; the new year begins at s. 7 ($\ddot{a}\mu a$ $\delta \dot{\epsilon}$ $\tau \hat{\omega}$ $\ddot{\epsilon}\alpha\rho\iota$ . . .). In the campaigning season of 393 Conon and Pharnabazus visited the allied armies at the Isthmus (s. 8), after which Pharnabazus went home and Conon to Athens to supervise the rebuilding of the fortifications (ss. 9–10) at the latest in the autumn of this year.[1] Xenophon's account of the conference in Asia (IV. viii. 12 ff.) indicates a close connexion with the events described in ss. 9 ff.; the present participle $\dot{a}\kappa o\acute{v}o\nu\tau\epsilon\varsigma$ has been noted by Accame and the present optative $\dot{a}\nu o\rho\theta o\acute{\iota}\eta$ is also significant, showing that the Athenians are still in the process of rebuilding their walls. The conference, then, was hardly later than the early months of 392.

In his account of the land fighting between the battle of Coronea and Agesilaus' campaign of IV. v. 1 ff. Xenophon is concerned wholly with events in the north-east Peloponnese, especially in and around Corinth. His account of the battle of Coronea runs to the end of IV. iii. The opening sentence of IV. iv concludes the campaign of 394: 'after this the rest of the armament was dismissed by cities, and Agesilaus sailed back home'. There follows the general remark: 'and after this the Athenians, the Boeotians, the Argives and their allies carried on the war based on Corinth, and the Spartans and their allies based on Sicyon.' From the third sentence of IV. iv. 1 to the end of IV. iv. 18 Xenophon gives a continuous narrative of what appears to be a year's fighting in the area of Corinth—unrest in Corinth, the massacre of the pro-Spartan oligarchs there at the feast of the Euclea (Feb./Mar.), the partial union of Corinth and Argos, the Spartan capture of Lechaeum, further fighting and the withdrawal of the main Spartan force (IV. iv. 13 end), siege warfare thereafter and Iphicrates' attack on Phlius, and finally the rebuilding by the Athenians of the Long Walls linking Corinth and Lechaeum. IV. iv. 19 describes how Agesilaus ravaged the Argolid for the first time, then proceeded to Corinth, where he found the Long Walls rebuilt, and recaptured them with the help of Teleutias, the admiral in the Corinthian Gulf; Agesilaus then disbanded his army and went home. The narrative of IV. v. 1 ff. follows directly with the connexion $\dot{\epsilon}\kappa$ $\delta\dot{\epsilon}$ $\tau o\acute{v}\tau ov$.

The Isthmian Games of IV. v. 1 could be either those of 392 or those of 390. There are, then, two possible chronological systems:

System I

If the games are those of 392, all the events of IV. iv must come between early 393 and May/June 392. Then IV. iv. 1–18 would be the

---

[1] Underhill (op. cit., introduction, p. xlvii) believed that the inscription which is now part B of Tod 107 recording expenditure on the rebuilding of the walls during the archonship of Eubulides (394/393) meant that Conon must have reached Athens by the end of that archon-year, midsummer 393. But part A of the same inscription records a similar payment in the last month of 395/394, before the battle of Cnidus even (cf. Tod's commentary).

campaign of 393 and IV. iv. 19 would belong either to the autumn of 393 or to the spring of 392. But neither time is wholly suitable. The disbanding of the main Spartan force at IV. iv. 13 is unlikely to have been before midsummer, and the events of IV. iv. 14–18 would leave Agesilaus' campaign very late and past the useful time for ravaging the Argolid. It is similarly a tight, though not impossibly tight, fit to make time for Agesilaus to invade the Argolid in spring 392 late enough to do damage, move on to Corinth, return to Sparta and disband his army, re-collect it and return to Corinth before the end of May. Under this system there is an even tighter fit for naval action in the Corinthian Gulf. In IV. viii. 10–11 Xenophon tells how the Corinthians manned a fleet under Agathinus from the money Pharnabazus left when he visited the Isthmus (late summer 393, see below); the Spartans also manned a fleet under Podanemus; Podanemus was killed, his successor Pollis wounded and Herippidas took over; he in turn was superseded by Teleutias, who under this system must be in command by April 392 at the latest (cf. IV. iv. 19).

Andocides' speech was after the Spartan victory at Lechaeum (s. 18) and before the invasion of the Argolid (s. 27); under this system the battle of Lechaeum was in the first half of 393 and the invasion of the Argolid early in 392; so the possible dates for the speech precede those for the conference in Asia, as speech and conference can hardly be simultaneous.

System II

If the games are those of 390, then the events of IV. iv. 1–19 must be spread over two more years, from early 393 to May/June 390. If this is right, Xenophon must have passed over at least one campaigning season in silence. That he should do so need occasion no surprise, for he was not interested in chronology and he recorded what happened, remaining silent when nothing happened. There are in fact some reasons for thinking that the second sentence in IV. iv. 1 quoted above does span the whole season of 393, and that the events of IV. iv. 1–18 belong to 392, allowing this year for the commands of Podanemus, Pollis and Herippidas with Teleutias taking over for the new season of 391.

(i) In the third sentence of IV. iv. 1 Xenophon says: 'the Corinthians, seeing their own land being ravaged and their men dying because they were always near the enemy, while the other allies themselves enjoyed tranquillity and had their fields under cultivation. . . .' The time is early in the year before the feast of the Euclea in February/March. It is true that there had been fighting near Corinth in 394, but there had also been fighting on a large scale in Boeotia in that year as in 395.

These Corinthian complaints would make better sense after a year in which Corinth had been exclusively in the front line.

(ii) Xenophon's account of the naval war after Cnidus in IV. viii. 1 shows that the visit of Pharnabazus and Conon to the Isthmus was late in the campaigning season of 393. He says that on this visit they encouraged the allies and Pharnabazus left them all the money he had before sailing home. There is no indication at all that any of the critical events described in IV. iv. 2–18 had taken or were taking place, and, if they were, one might expect some succour from the fleet other than words and money.

(iii) From the Isthmus Pharnabazus went home and Conon to Athens to assist in the reconstruction of the walls of Athens which had already begun. It is hard to say how long the reconstruction would take; at any rate it was not satisfactorily finished, as Piraeus was still inadequately fortified in 378 (Xen. *Hell.* v. iv. 20). It does not seem likely that the Athenians would have sent their workmen to Corinth in the autumn or winter of 393.

(iv) In IV. iv. 2 Xenophon speaks of *both* those Corinthians who had received the King's money *and* those who had been most to blame for the war ($o\ddot{\imath} \tau\epsilon \ldots \kappa a\dot{\imath} o\dot{\imath} \ldots$). This expression should mean two different groups of Corinthians, and those who had received the King's money from Timocrates (Xen. *Hell.* III. v. 2) had been just those who had been most to blame for the war. It should, then, be Pharnabazus' money which is referred to here; and so the events of IV. iv. 2 ff. should be after Pharnabazus' visit and belong to 392.

There are two further points about this narrative of the land fighting which suggest that it covers four years rather than two:

(i) Xenophon on three occasions (IV. iv. 1, 13 end and 19 end) appears on a normal interpretation of his words to refer to the end of a campaigning season and the disbanding of the Spartan army for the winter.

(ii) As Griffith pointed out ('The Union of Corinth and Argos', *Historia*, i (1950), 242, note 26): 'there are at least four occasions where a considerable lapse of time is expressed or implied, time which simply is not available in Judeich's two campaigning seasons.' He instanced IV. iv. 1, 14, 15 ff., and 19 taken together with v. 1.

Under this system the terminal points for Andocides' speech are summer 392[1] and spring 391, a period which accords with Philo-

---

[1] The capture of Lechaeum could still have been before the end of archon-year 393/392, and so Aristeides' statement (ed. Dindorf, ii. 370) that the archonship of Eubulides (394/393) lay between the battles of Corinth (Nemea) and Lechaeum

chorus' date (Attic Year 392/391) for the conference at Sparta, Andocides' speech and his trial and exile (Didymus vii. 20) and with Andocides' own statement (s. 20) that the Boeotians had been at war for four years;[1] and so the conference in Asia under this system well-nigh certainly precedes that at Sparta.

As between the two systems there can be no certainty, but on balance System II is preferable and, as a choice must be made, it should be taken that the conference in Asia preceded that at Sparta.

Note. Many of the arguments used in this controversy depend to a great extent on exact interpretations of Xenophon's words. Accame produced another, which, if it were acceptable, would give priority to the conference in Asia, whatever chronological system were followed. He suggested that Xenophon's wording at iv. viii. 15, where he described Argive opposition to the terms proposed in Asia—'the Argives did not think that they would be able as they wanted to have Corinth as Argos'—means that the partial union of the two cities (iv. iv. 6) had not yet taken place; the partial union preceded the capture of Lechaeum, the *terminus post quem* of Andocides' speech.

Diodorus is virtually useless for this problem, his dates being demonstrably unreliable; he puts Cnidus, Coronea and the fleet's visit to the Isthmus all in 395/394. He does, however, achieve what seems to be the correct order of events by completing this sequence before going on to the stasis in Corinth and the fall of Lechaeum.

could be accurate. Judeich and Momigliano take Aristeides to mean that the capture of Lechaeum must have fallen *directly* after the end of Eubulides' year, in summer 393. But nothing more should be assumed than that in an annalistic source the battle of Corinth was listed under 395/394 and the capture of Lechaeum under 393/392.

[1] If the war had started at the very end of 396/395, it might theoretically be possible early in 392 to say that it had lasted four years, reckoning in Attic years inclusively, but it would be a most unnatural way of reckoning. This statement and the consideration of Xenophon's narrative mentioned above (ii) are the points made by Griffith (l.c.) in rejecting Judeich's chronology.

APPENDIX XIII

The Chronology of the Years 370–364

THE period of six years between the death of Jason of Pherae and the death of Pelopidas was one of almost continuous warfare in Greece, during which there were two separate attempts to re-establish the Peace and one treaty actually concluded which is widely thought to have been a Common Peace. If these agreements, projected or realized, are to be put in their historical contexts, some attempt must be made to reach a satisfactory chronological system for this period.

Niese made such an attempt in his 'Beiträge zur griechischen Geschichte 370–364' published in *Hermes*, xxxix (1904), 84 ff. There he argued that the second Theban invasion of the Peloponnese must have taken place in 368, that Philiscus' mission to Greece, Pelopidas' second expedition to Thessaly and the two attempts to rescue him were in 367, and that Pelopidas' return from Persia, the subsequent conference and the invasion of Achaea were in the first half of 366 before the capture of Oropus, which he assigned to the midsummer of that year.

Beloch (*Griechische Geschichte*, 2nd ed., III. ii. 238 ff.) refuted Niese's arguments about the second Theban invasion of the Peloponnese, and established a chronology for the years 369 and 368, which fixes the chief events as follows:

> End of April 369. Return of the first Theban expedition from the Peloponnese (four months after the Boeotian year began—Plut. *Pelop.* 25. 1).
>
> May–June 369. Negotiations at Athens on the details of the alliance with the Spartans ('in the next year' at Xen. *Hell.* VII. i. 1 must mean the year starting that spring, the campaign just described having been in the winter).
>
> July–September 369. Second Theban expedition into the Peloponnese; first supporting force from Dionysius round Corinth (Dionysius' mercenaries left Greece at the end of summer—Diod. xv. 70. 1; that they received five months' pay from Dionysius—Diod. l.c.— does not mean that they served five months, still less that they were five months in Greece).
>
> July–September 369. First mission of Pelopidas to Thessaly (at the same time as the above—Diod. xv. 67. 3; Plut. *Pelop.* 26. 1).

Winter 369/368. Attacks on Pelopidas and Epaminondas at Thebes; Epaminondas not re-elected Boeotarch (after Epaminondas' failure at Corinth—Diod. xv. 72. 2; cf. Beloch, p. 247, and above p. 79, n. 3).

Spring 368. Philiscus' embassy.

Early summer 368. Second mission of Pelopidas to Thessaly; second supporting force from Dionysius arrived.

Summer 368. Pelopidas imprisoned in Thessaly; no Theban expedition into the Peloponnese; the 'tearless' battle (all the events of the last three paragraphs must have occurred in the same year— cf. Xen. *Hell.* vii. i. 27–28).

Autumn 368. First expedition to rescue Pelopidas failed (Epaminondas still out of office—Diod. xv. 71. 6).

Winter 368/367. Pelopidas rescued.

From this point Beloch's system seems less convincing. Though he had rightly disregarded Diodorus' placing of the rescue of Pelopidas in 367/366, he extended the negotiations in Persia over the whole of 367 and put the conference at Thebes in summer 366, to fit in with Diodorus' statement (xv. 76. 3) that in 366/365 the King sent ambassadors to Greece to promote peace. But there is no hint of Persian ambassadors in Greece at the time of the conference at Thebes, and, as Diodorus seems to be confusing the peace terms brought back by Pelopidas and rejected by the Greeks (Xen. *Hell.* vii. i. 33–40) with those later proposed by the Thebans and accepted by the Corinthians and others (Xen. *Hell.* vii. iv. 6–11, cf. Appendix VII), he may easily have ascribed his hotch-potch to the archon-year of the latter and not to that of the former.

Beloch further had to place Epaminondas' invasion of Achaea during the time when Pelopidas was in Persia, though in Xenophon's narrative it comes after the rejection of Pelopidas' terms. He argued that the motive for the invasion given by Xenophon (*Hell.* vii. i. 41)— to coerce the Arcadians and their other allies—indicates an early date, because in winter 369/368 there had already been enmity between the Arcadians and the Thebans (Xen. *Hell.* vii. i. 26); but the Arcadians seem to have sent their ambassador to Persia with Pelopidas (ibid. 33), and their alliance was apparently still regarded as valid at the time of the conference at Thebes (ibid. 39).

Beloch's system also made the conference at Thebes take place at about the same time as the capture of Oropus (which he, like Niese, assigned to about midsummer 366 on the basis of Schol. Aeschines iii. 85 and Diod. xv. 76. 1), although Xenophon's account of the conclusion of the alliance between the Athenians and the Arcadians (vii. iv. 2 ff.) suggests that the capture of Oropus was the most important recent event that prompted this change of Athenian policy. Moreover, Timotheus was general at Athens in December 366 (*IG* i^2. 108, vv. 9–10), and must have been elected, for the first time since 373, in January 366; his return to office after his disgrace would indicate some change in the Athenian attitude to the naval hegemony, such as that brought about by the failure of the Persians to support Pelopidas' settlement with force.

If Pelopidas was rescued in winter 368/367, there is no reason why the embassies to Persia and the conference at Thebes should not have taken place in the spring and summer of 367, during which little fighting is reported. After the failure of the conference Epaminondas invaded Achaea, to coerce the Arcadians and others who had wrecked the settlement; the decision to alter his arrangements in Achaea (Xen. *Hell.* VII. i. 43) may well have been caused, as Beloch suggested, by a change in Boeotarchs (winter 367/366), and so the pro-Spartan revolutions in Achaea probably took place in early 366.

The loss of Oropus (midsummer 366) was followed by the alliance between the Athenians and the Arcadians and by the abortive Athenian attempt on Corinth (Xen. *Hell.* VII. iv. 2–6); the peace negotiations between the Corinthians and the Thebans followed (ibid. 6–10), and an agreement was finally reached (ibid. 10). This agreement evidently belongs to early 365, as the arrival of the third supporting force from Syracuse at about the same time (ibid. 12) must have been for the new campaigning season; not long after it war broke out between the Arcadians and the Eleans (in 365/364 according to Diod. xv. 77. 1) and in the next year interrupted the Olympic festival of August/September 364 (Xen. *Hell.* VII. iv. 28 ff.). Pelopidas' fatal expedition to Thessaly had been delayed by the eclipse of the sun of 13 July 364 (Plut. *Pelop.* 31).

APPENDIX XIV

The Geographical Limits of the Common Peace Treaties

IT has been seen that one of the notable features of the Common Peace treaties was that, because their terms were general principles, they were deemed to apply to all Greek cities whether or not they had actually sworn an oath to the particular treaty; only definite refusal to accept a treaty's conditions rendered a city ἔκσπονδος (as the Spartans in 362/361), and a city in such a position could be regarded as still at war (cf. the threats to the Thebans in 387/386 and 371).

Unfortunately a detailed list of signatories is given for none of the treaties, and the best that the sources provide is the sort of incomplete and vague statement made by Xenophon (*Hell.* vi. iii. 18) about the Peace of 371 at Sparta: the Spartans, he says, took the oath for themselves and their allies, the Athenians and their allies swore separately. Diodorus says simply that 'the Greeks' (xv. 38. 1–2, 70. 2, 76. 3, 89. 1) or 'the cities' (xv. 50. 4, 51. 1) made Common Peace.

It is therefore impossible to produce a certain example of a city which did not swear to a particular treaty, but was later deemed by other Greeks to be bound by it. The Olynthians may not have attended the conferences of 387/386 or taken the oath, yet they were made the victims of a war carried out, most likely, in support of the autonomy principle (cf. above, pp. 47 ff.).

The treaties were then theoretically binding on all Greeks. By this the most that were meant were the mainland Greeks, the islanders of the Aegean and Ionian seas and the coastal cities as far as Corcyra in the west and Byzantium in the east. The Asiatic Greeks were specifically excluded from the King's Peace, as being the property of the King, and remained outside subsequent treaties, even that of 362/361 when the King had no part in the treaty; it is not clear whether or not they were enrolled in the treaty of 338/337 after their liberation by Alexander (cf. above, p. 106, n. 5). The affairs of the western Greeks never came into the question.

As to barbarians, there is no evidence that any were included in any treaty. The Second Athenian confederacy was in theory open to barbarians as well as to Greeks (Tod 123, v. 16) and the semi-barbarian Alcetas of the Molossi and his son, Neoptolemus, were members of it (ibid., vv. 109 ff.), but they need not necessarily have been included among the allies of the Athenians who swore to the Peace of 371 at Sparta.

BIBLIOGRAPHY OF WORKS
REFERRED TO

(For abbreviations see p. ix)

I. BOOKS

S. ACCAME, *La lega ateniense del secolo IV a. C.*, Rome, 1941.
—— *Ricerche intorno alla guerra corinzia*, Turin, 1951.
K. J. BELOCH, *Griechische Geschichte*, vol. iii (2nd ed.), Strasbourg, 1922–3.
H. BENGSTON, *Die Strategie in der hellenistischen Zeit*, Munich, 1937.
—— *Griechische Geschichte* (2nd ed.), Munich, 1960.
E. BUCHNER, *Der Panegyrikos des Isokrates*, Historia Einzelschriften, ii, 1958.
A. R. BURN, *The Lyric Age of Greece*, London, 1960.
I. CALABI, *Ricerche sui rapporti tra le poleis*, Florence, 1953.
W. E. CALDWELL, *Hellenic Conceptions of Peace*, New York, 1919.
P. CLOCHÉ, *La Politique étrangère d'Athènes de 404 à 338 a. C.*, Paris, 1934.
—— *Thèbes de Béotie*, Namur, 1952.
H. DIELS and W. KRANZ, *Fragmente der Vorsokratiker*, vol. ii (6th ed.), Berlin, 1952.
J. G. DROYSEN, *Geschichte des Hellenismus*, vol. i (2nd ed.), Gotha, 1877.
V. EHRENBERG, *Alexander and the Greeks*, Oxford, 1938.
—— *The Greek State*, Oxford, 1960.
A. W. GOMME, *Essays in Greek History and Literature*, Oxford, 1937.
—— *A Historical Commentary on Thucydides*, 3 vols., Oxford, 1945–56.
G. GROTE, *Plato and the Other Companions of Socrates*, vol. iii, London, 1867.
—— *History of Greece*, vols. viii and ix (new ed.), London, 1888.
N. G. L. HAMMOND, *A History of Greece to 322 B.C.*, Oxford, 1959.
F. HAMPL, *Die griechischen Staatsverträge des 4. Jahrhunderts v. Christi*, Leipzig, 1938.
B. V. HEAD, *Historia Nummorum* (2nd ed.), Oxford, 1911, reprinted London, 1963.
G. L. HUXLEY, *Early Sparta*, London, 1962.
W. JAEGER, *Demosthenes*, Cambridge, 1938.
A. H. M. JONES, *Athenian Democracy*, Oxford, 1957.
F. KLEINE-PIENING, *Quo tempore Isocratis orationes quae* περὶ εἰρήνης *et* Ἀρεοπαγιτικός *inscribuntur compositae sunt* (Diss. Münster), Paderborn, 1930.
M. L. W. LAISTNER, *Isocrates: De Pace and Philippus*, Cornell Studies in Classical Philology, xxii, 1927.
H. G. LIDDELL and R. SCOTT, *A Greek–English Lexicon* (revised by H. S. Jones), Oxford, 1925–40.
F. H. MARSHALL, *The Second Athenian Confederacy*, Cambridge, 1905.
G. MATHIEU, *Les Idées politiques d'Isocrate*, Paris, 1925.

L. Méridier, *Platon V* (Budé ed.), Paris, 1931.

B. D. Meritt, H. T. Wade-Gery and M. F. McGregor, *The Athenian Tribute Lists*, 4 vols., Princeton, 1939–53.

E. Meyer, *Theopomps Hellenika*, Halle, 1909.

—— *Geschichte des Altertums*, vol. v, Stuttgart–Berlin, 1921.

A. Momigliano, *Filippo il Macedone*, Florence, 1934.

F. Nolte, *Die historisch-politischen Voraussetzungen des Königsfriedens*, Bamberg, 1923.

H. W. Parke, *Greek Mercenary Soldiers*, Oxford, 1933.

H. Raue, *Untersuchungen zur Geschichte des korinthischen Bundes*, Diss. Marburg, 1937.

R. von Scala, *Die Staatsverträge des Altertums*, Leipzig, 1898.

A. Schaefer, *Demosthenes und seine Zeit*, 2 vols. (2nd ed.), Leipzig, 1885–6.

M. Scheele, στρατηγὸς αὐτοκράτωρ, Diss. Leipzig, 1932.

E. von Stern, *Geschichte des spartanischen und thebanischen Hegemonie vom Königsfrieden bis zur Schlacht bei Mantineia*, Dorpat, 1884.

F. Taeger, *Der Friede von 362/1*, Stuttgart, 1930.

W. W. Tarn, *Alexander the Great*, vol. ii, Cambridge, 1948.

A. E. Taylor, *Plato: the Man and his Work*, London, 1926.

J. Thiel, *Xenophon de vectigalibus*, Amsterdam, 1922.

M. N. Tod, *Greek Historical Inscriptions*, 2 vols. (vol. i, 2nd ed.), Oxford, 1946–8.

G. E. Underhill and F. C. Marchant, *Xenophon Hellenica*, Oxford, 1906.

C. A. Volquardsen, *Untersuchungen über die Quellen der griechischen und sizilischen Geschichte bei Diodoros XI bis XVI*, Kiel, 1868.

F. W. Walbank, *A Historical Commentary on Polybius*, vol. i, Oxford, 1957.

C. B. Welles, *Royal Correspondence in the Hellenistic Period*, New Haven and Prague, 1934.

U. von Wilamowitz-Möellendorf, *Platon*, vol. i (3rd ed.), Berlin, 1867.

F. Wüst, *Philipp von Makedonien und Griechenland in den Jahren von 346 bis 338*, Munich, 1938.

II. ARTICLES, ETC.

F. E. Adcock, 'The Archidamian War', Chap. VIII of *C.A.H.* v (1927).

R. P. Austin, 'Athens and the Satraps' Revolt', *J.H.S.* lxiv (1944).

E. Badian, 'Harpalus', *J.H.S.* lxxxi (1961).

J. P. V. D. Balsdon, 'The "divinity" of Alexander', *Historia*, i (1950).

H. Berve, Review of F. Taeger, 'Der Friede von 362/1', *Gnomon*, ix (1933).

E. Bickermann, 'Alexandre le Grand et les villes d'Asie', *Rev. d'étud. grec.* xvii (1934).

—— 'Les préliminaires de la seconde guerre de Macédoine, la Paix de Phoenicé', *Rev. de philologie*, 3rd ser. ix (1935).

D. W. Bradeen, 'The Popularity of the Athenian Empire', *Historia*, ix (1960).

P. A. Brunt, 'The Hellenic League against Persia', *Historia*, ii (1953–4).

C. D. Buck, 'Interstate Use of the Greek Dialects', *Class. Phil.* viii (1913).

A. P. Burnett, 'Thebes and the Expansion of the Second Athenian Confederacy', *Historia*, xi (1962).

I. Calabi, 'Il sinedrio della lega di Corinto e le sue attribuzioni giurisdizionali', *Riv. di filol.* lxxviii (1950).

M. Cary, 'The Alleged Achaean Arbitration after Leuctra', *C.Q.* xix (1925).

—— 'The Ascendancy of Sparta', Chap. II of *C.A.H.* vi (1927).

G. L. Cawkwell, 'Aeschines and the Peace of Philocrates', *Rev. d'étud. grec.* lxxiii (1960).

—— 'The Common Peace of 366/5 B.C.', *C.Q.* n.s. xi (1961).

—— 'The Defence of Olynthus', *C.Q.* n.s. xii (1962).

—— 'The ΣYN coins again', *J.H.S.* lxxxiii (1963).

—— 'Notes on the Peace of 375/4', *Historia*, xii (1963).

P. Cloché, 'Notes sur la politique athénienne au début du IV siècle', *Rev. d'étud. anc.* xliii (1941).

K. Dienelt, 'Der korinthische Bund', *Jahreshefte Oesterr. Arch. Inst.* xliii (1956).

W. G. Forrest, 'Themistocles and Argos', *C.Q.* n.s. x (1960).

A. W. Gomme, '*IG* i² 60 and Thucydides iii. 50. 2', *Robinson Studies*, ii (1953).

G. T. Griffith, 'The so-called κοινὴ εἰρήνη of 346 B.C.', *J.H.S.* lix (1939).

—— 'The Union of Corinth and Argos', *Historia*, i (1950).

N. G. L. Hammond, 'The Sources of Diodorus Siculus XVI', *C.Q.* xxxi (1937).

F. Hampl, 'Zur angeblichen κοινὴ εἰρήνη des 346 und zum philokrateischen Frieden', *Klio*, xxxi (1938).

J. Hatzfeld, 'Jason de Phère a-t-il été l'allié d'Athènes', *Rev. d'étud. anc.* xxxvi (1934).

A. Heuss, 'Antigonos Monophthalmos und die griechischen Städte', *Hermes*, lxxiii (1938).

P. Huby, 'The Menexenus Reconsidered', *Phronesis*, ii (1957).

H. Ll. Hudson-Williams, 'Isocrates and recitations', *C.Q.* xlii (1949).

W. Jaeger, 'The Date of Isocrates' Areopagiticus and the Athenian Opposition', *Harv. Class. Stud. Suppl.* i (1940).

W. Judeich, 'Der Zeit der Friedensrede des Andokides', *Philologus*, lxxxi (1926).

A. Kaerst, 'Der korinthische Bund', *Rh. Mus.* lii (1897).

D. Kagan, 'Corinthian Politics and the Revolution of 392 B.C.', *Historia*, xi (1962).

C. H. Kahn, 'Plato's Funeral Oration', *Class. Phil.* lviii (1963).

B. Keil, 'Εἰρήνη', *Berichte über die Verhandlungen des Königlichen sächsischen Gesellschaft der Wissenschaften*, lxviii (1916).

U. Köhler, 'Die griechische Politik Dionysius des älteren', *Ath. Mitt.* I. xv (1876).

J. A. O. Larsen, 'Representative Government in the Panhellenic Leagues', *Class. Phil.* xx (1925) & xxi (1926).

—— 'Sparta and the Ionian Revolt', *Class. Phil.* xxvii (1932).

J. A. O. LARSEN, 'The Constitution of the Peloponnesian League', *Class. Phil.* xxviii (1933).

—— Review of F. Hampl, 'Die griechischen Staatsverträge', *Class. Phil.* xxxiv (1939).

—— 'The Constitution and Original Purpose of the Delian League', *Harv. Class. Stud.* li (1940).

—— 'Federation for Peace in Ancient Greece', *Class. Phil.* xxxix (1944).

—— 'The Early Achaean League', *Robinson Studies*, ii (1953).

—— 'Orchomenus and the Formation of the Boeotian Confederacy', *Class. Phil.* lv (1960).

S. LAUFFER, 'Die Diodordublette XV 38 = 50 über die Friedensschlüsse zu Sparta', *Historia*, viii (1959).

T. LENSCHAU, 'Alexander der grosse und Chios', *Klio*, xxxiii (1940).

V. MARTIN, 'Le traitement de l'histoire diplomatique dans la tradition littéraire du IVᵐᵉ siècle', *Museum Helveticum*, i (1944).

G. MATHIEU, 'Les premiers conflicts entre Platon et Isocrate et la date de l'Euthydème', *Mélanges Glotz*, ii (1932).

H. B. MATTINGLY, 'The Date of Plato's Symposium', *Phronesis*, iii (1958).

—— 'The Athenian Coinage Decree', *Historia*, x (1961).

B. D. MERITT, 'Athenian Covenant with Mytilene', *A.J.Ph.* lxxv (1954).

F. MILTNER, 'Die Datierung des Areopagitikos', *Mitteilungen des Vereins klassischen Philologen in Wien*, i (1924).

—— 'Die staatsrechtliche Entwicklung des Alexanderreiches', *Klio*, xxvi (1933).

A. MOMIGLIANO, 'La κοινὴ εἰρήνη dal 386 al 338 a. C.', *Riv. di filol.* n.s. xii (1934).

—— 'Per la storia pubblicistica sulla κοινὴ εἰρήνη nel IV secolo a. C.', *Annali di Pisa*, II. v (1936).

—— 'Un momento di storia greca', *Athenaeum*, N.S. xiv (1936).

D. J. MOSLEY, 'The Athenian Embassy to Sparta in 371 B.C.', *Proceedings of the Cambridge Philological Society*, N.S. viii (1962).

W. NESTLÉ, 'Der Friedensgedanke in der antiken Welt', *Philologus Suppl.* xxxi, no. 1 (1938).

B. NIESE, 'Beiträge zur griechischen Geschichte 370–364', *Hermes*, xxxix (1904).

J. PAPASTAVROU, 'Τὸ ἐν Ἀθήναις συνέδριον τῶν συμμάχων τὸ κατὰ τὸ ἔτος 370 π.Χ.' *Hellenika*, x (1937–8).

H. W. PARKE, 'The Development of the Second Spartan Empire', *J.H.S.* l (1930).

S. PAYRAU, 'Sur un passage d'Andocide', *Rev. d'étud. anc.* lxiii (1961).

S. PERLMAN, 'Isocrates' Philippus—a reinterpretation', *Historia*, vi (1957).

A. W. PICKARD-CAMBRIDGE, 'The Rise of Macedonia', Chap. VIII of *C.A.H.* vi (1927).

D. M. ROBINSON, 'Inscriptions from Macedonia 1938', *Transactions of the American Philological Association*, lxix (1938).

C. ROEBUCK, 'The Settlements of Philip II of Macedon with the Greek States in 338 B.C.', *Class. Phil.* xliii (1948).

A. ROOS, 'The Peace of Sparta of 374 B.C.', *Mnemosyne*, N.S. ii (1949).

F. Rühl, 'Vermischte Bemerkungen', *Neues Jahrbuch für Philologie und Pädagogik*, i (1888).

T. T. B. Ryder, 'The Supposed Common Peace of 366/5 B.C.', *C.Q.* N.S. vii (1957).

—— 'Spartan Relations with Persia after the King's Peace; a Strange Story in Diodorus 15. 9', *C.Q.* N.S. xiii (1963).

—— 'Athenian Foreign Policy and the Peace-conference at Sparta in 371 B.C.', *C.Q.* N.S. xiii (1963).

G. de SteCroix, 'The Character of the Athenian Empire', *Historia*, iii (1954–5).

G. De Sanctis, 'La pace del 362/1', *Riv. di filol.* N.S. xii (1934).

F. Schehl, 'Zum korinthischen Bund vom Jahr 338/7 v. Chr.', *Jahreshefte Oesterr. Arch. Inst.* xxvii (1932).

H. Schwahn, 'Heeresmatrikel und Landfriede Philipps von Makedonien', *Klio*, Beiheft xxi (1930).

E. Schwartz, 'Diodoros (38)', *Paulys Realencyclopädie der classischer Altertumswissenschaft*, cols. 679–82.

R. Sealey, 'Callistratus of Aphidna and his Contemporaries', *Historia*, v (1956).

—— '*IG* ii² 1609 and the Transformation of the Second Athenian Sea-League', *Phoenix*, xi (1957).

R. H. Simpson, 'The Historical Circumstances of the Peace of 311', *J.H.S.* lxxiv (1954).

R. E. Smith, 'The Opposition to Agesilaus' Foreign Policy', *Historia*, ii (1953–4).

M. Sordi, 'I carattori dell'opera storiografica di Senofonte nelle Elleniche: II. Le Elleniche come opera storica', *Athenaeum*, xxix (1951).

—— 'La pace di Atene del 370 a. C.', *Riv. di filol.* lxxix (1951).

H. Swoboda, 'Der hellenische Bund des Jahres 371 v. Chr.', *Rh. Mus.* xlix (1894).

W. W. Tarn, 'Alexander: the Conquest of the Far East', Chap. XIII of *C.A.H.* vi (1927).

P. Treves, 'Dopo Ipso', *Riv. di filol.* N.S. ix (1931).

—— 'Note sulla guerra corinzia', *Riv. di filol.* N.S. xv (1937).

W. P. Wallace, 'Kleomenes, Marathon, the Helots and Arcadia', *J.H.S.* lxxiv (1954).

J. Walz, 'Der lysianische Epitaphios', *Philologus Suppl.* xxix, no. 4 (1936).

H. D. Westlake, 'Hermocrates the Syracusan', *Bulletin of the John Rylands Library*, xli (1958–9).

—— 'Athenian aims in Sicily, 427–424 B.C.', *Historia*, ix (1960).

U. Wilcken, 'Beiträge zur Geschichte des korinthischen Bundes', *Sitzb. München*, 1917, iii, Abh. x.

—— 'Alexander der grosse und der korinthische Bund', *Sitzb. Berlin*, 1922.

—— 'Zu der epidaurischen Bundesstele vom J. 302 v. Chr.', *Sitzb. Berlin*, 1927.

—— 'Philipp II von Makedonien und die panhellenische Idee', *Sitzb. Berlin*, 1929.

U. Wilcken, 'Über Entstehung und Zweck des Königsfriedens', *Abh. Berlin*, 1941, no. 15.

A. Wilhelm, 'Ein Friedensbund der Hellenen', *Jahreshefte Oesterr. Arch. Inst.* iii (1900).

—— 'Attische Urkunden', *Sitzb. Wien*, clxv, no. 6 (1911).

A. G. Woodhead, '*IG* ii² 43 and Jason of Pherae', *A.J. Arch.* xli (1957).

—— 'The Aegean Allies 375–373 B.C.', *Phoenix*, xvi (1962).

F. Wüst, 'Amphiktyonie, Eidgenossenschaft, Symmachie', *Historia*, iii (1954).

INDEX

Greek states are indicated by the names of the people. References to an actual city are included with those to its people. The Athenians and the Spartans, who pervade the whole book, are not included.